INNOVATION AND CHANGE
IN ENGLISH LANGUAGE EDUCATION

Questions about what to teach and how best to teach it are what drive professional practice in the English language classroom. *Innovation and Change in English Language Education* addresses these key questions so that teachers are able to understand and manage change to organise teaching and learning more effectively. The book provides an accessible introduction to current theory and research in innovation and change in ELT and shows how these understandings have been applied to the practical concerns of the curriculum and the classroom. In specially commissioned chapters written by experts in the field, the volume:

- sets out the key issues in innovation and change and shows how these relate to actual practice.
- offers a guide to innovation and change in a range of key areas grounded in research.
- relates theory to practice through the use of illustrative case studies and examples.
- brings together the very best scholarship in TESOL and language education from around the world.

This book will be of interest to upper undergraduate and graduate students in applied linguistics, language education and TESOL as well as pre-service and in-service teachers, teacher educators, researchers and administrators keen to create and manage teaching and learning more effectively.

Ken Hyland is Chair Professor of Applied Linguistics and Director of the Centre for Applied English Studies at the University of Hong Kong. He has published over 160 articles and 20 books on language teaching and academic writing and is co-editor of *Applied Linguistics*.

Lillian L. C. Wong is a senior lecturer in the Centre for Applied English Studies at the University of Hong Kong. She also researches innovations in English language teaching and learning and is a member of the Board of Directors of *TESOL International Association*.

INNOVATION AND CHANGE IN ENGLISH LANGUAGE EDUCATION

Ken Hyland and Lillian L. C. Wong

Routledge
Taylor & Francis Group

LONDON AND NEW YORK

First published 2013
by Routledge
2 Park Square, Milton Park, Abingdon, Oxon OX14 4RN

Simultaneously published in the USA and Canada
by Routledge
711 Third Avenue, New York, NY 10017

Routledge is an imprint of the Taylor & Francis Group, an informa business

British Library Cataloguing in Publication Data
A catalogue record for this book is available from the British Library

Library of Congress Cataloging in Publication Data
A catalog record for this book has been requested

ISBN: 978-0-415-82686-0 (hbk)
ISBN: 978-0-415-82687-7 (pbk)
ISBN: 978-0-203-36271-6 (ebk)

Typeset in Galliard
by Saxon Graphics Ltd, Derby

MIX
Paper from
responsible sources
FSC
www.fsc.org   FSC® C013056

Printed and bound in Great Britain by
TJ International Ltd, Padstow, Cornwall

CONTENTS

LIST OF ILLUSTRATIONS

Figures

Tables

CONTRIBUTORS

Kathleen M. Bailey received her M.A. in TESL and her Ph.D. in Applied Linguistics from UCLA. She is a Professor of Applied Linguistics at the Monterey Institute of International Studies as well as a Professor in the TESOL masters program at Anaheim University. From 1998–1999, she was the President of the international TESOL association. She currently serves as the President of the International Research Foundation for English Language Education (TIRF) and is the Chair of its Board of Trustees. Her research interests include teacher education, supervision and development, second language acquisition, language testing, classroom research and research methodology.

Joseph Lo Bianco is Professor of Language and Literacy Education at the University of Melbourne. He is a language planning practitioner, working on national language policies in many countries, especially language in education planning. He is well known for the National Policy on Languages, adopted in 1987 by the Australian government as a comprehensive plan to cover all of Australia's language needs and interests. His most recent books are *China and English: Globalisation and Dilemmas of Identity* (Multilingual Matters, 2009) and *Second Languages and Australian Schooling* (ACER Press, 2009) but he has 120 refereed publications. In 2009 he was elected President of the Australian Academy of the Humanities.

Anne Burns was formerly Professor of Linguistics, Dean of Linguistics and Psychology, and Associate Director of the National Centre for English Language Teaching and Research (NCELTR) at Macquarie University, Sydney. She currently holds two part-time positions, as Professor of Language Education at Aston University, Birmingham, and Professor of TESOL at the

University of New South Wales, Sydney. She has published extensively on action research in English language teaching.

David Carless is Professor of Educational Assessment in the Faculty of Education, University of Hong Kong. His recent Routledge-published books are: *From Testing to Productive Student Learning: Implementing Formative Assessment in Confucian-heritage Settings*; and *Reconceptualising Feedback in Higher Education: Developing Dialogue with Students* (co-edited by S. Merry, M. Price, D. Carless and M. Taras).

Chris Davison is Professor of Education and Head of the School of Education, University of NSW, Sydney, Australia and an Honorary Professor at the University of Hong Kong. She has been researching and developing various assessment for learning initiatives in Hong Kong, Singapore, Brunei and Australia, and has published widely on English language assessment and innovation.

Beverly Derewianka is Professor of Language Education at the University of Wollongong, Australia. Her research interests include the identification of key indicators of development in adolescent writing; the writing demands of the various curriculum areas; a genre approach to writing pedagogy; and the relationship between research, policy and practice in literacy education. Several of these projects have been supported by major national competitive grants.

Donald Freeman is on the faculty at the School of Education, University of Michigan, where he works with undergraduate and postgraduate teacher preparation in all subjects K12. For 25 years, he was on the graduate faculty at the School of International Training, where he chaired the Department of Language Teacher Education and founded and directed the Center for Teacher Education, Training, and Research, a research and development unit that designed and implemented teacher education projects around the world. His research and design interests focus on creating new, atypical professional environments to support individual learning and institutional transformation.

Yafu Gong is a research fellow and Director in the Foreign Language Education Research Center at the China National Institute for Educational Research (SNIER). He is also President of the National Association of Foreign Language Education, China Education Society (NAFLE). He has been involved with the development of several national English syllabi for primary and secondary schools of China.

Gary Harfitt is an Assistant Professor in the Division of English Language Education, Faculty of Education, University of Hong Kong. His main research interests are how class size impacts on teaching and learning; and the use of literature and language arts in ELT.

Adrian Holliday is Professor of Applied Linguistics at Canterbury Christ Church University, where he supervises doctoral research in the critical sociology of language education and intercultural communication. His publications include *The Struggle to Teach English as an International Language* (Oxford 2005), and *Intercultural Communication & Ideology* (Sage 2011), which deals with the Western ideologies that inhibit our understanding of non-Western cultural realities.

Ken Hyland is Professor of Applied Linguistics and Director of the Centre for Applied English Studies at the University of Hong Kong. He has taught Applied Linguistics for over 30 years and published over 170 articles and 20 books on language education and academic writing. His most recent book is *Disciplinary Identities* published by Cambridge University Press in 2012. He is a foundation member of the Hong Kong Academy of the Humanities, was founding co-editor of the *Journal of English for Academic Purposes* and is currently co-editor of *Applied Linguistics*.

Karen E. Johnson is Liberal Arts Research Professor of Applied Linguistics in the Department of Applied Linguistics at The Pennsylvania State University, and Co-director of the Center for Advanced Language Proficiency Education and Research. Her research interests include narrative inquiry as professional development, teacher learning in second language teacher education and a sociocultural theoretical perspective on teacher professional development.

Chris Kennedy has worked as teacher, trainer, adviser, academic and manager in Africa, Europe, the Middle East, South-East Asia and South America. His research and publications focus on curriculum innovation, language policy and English as a global language, and the inter-relationships between them, with interests also in primary ELT, professional communication and applied corpus linguistics. He is a Past President of IATEFL, and was Chair of the British Council English Teaching Advisory Committee for many years. He is Director of the Centre for English Language Studies at the University of Birmingham UK, which runs Masters and Ph.D. programmes in TEFL, Applied Linguistics and Translation.

Numa Markee teaches Applied Linguistics courses on (innovative) curriculum design, second language acquisition, and conversation analysis at the University of Illinois at Urbana-Champaign. He is the author of *Managing Curricular Innovation* (Cambridge University Press 1997) and *Conversation Analysis* (Lawrence Erlbaum 2000) and also numerous articles and books. His current interests include working on a synthesis of insights from these two fields of inquiry.

Denise E. Murray is Professor Emeritus at Macquarie University, Australia and San José State University, California. She was founding chair of the Department of Linguistics and Language Development at San José State University for nine years and Director of the National Center for English Language Teaching and Research at Macquarie University for six years. She was on the TESOL Board of Directors for seven years, being President in 1997–1998. Her research and publications include CALL; cross-cultural literacy; use of L1 in the second language classroom; intersection of language, society and technology; settlement of adult immigrants; language education policy; and leadership in language education.

David Nunan is Emeritus Professor of Applied Linguistics at the University of Hong Kong and Vice-President for Academic Affairs at Anaheim University. He has worked as a teacher, researcher and consultant in many countries, including Australia, the United Kingdom, Thailand, Singapore, Oman, Japan, China and the United States. He has published over 100 books and articles. He is a former President of TESOL and currently serves on the Board of Trustees of The International Research Foundation for Language Education.

Sarah E. Springer has been teaching core and elective CALL courses in the Monterey Institute's M.A. in Teaching Foreign Languages (TFL) and Teaching English as a Second Language (TESOL) since 2005. She has lived, taught and trained teachers in the United States, Brazil, Switzerland, Guatemala and Mexico. She wrote her first educational software program in 1983 on an Apple IIe and has been engaged in curriculum development, teacher training and materials development projects ever since. Her research is focused on teacher education and the development of expertise in pre- and in-service educators across a wide range of subject areas and contexts.

Brian Tomlinson is Visiting Professor at Leeds Metropolitan University. He has worked in Japan, Indonesia, Nigeria, Oman, Singapore, the UK, Vanuatu and Zambia and has given presentations in over 60 countries. He is Founder and President of MATSDA (the international Materials Development Association) and has published many articles and books on language acquisition, language awareness, language through literature and materials development for language teaching.

Maria Luz C. Vilches is Associate Professor of English and Dean of the School of Humanities at Ateneo de Manila University. Under the auspices of the Ateneo Center for ELT, the Department of Education, the Commission on Higher Education, and the British Council, she has had an extensive involvement in running ELT projects in the Philippines and in other parts of South East Asia. Her research interests are ELT teacher/trainer education and development as well as ELT management – both with focus on experiences in the Asian context.

Alan Waters is a senior lecturer in the Department of Linguistics and English Language at Lancaster University, UK. He has taught EFL and trained teachers in several other parts of the world and published a number of books and articles on a range of ELT topics. His main research interests are in language teaching methodology, teacher learning and curriculum innovation.

Lillian L. C. Wong has a Ph.D. in Applied Linguistics teaches in the Centre for Applied English Studies at the University of Hong Kong. She has taught English in primary and secondary schools and has extensive experience developing, teaching and coordinating undergraduate, postgraduate and teacher education programmes. She is Coordinator of the English Programme in the Graduate School and Chair of the Research and Professional Development Committee for the Centre. Her research includes curriculum innovation and development, language education planning and policy, motivation, autonomous learning, student e-portfolios and assessment, teacher professional development and IT in ELT. She was Chair of the Professional Development Committee (2005–2006) and is on the Board of Directors (2012–2015) of TESOL International Association. She is also Chair of the Research and Professional Development Committee for the Centre and Coordinator of the English Programme in the Graduate School.

PREFACE

The impetus for this book came from Lillian's long research interest in curriculum innovation and teacher professional development. She also brought to the book a list of potential authors that included many of the established players in the field, and to this we added names of people we thought had made a substantial contribution to recent discussions of language innovation in various areas. We are delighted to say that all of them accepted to join us in the project – allowing us, in this book, to explore a diverse array of innovative projects, methodologies and theoretical positions across a broad canvas of contexts.

Change seems to be fundamental to our professional lives as teachers and in Hong Kong it is almost constant. Trends are picked up by the education bureau and introduced with fanfare and considerable funding into schools, and then put down again before harassed teachers have a chance to understand or assimilate them. Tasks, CALL, genre, e-portfolios and online corpus information all ripple the surface of classroom practice and are gone, often leaving no lasting impression on professional practice or the consciousness of those asked to implement them. It is this curiosity about how innovations come into being, are introduced, taken up (or not) and how they effect change in teachers, practice or policy which informs the chapters of this book.

Our aim in selecting papers was to represent as wide a range of approaches and contexts as possible, while being as comprehensive as we could in terms of the kinds of innovation and change we included. We wanted to present a multiform view of innovation and change, looking at different conceptions, models, influences and contexts; exploring how it emerges in teacher education, action research and reflective practice; the role it plays in different stages of the language curriculum; and how it impacts on classroom practice. We asked all our authors to provide a case study to illustrate their themes and, if possible, for this to illustrate a positive implementation of change. While this has not always been feasible, we think an understanding of why innovations fail to take root as change can be instructive and help ensure we do not repeat mistakes.

We hope the reader will come away from this book with an increased understanding of the importance of innovation in language education and how it works to effect change in language education. We also hope that it encourages teachers to explore innovations in their own classrooms and embrace the possibilities that change offers both to themselves and their students.

ACKNOWLEDGEMENTS

We wish to thank our authors for (mainly!) being easy to work with, for their enthusiastic commitment to this project, for their insights, and for teaching us more than they will know about innovation and change in language education.

1

INTRODUCTION: INNOVATION AND IMPLEMENTATION OF CHANGE

Ken Hyland and Lillian L. C. Wong

Innovation and change in language education has been a subject of interest for both teachers and researchers since the early days of English language teaching. Driven by professional dissatisfaction with the status quo in local contexts or, increasingly, by the imperatives of quality audits and external course assessments, questions concerning the design, implementation and maintenance of innovation and change are, perhaps more than ever before, of central concern to teachers. As a result, there have been many initiatives by teachers, researchers and administrators to create and manage teaching and learning more effectively. Despite this interest, however, research does not seem to filter down to practitioners in a way which always allows them to draw on this activity to inform their own work. This book addresses this need by providing a clear and comprehensive introduction to the theoretical and research issues that inform this area and, at the same time, ground the discussion in practical examples of implementation. It brings together an impressive array of experts from around the world who, in a series of specifically commissioned chapters, link theory and practice in ways which illustrate both the findings of research and the processes of innovation and change in different domains of language education.

Innovation and change

Change seems to be a constant in our professional lives as teachers. There is almost a continuous progression of modifications to our current situation, sometimes improving matters and sometimes not, sometimes having beneficial effects, and at other times worsening things. But change can be unplanned and chaotic, a random process that occurs to us rather than being controlled by us and for this reason some observers prefer to talk of innovation, a process which 'implies some deliberation and consciousness' (Kennedy, 1996: 4). Constructive change involves an aim, which makes innovation a key part of the process of educational change, initiating and driving change in many different areas.

According to Rogers (2003: 12), an innovation is 'an idea, practice, or object perceived as new by an individual or other unit of adoption'. Novelty resides in perception; how something is seen by teachers, headmasters, administrators or others involved in its implementation. Sometimes these are mandated from above by policy-makers in government offices and at other times by classroom practitioners trying something new to make their students more active or their lessons more effective. As the contributors to this book make clear, such innovations can appear in a variety of guises and at various levels of performance. They are found in classrooms, materials and exam halls, and in the heads of teachers, in-service trainers, planners, policy-makers, materials developers and curriculum designers.

Rogers also talks of 'diffusion' to denote the process through which an innovation is communicated and made real. This is how those at the sharp end learn about innovations and attempt to understand them and put them into practice, however expertly or clumsily. It is where innovation becomes change and we can see the fruits of novelty. As our authors make clear, however, the stages through which innovation might move can be messy, with reinterpretations and additions made along the way which accommodate individual preferences, institutional ideologies and fiscal necessities. Teachers get different versions of the same story and are motivated to different degrees. Innovation, in other words, does not always mean change, or at least the kind of change that may have been intended. It is successful to the extent that targeted clients are reached, informed and persuaded to buy into it. Not all teachers are ready for change and not all institutions are prepared to support it. Stories of failed innovations are legend and the literature groans with detailed case studies where innovations are either unsuccessful or have limited effect.

In this book, we have tried to offer readers a range of different ways of thinking about innovation in English languge education, and different methods of investigating the impact of innovation. One theme that does recur in different guises throughout the book, however, is the importance of teacher-initiated innovation, and the practical difficulties associated with fostering this kind of bottom-up perspective. We hope this emphasis is welcomed by teachers who read the volume and who may not, for the moment at least, be in a position to influence or participate in top-down decision-making on innovation. Ultimately, however, it is the EFL teacher who decides what innovations find their way into the classroom: how new methods are implemented, new technologies deployed and new textbooks used. Innovations can, and should, be supported from above and forced through by clear policies, adequate funding and professional development initiatives, but if teachers have not fully embraced the concepts, then the innovation will die.

Some readers may wonder why this introduction does not attempt to more explicitly set the scene for the current state of ELT provision in the world, why it does not outline what the existing literature agrees to be the main features that need to be considered by those planning innovation and seeking to initiate change to such provision. It would, of course, be a useful undertaking to provide a checklist of innovations so that educators could just tick off what was needed. We are, however, unsure how to characterize the way ELT is offered worldwide and doubt this is even possible. The case studies in the book show a tremendous diversity in contexts, provision, expertise, resources and so on, which defy such simple characterization. *Context* is one of the key terms which inform this book and local conditions have a central locus of innovation which occurs in every one of the following chapters. It is not possible to establish a generic, universal yardstick by which to evaluate changes. Instead, we prefer to let the discussions and reflections by each author speak for themselves and allow readers to draw their own conclusions about what is relevant to them.

What we learn from these chapters is that only if change agents recognize the complexity and importance of local situations can innovations be successfully introduced and sustained. What is also clear is the systemic and holistic nature of educational change: that underpinning successful change, at any level, is the fact that the parts are interdependent and inseparable. It is futile, as many innovators have found, to change just one aspect of a national policy, institutional plan, classroom approach or beliefs of one group. Stakeholders need to 'learn change' together.

As editors, we believe that a better understanding of change, and the processes of change, will help teachers, administrators and policy-makers to implement more effective innovations, and this view is shared by the contributors to this volume. The authors are all established experts, well-published in their fields and bringing to the book a measured sense of what potential different innovations have and how they might develop. While predominantly 'Western', many of these contributors have spent years working overseas and several have collaborated with a 'non-Western' co-author to cover a dozen different countries. There is, however, a certain emphasis on South East Asian countries, as this is where many of the exciting attempts at innovation and change are happening, given increased funding by governments and attempts to break away from traditional teaching and assessment methods which have dominated the region for decades.

Each author focuses on a different area of innovation and change and provides a state-of-the-art review of the key ideas and concepts about that area, reflecting on how innovation has been conceived of and change undertaken. Where relevant, we have asked authors to include a case study of research to illustrate the points they are making, setting out in an accessible way the challenges, pitfalls and opportunities that educational innovations can present in particular instances of implementation. We have also asked authors to provide a reflection on their case study, considering its value and wider significance. Each chapter, therefore, offers an attempt to conceptualise, synthesise and illustrate what is meant by innovation in that field. The chapters conclude with annotated recommendations for further readings on the topic discussed.

Theoretical discussion is therefore set alongside case studies. In this way we hope to not only provide a sense of coherence to the volume, but also to encourage readers to think consistently in terms of applications and, while reflecting on conceptual dimensions of innovation, to understand these in terms of concrete examples.

Structure of the book

The book is divided into four sections with four or five chapters in each. The first introduces key ideas and perspectives on innovation and change in language education. Here the principles, models, contexts, cultures and management of change are presented and discussed. Section Two explores how change is initiated and implemented in teacher education and the effects this can have on teachers' thinking, practices and self-conceptions. In Section Three, the authors investigate and illustrate aspects of innovation and change in the language curriculum, looking respectively at innovation in language policy and at primary, secondary and higher education in Hong Kong, Malaysia, the US, Australia and other contexts. Section Four brings ideas about change down from these broad areas of planning and curriculum innovation to show what it means in particular contexts of practical implementation. Here, the focus is on the classroom, the development of materials and the introduction of technology to teaching. We have, then, sought to shape a movement from theoretical frameworks, through teacher training to curriculum to classroom practice, focusing on a variety of areas in a range of different ways, from detailed analysis of individual exchanges in the classroom, to overviews of large-scale decision-making at governmental level.

Section One seeks to define change and introduce the principal ideas and concepts which are central to understanding it in educational contexts.

In Chapter 2, Chris Kennedy discusses models of change and argues that innovation projects often fail because they follow simplistic linear views. Instead, he proposes that models should be informed by a view of change as processes that continue to develop over time rather than have a definite start and end point. He stresses that we need to understand the central role of context in effecting change and the influence of social-psychological theories of behaviour, including the importance of cognition, attitudes, beliefs and social influences, to integrate relevant theories of behaviour into models of change. In this way, it should be possible to develop models that guide the implementation of change rather than seek to determine it. Drawing on examples, he explores the extent to which change in ELT has been influenced by such models, and whether best practice can suggest other aspects to be included in developing models of change.

Numa Markee takes up the issue of context in more detail in Chapter 3. Building on Kennedy's (1988) earlier 'onion skin' model of how various socio-cultural factors (cultural, political, administrative, educational and institutional) play in influencing classroom change, Markee focuses on more emic, or participant-oriented, accounts of context. Here, he reviews recent discussions of context in the applied linguistics and ethnomethodological literatures on talk-in-interaction, and shows how these perspectives may allow us to gain novel insights into how innovative a project on iterative curriculum design, implementation and evaluation carried out at an American university actually was.

In Chapter 4, Yafu Gong and Adrian Holliday again turn to the crucial issue of context and consider the major question of making curriculum change appropriate to the cultural makeup of the target setting. Rejecting common conceptualizations of 'context' as essentialist and the 'native speaker' model as dependant on views which posit a deficient non-Western cultural Other, the authors present a critical cosmopolitan approach, taken from sociology, which recognises the positive contribution of wider cultural realities to curriculum renewal. The authors exemplify this through a case study of recent research into the attitudes of rural Chinese secondary school students to English language textbooks, revealing an inner cultural reality which connects with long-standing issues of authenticity and suggests a key to wider ranging curriculum renewal.

The final chapter in this section explores the difficulties involved in change management. Here Alan Waters and Maria Luz C. Vilches survey some key aspects of managing change, such as the structure of the change process, innovation design features and contexts, and implementation processes. They then go on to examine the application of these concepts in the management of a recent major ELT in-service initiative for teachers in the Philippines. By describing the project's main features and the findings of research into its operation, they evaluate its success in terms of the literature reviewed in the first part of the chapter. They then draw conclusions for the management of change in ELT and how these conclusions might help teachers avoid some of the pitfalls of implementing change.

Section Two of the book contains four chapters which look at the implementation of change in teacher education and the possible consequences of this on teachers' identities and practices.

In Chapter 6, Karen E. Johnson discusses the most explicit form of developing teaching expertise: innovation through teacher education programmes. She points out that many of these programmes are predicated on sociocultural principles which understand cognition as originating in and shaped by engagement in social activities, and this requires us to critically examine how teachers are expected to engage in such programmes. She argues that we have to scrutinize the nature of the activities in teacher education programmes, the sort of assistance that is provided for teachers as they engage in these activities, and how participation supports and enhances the development of teaching expertise. She then shows how a restructured microteaching simulation in a TESL methodology course addresses these issues to create spaces for strategic mediation in teacher learning and opportunities for teachers to practise their emerging understandings of both pedagogical and subject matter concepts within authentic activities of teaching.

Another means of initiating change and innovation in teaching practices is through action-research, which Anne Burns explores in Chapter 7. Burns sees action research as a means of empowering teachers and enabling them to acquire deeper insights and understanding of their practices through a systematic approach that brings together classroom action, research and reflection. This chapter describes the central philosophies and principles informing action research as a research approach and describes the main steps, procedures and methods used in conducting action research. Addressing the criticisms and debates surrounding action research, she considers issues such as how feasible it is for teachers to carry out action research, the conditions which can encourage or hinder action research, and how action research promotes change in teaching practice. To illustrate these points, she draws on a case study from a recent project involving teachers on intensive English programmes for overseas students in Australia.

Kathleen M. Bailey and Sarah E. Springer examine the important issue of reflection in Chapter 8, focusing on reflective teaching as an example of an educational innovation. Here, they define reflective teaching as a collection of practices 'in which teachers and student teachers collect data about teaching, examine their attitudes, beliefs, assumptions, and teaching practices, and use the information obtained as a basis for critical reflection about teaching' (Richards and Lockhart, 1994: 1). Drawing on Wallace's (1991) three models of teacher development – (1) the craft model, (2) the applied science model and (3) the reflective model – they see reflective teaching as innovative because it is disseminated through grassroots means as well as through official channels and because it can lead to the development of teaching skills, greater awareness, and enhanced professional satisfaction.

In Chapter 9, Donald Freeman takes a very different perspective on the complexity of educational change, turning to look at teacher thinking, learning and identity in the process of change. His focus is the critical importance of how the process of change is framed, which, he argues, is central from both the standpoints of designing and implementing educational change projects and researching them. From this perspective, he examines three interrelated constructs: teacher thinking (Borg, 2006), professional learning (Freeman, 2002), and professional identity (Lortie, 1975), showing how these constructs contribute to and are constrained in the educational change process. Each of the constructs is elaborated historically, with reference to the recent literatures in second language teacher education and general education, and operationally, through reference to specific educational change projects. Taken together, he shows that the three constructs can map out key elements and so help us make better sense of the educational change process.

Section Three moves from innovation in teacher education to the broader level of curriculum change, examining the planning and implementation of large-scale policy innovations.

Joseph Lo Bianco opens this section with Chapter 10 by looking at innovation in language policy and planning, confronting the geo-political forces which seem to be driving language planning in countries across the globe. He sees an explosion of the actual practice of language planning almost everywhere, despite a decade or more of savage criticism of its methods, concepts and operations. He finds explanations for this in the increasingly closer integration of economies and laws in Europe, partly in response to the economic growth of China, and in the continuing pressure, in post-colonial and immigrant receiving contexts, for the recognition of language rights. These major changes are occurring against the backdrop of the intensification of the role of English as an international lingual franca. He then discusses the innovations required and that are beginning to be felt within language planning scholarship and practice in this context.

In Chapter 11, Beverly Derewianka discusses innovation in English language teaching in the primary sector, examining the kinds of decisions involved in developing a national English curriculum at this level, the influences on those decisions and their implications for teachers. The focus here is on Australia, where the federal government has recently been able to implement a national curriculum after years of state independence. She points out that one of the requirements of this consensus was that the curriculum be innovative, and in this spirit, the English curriculum placed 'knowledge about language' at the centre of learning, along with an informed appreciation of literature and an evolving repertoire of literacy uses. This was a radical departure and, for a generation of teachers who had not been exposed to explicit teaching about language, it posed considerable challenges. After reviewing such issues as the nature of the subject English as a discipline, an appropriate model of language for today's students and the integration of the language, literature and literacy strands, Derewianka investigates how teachers make sense of the new curriculum in their classes.

In Chapter 12, the spotlight turns on innovation in secondary education, and here David Carless and Gary Harfitt explore ongoing reforms to the structure and content of the senior secondary curriculum in Hong Kong. The structural aspect involves a move from a four-year to a three-year course of study, with students entering university one year earlier than previously. The content aspects include: stronger synergies between schooling and future career or higher education; diversification of assessment modes and processes; and greater emphasis on preparation for lifelong learning. The authors undertake a critical analysis of the English language components of this new senior secondary school curriculum, building on the work of Paul Morris (1995; 2002). This wide-ranging discussion reveals mismatches between intentions and realities in educational reform; continuities and discontinuities in educational change; tensions between new modes of assessment and examination-oriented Chinese traditions; and policy borrowing versus contextually grounded approaches.

Denise E. Murray looks at innovation in two higher education contexts, the United States and Australia, in Chapter 13. Following Stoller (1997) in distinguishing between innovation and change, and seeing change as resulting in alterations in the status quo but not necessarily in improvements, Murray shows how change is adapted and revised in local contexts. Focusing on two very different institutions, she demonstrates that English language education in public higher education can respond innovatively and creatively to changes in government policy such as immigration, international student visas, reduced public funding, and competition from for-profit higher education colleges. She argues that for innovations to be fully implemented and sustained over time requires going beyond the immediate English language faculty to break down organizational and cultural structural barriers endemic to higher education. It requires sustained leadership from higher level administrators.

Section Four returns the discussion of innovation in language education to practical implementations of change, through classroom practice, materials and technological delivery.

In Chapter 14, the first chapter in this section, Brian Tomlinson discusses innovation in materials development, arguing that course books for teaching English as a second language have remained largely unchanged in the past 30 years. Although many commercially produced textbooks continue to emphasise Presentation Practice Production activities, Tomlinson discusses some innovations that have been pioneered in institutional and Ministry materials development projects around the world. These innovations involve collaborative materials development in Japan, discovery-driven materials in Oman, extensive reading materials in Lebanon and Japan, new technology supported materials in India and Sri Lanka, task-driven materials in Belgium, task-free activities in the UK and text-driven materials in Ethiopia and Namibia. He also considers the possibilities offered by generic tasks, individualised routes, menus of texts and multi-dimensional activities, and reports a case study of a project in a South Korean secondary school in which the course book was replaced by process drama materials.

In Chapter 15, Ken Hyland points out that corpora have been at the vanguard of two of the most significant changes in language education in recent years. On the one hand, they have provided teachers and materials designers with new ways of understanding how language is patterned and used and, on the other, they have given students the means to take a more active and reflective part in their learning. New descriptions of language based on phraseology and collocation have informed syllabus design, dictionaries, reference grammars, teaching materials and assessment. In the classroom itself, corpora have contributed to the shift from teaching as imparting knowledge to teaching as mediating learning by providing a way for students to explore authentic examples of language. This chapter describes some of these changes in language education and illustrates one approach offered by an online reference tool for second language writers. This resource encourages autonomy and learning by providing students with access to collocational information and examples of real language use as they write.

David Nunan explores the development of two innovative pedagogical practices in the teaching of English to younger learners in Chapter 16. Nunan begins by reviewing some of the current literature on the teaching of English to younger learners and on current educational policies on the teaching of foreign languages to younger learners. He then presents a number of case studies of innovative pedagogical practices in the teaching of English to younger learners in a range of educational and geographical contexts, focusing in particular on technological innovations. In the chapter, he looks at published data sources as well as carrying out research which draws on elicited data from questionnaires and interviews as well as case studies and classroom observation.

In Chapter 17, Lillian L. C. Wong looks at the implementation of information technology (IT) in schools and explores the considerable challenges this can pose to teachers. In reviewing the factors which affect the incorporation of technological innovation in language teaching, she argues that the decisive factor for successful change lies with the teachers who are asked to implement the changes. Taking an innovative programme by the Hong Kong government to help over 1,800 English teachers develop IT skills as a case study, she reports a two-year longitudinal investigation into the ways in which English teachers sought to integrate their use of IT into their classroom practice. The study shows how teachers took up the innovation in their classrooms while remaining in control of their professional practices. The study points to important relationships between pedagogy and technology and between the adoption of the innovation and teachers' beliefs and practices, suggesting ways in which teachers can empower themselves in the area of IT in ELT.

The final chapter in the collection, Chapter 18, examines innovation in assessment. Here, Chris Davison takes a close look at *Assessment for learning (AfL)*, a concept referring to any assessment in which the primary purpose of the information being collected is to improve learning (Black & Wiliam, 1998). Davison points out that despite the demonstrated learning gains that can be achieved through well-focused, teacher-based formative assessment in different contexts, the process of implementing such innovative assessment approaches in English language education can pose particular challenges. Drawing on data from a range of questionnaires, interviews with key stakeholders and teachers, and the analysis of policy documents collected as part of various studies she has conducted in Hong Kong, Singapore and

Brunei, Davison explores some of the common misunderstandings and conceptual confusions that arise in educational communities during the process of innovation. She also discusses the implications of the findings for assessment reform and professional development.

Readers will no doubt notice that innovations in second and foreign language education do not differ dramatically from innovations in other fields of education. They require the same sustained effort and support of those involved in devising, initiating and maintaining change as we find in other domains. Readers will also note, moreover, that it is teachers who are at the heart of this process as it is he or she who decides what will happen to initiatives. A sensitivity to teachers' concerns and beliefs and an awareness of local contexts are at the heart of many of the cases discussed above. This sensitivity marks the difference between successful transformations of practice and superficial adjustments to the status quo: it determines whether innovations result in change.

References

Black, P. and Wiliam, D. (1998). Assessment and classroom learning. *Assessment in Education*, 5 (1), 7–74.

Borg, S. (2006). *Teacher Cognition and Language Education*. London: Continuum.

Freeman, D. (2002). The hidden side of the work: Teacher knowledge and learning to teach. *Language Teaching*, 35(1), 1–14.

Kennedy, C. (1988). Evaluation of the management of change in ELT projects. *Applied Linguistics*, 9, 329–342.

Kennedy, C. (1996). *MA TEFL/TESL Open Learning Programme: ELT Management*. University of Birmingham: Centre for English Language Studies.

Lortie, D. (1975). *Schoolteacher: A Sociological Study*. Chicago: University of Chicago Press.

Morris, P. (1995). *The Hong Kong School Curriculum: Development, Issues and Policies*. Hong Kong: Hong Kong University Press.

Morris, P. (2002). Promoting curriculum reforms in the context of political transition: An analysis of Hong Kong's experience. *Journal of Education Policy*, 17(1), 13–28.

Richards, J. C. and Lockhart, C. (1994). *Reflective Teaching in Second Language Classrooms*. Cambridge: Cambridge University Press.

Rogers, E. (2003). *Diffusion of Innovations*, 5th edn. New York: Free Press.

Stoller, F. L. (1997). The catalyst for change and innovation. In M. A. Christison and F. Stoller (eds), *A Handbook for Language Program Administration. Alta Book Center*. West Provo, UT. (pp. 33–48).

Wallace, M. J. (1991). *Training Foreign Language Teachers: A Reflective Approach*. Cambridge: Cambridge University Press.

SECTION 1

Conceptions and contexts of innovation and change

2

MODELS OF CHANGE
AND INNOVATION

Chris Kennedy

The process of innovation occurs within social and cultural contexts situated in time and space, and models of innovation derive from these social development contexts. I have suggested elsewhere (Kennedy 2011) three categories of social development, the traditional, the contemporary and the emergent (Table 2.1). Each category influences the design of innovation models, and different types of education system, the didactic, the authentic and the transformative, can in turn be linked to the three categories of social development (Table 2.2). Thus, the traditional category and its educational corollary, the didactic, reflect a mechanistic view of social development and a teacher-controlled view of learning; the contemporary/authentic categories more communicative and autonomous approaches; and the emergent/ transformative categories view of society as inherently complex with a greater interest in micro-agency and collaboration.

Tables 2.1 and 2.2 represent generalisations and we should not automatically place societies or educational systems in any one category, since a society or institution will show characteristics in different domains spread over the categories. There is always a danger of 'a priori' classification and it is more valid in any analysis of social development to investigate from micro levels, working up the system to reveal the complexity of classification.

However, the content of such tables can be useful guides to any potential mismatches between an innovation and the socio-cultural or educational context in which it is to be introduced. If current practice indicates rational, centralised top-down processes (the Traditional stage A in Table 2.1) and an innovation has as its aim the promotion of collaborative participative micro-cultures (Emergent stage C) then when planning interventions, change agents have to consider strategies for bridging or minimising the gap between current practices and desired outcomes.

TABLE 2.1 Three stages of social development

Traditional – A	Contemporary – B	Emergent – C
rationalist economics	behavioural economics	knowledge society
rational	romantic	criticality
highly structured	neo-liberalism	distributed knowledge
top down	soft power	collaboration
centralisation	decentralisation	micro-agency
nationism/nationalism	globalisation	diversity
state power	localisation	public/private partnership
predictability	uncertainty	fuzziness/complexity
mass production 'Fordism'	choice/market-driven	mobility/flexibility
stratified society	less stratified society	multiple identities
collectivist cultures	individualism	participation

Adapted from Kalantzis and Cope (2008)

TABLE 2.2 Three types of educational system

Didactic	Authentic	Transformative
structural approaches	communicative approaches	task-based approaches
skills for the many – education for the few	transferable skills	variety of learning
institutions	institutions/off-site	new technologies
teacher control	learner autonomy	collaborative learners
transmission	interpretation	enquiry
book culture	book plus IT	greater variety of media
knowing that	knowing how	knowing why
defined role for teachers	greater teacher roles	teachers as educators catalysts agents
uniform learners	individuality	learner differences

Terms and categories from Kalantzis and Cope (2008)

Designers of models of change select from the several dimensions listed in Table 2.3 and ignore others, since each model serves to answer specific questions, such as what the attributes of the innovation are and what configurations will work (Havelock 1971); how change agents can promote change (Buchanan and Boddy 1992); what stages teachers go through in an innovation (Hord et al. 2004); how the innovation can be embedded (Rogers 1995); and how we can effect systemic change and create learning organisations (Senge 2006).

Models are generalisations and they are not specific to groups or individuals. They should be used with caution as guides and tools for action but not necessarily applied directly to a situation. No model can capture the reality and complexity of change, its messiness and its unpredictability and, since change is context-specific, models should only be developed and used in conjunction with ongoing fact-finding research.

I wish to consider three models of change as examples (adapted from Slater 1985). Their characteristics together cover many of the dimensions in Table 2.3 and go some way to providing answers to the questions raised above. Figure 2.1 illustrates the three models – the mechanistic, the ecological and the individual.

TABLE 2.3 Dimensions of change

scale – small or large
location – at micro; meso; macro levels
time span – short or long term

control – centralisation or decentralisation
strategies – coercive; rational; cognitive
top-down or bottom-up management

participants – stakeholders and agents and their roles
attitudes and beliefs
social norms
cost–benefit calculations

purpose
outcomes
effect – intake; uptake; sustainability; spread

type of change – incremental continuous discontinuous
complexity – convergent (single permanent solution)/divergent (multiple continuing solutions)

content – e.g. curriculum; methods and materials; teacher training and development

conditions necessary for change –
user-centred; ownership; acceptability (beliefs); relevance (needs and wants); feasibility; flexibility and trialability; communication

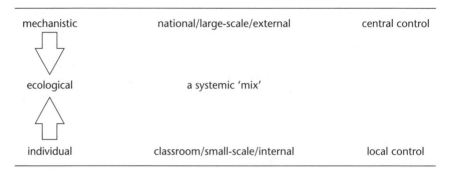

mechanistic	national/large-scale/external	central control
ecological	a systemic 'mix'	
individual	classroom/small-scale/internal	local control

FIGURE 2.1 Three models of change

The three models should be interpreted as a cline from macro national change at one end of the scale, to micro classroom-based change at the other; from large-scale to small-scale change; from external change to internal change led by teachers themselves; and from central to local control. The arrows indicate the likely direction of change, top-down in the case of mechanistic change, and a potential for bottom-up change in individual change.

Mechanistic change

Mechanistic change is a top-down approach based on hierarchical roles and functions, and introduces institutional change from the outside. Coercive strategies in the form of rules and regulations pass down decisions for implementation so that each level (e.g. government, ministry, curriculum centre, district education board, training colleges, schools, departments, principals, inspectors, teachers, learners and parents) is both implementing a policy made above it and making policy for implementation at the next level below. Much national curriculum change takes this form since it is a potentially effective way of ensuring implementation of a common national policy throughout a nation, at least in theory, if not in practice.

Those responsible for mechanistic change may regard curriculum renewal as a product to be implemented irrespective of context. In its more extreme version, curriculum outcomes in the form of materials and methodologies are presented to teachers as a pedagogic 'package' generally in the form of textbooks written within the Ministry or under Ministry guidelines. It is not difficult to get institutions to accept such packages (they have to) but it is less clear how the package is implemented in the classroom as there can be a mismatch between the originators of the curriculum outside the classroom and the teachers, the implementers (Chang 2007).

Such mismatches occur because the hierarchical nature of mechanistic change prevents maintenance of the linkages required at each level to ensure the original ideas and thinking behind the innovation are preserved when implementation faces the realities of the classroom. The mismatches are compounded if, using terms from Table 2.2, an innovation is attempting to move teachers from a didactic tradition towards an authentic or transformative system. The intervention may not take account of teachers' beliefs (acceptability), or their students' needs and wants (relevance) and as a consequence denies teachers ownership of the innovation (Prapaisit and Hardison 2009). In such instances, costs to teachers (emotional, intellectual and practical) may be higher than perceived benefits and the result will be resistance, subversion or simply indifference.

I have given some idea of the potential problems in the mechanistic model especially when the majority of curriculum decisions are taken outside the classroom by those who might be operating a different educational ideology from that of the teachers, and where the possibility of feedback from teachers is minimal.

This is not to say that there are no advantages to a mechanistic model. The authors of a report on the Middle East (World Bank 2008) suggest that any educational reform needs 'engineering', which is best undertaken centrally. Engineering would include the provision of physical and human resources, establishing a curriculum and teaching standards so that national criteria may be set, and providing finance and management so that resources are distributed equally across a national system. Hu (2005), drawing on case studies from China, demonstrates the resource disparities that can emerge between rural and urban schools if a national government is unable or unwilling to ensure an equal resources distribution, and how such contextual inequalities can adversely affect curriculum innovation.

The World Bank report's authors suggest, however, that engineering, though necessary, is not sufficient, and two further management strands are required: 'incentives' and 'public accountability'. Incentives, not always financial, are used for staff recognition and promotion to increase the motivation of principals and teachers. Central monitoring and evaluation systems should also be set up, not, however, as sanctions but as incentives for better performance. The third strand, public accountability, implies a relaxation of a strictly command-and-control model, since centralised systems should be more prepared to accept feedback from parents, teachers and learners on innovation policy and should increase the voice of these actors at national and local levels. Strand 1 (engineering) is relatively easy to undertake at government level; strands 2 (incentives) and 3 (public accountability) are more difficult to implement and are generally not popular with governments as they involve a lessening of central control.

Similar conclusions were drawn by Mourshed et al. (2010). Surveying educational change in 17 countries, the authors conclude that higher system performance occurs when the student learning experience improves. Schools achieve this by changing management structures to create more efficient operations and by providing greater resources for teaching. These actions are similar to the engineering strand mentioned above in the World Bank report, looking at change as a product. However, improving schools also change their curriculum processes to encourage better teaching and learning and ensure that their principals lead those processes. The first two strategies (changing management structures and providing resources) are mechanistic, and the third strategy (changing curriculum processes) is more behavioural and as a consequence more difficult to achieve.

The data appear to show that such interventions, the mechanistic and the behavioural, occur in all improving institutions, but the context dictates which take precedence and how they are implemented, whether by mandating or persuading. As schools improve over time, there is less requirement for mechanistic strategies. Teachers begin to take on more responsibilities and become more amenable to collaboration. In addition to improving student assessment, revising standards and changing the curriculum, recognising the work of teachers and principals and improving their remuneration structure is also important, an aspect often overlooked in the change literature. A similar questionnaire survey (OECD 2010) conducted in 24 countries with lower secondary teachers and principals, also highlighted the important role of principals, both pedagogic and managerial, especially in giving feedback to teachers, recognising their achievements and developing their skills.

I began this section of the chapter by describing mechanistic change and have shown that such a model has its benefits. However, the literature reviewed thus far has shown its limitations especially in its unmodified form. Control of an innovation cannot be left entirely at macro levels but must be pushed down at least to the level of educational institutions so that principals and teachers can be given more autonomy, creating a more hybrid form of action, involving the macro, but also the meso and micro levels, which I shall discuss later under the ecological model of change. What is also emerging is the fact that successful change is as much a behavioural process as an instrumental set of procedures and I should like now to turn to the change model at the other end of the cline from mechanistic change—individual change—before dealing with the third, ecological model.

Individual change

A model of individual change is centred around the classroom and the agents are teachers and learners acting locally and internally. Changes are smaller scale than national change though they are not insignificant as they may contribute to national change, and, as we have seen, the actors can influence the success of national interventions.

There are three possible types of change operating within the model. The first, already mentioned, has the classroom as the site for final implementation of a national reform. The freedom of teachers to innovate in this situation will be more or less limited depending on the amount of control from those higher up the system. The second type occurs when teachers innovate and their innovation is influential outside their own classroom. This may occur, for example, when a teacher innovation is spread throughout a school or, in the case of local school clusters, throughout a cluster area. It is rare for a teacher innovation to spread any further up the system to national level; that is to say, for bottom-up innovation to occur, though it can take place when a project, initially limited in scale, is replicated at national level. The third type remains at the level of individual classrooms where the intention is personal development. This latter type is familiar as a form of exploratory research (Allwright 2005), action learning (Aubusson et al. 2009), and action research (Burns 2010).

All three types of innovation belonging to the individual model involve some kind of micro-agency (see Emergent stage C in Table 2.1). The study of micro-agency in innovation is interested in what motivates teachers (and learners) to change, their reactions to change, and why some individuals change and others not. Models of behavioural change are useful to investigate these aspects and help to guide innovation planning. For example an analysis of behavioural characteristics might influence the type of strategies used to change an individual or a group, whether coercive, rational through informing and persuading, or cognitive strategies by engaging with deeper beliefs and attitudes.

Most behavioural models (Budge et al. 2009) contain the following factors: individuals' personal attitudes and beliefs, habits, emotions, previous experience, biases and knowledge; social relationships between the individuals and those they associate with or are influenced by (social norms); and local or more remote environmental factors. A model widely used in social psychology that has been used in education and ELT is Ajzen's theory of planned behaviour (Figure 2.2).

The model seeks to explain the influences behind intention which will lead to the desired behaviour (the innovation). It suggests three sets of beliefs which interact together to produce intention and action. Strength of beliefs about the outcomes of an action, together with a positive or negative

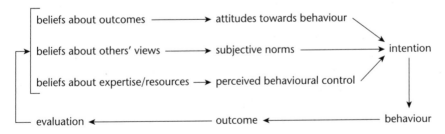

FIGURE 2.2 A theory of planned behaviour (Ajzen 1991)

evaluation of the outcomes, will lead to attitudes towards the behaviour. Beliefs about what influential others, such as peers, learners, parents, principals and officials, think of the behaviour will lead to positive or negative subjective norms and will influence intention. Finally, beliefs will influence the degree of behavioural control individuals perceive they have over an innovation. Behavioural control factors may be internal (teachers may believe they do not have the knowledge or the skills to implement an innovation) or external (factors such as examinations or provision of resources). Outcomes of any implemented behaviour will be evaluated by the individual and will feed back once more into the model. A fuller description of the model applied to ELT and education is given in Kennedy and Kennedy (1996), by D. Kennedy (1999) to explain trainees' differential take-up of a teacher-training programme and by Bullock (2011) who investigated teacher beliefs towards learner self-assessment.

The strength of the theory lies in its multi-dimensional nature and the combination of the three elements—attitudes, social norms and behavioural control—all three deriving from beliefs. It explains, for example, why a teacher with a positive attitude towards a new teaching methodology might nevertheless not implement it because social norms are strongly against it (perhaps peers do not agree with the methodology or a principal is critical of it) or the teacher feels more training is necessary or discipline will be problematic (negative perceived behavioural control). With circumspection, the theory can be used diagnostically to reveal where problems might lie in the design of an innovation, and steps can then be taken to solve the problems or accept them and re-design the innovation accordingly. It can also be used for evaluation purposes to establish reasons for success or failure of an innovation.

Investigating teachers' personal histories and narratives is another potentially fruitful methodology for researching micro-agency. Kiernan (2010) interviews both Japanese and Western teachers working in Japan about their personal and professional lives and how the perception of their multiple identities affects their teaching. Kalaja et al. (2008) provide a rich array of cross-national personal data to explain classroom behaviours and demonstrate effectively that there is much more than language 'going on' in language learning classrooms. Tsui (2007) explores the development of one Chinese teacher's identity over his six years of teaching in China and, although making no reference to Ajzen's theory (Ajzen 1991), demonstrates the powerful influence of social norms (particularly those of students and superiors) and behavioural control on the teacher's methods. Hayes (2010) similarly uses a case study of one teacher, a Tamil in Sri Lanka, to show why he became a teacher and how he survived in the classroom and in his community during the stress of the Sri Lankan civil war.

I have now introduced two of the three models of change: the mechanistic and the individual. They constitute two ends of a cline, the mechanistic model being top-down with innovation delivering a product, and the individual model concerned with processes and the influence of teacher behaviours and identities on classroom innovation. I should now like to introduce the third model of change, the ecological, looking at some alternative but complementary concepts of the model.

The ecological model

It is clear that both mechanistic and individual models of change have their advantages and I suggest an ecological model of change can build on these while minimising their disadvantages. Combining the advantages of the mechanistic approach with those of the individual approach produces a model whereby roles and functions in curriculum design and implementation are allocated throughout the levels of an educational system according to the skills and expertise of the participants. This is a strategy of deconcentration (Kennedy 1996; Turner 2002; Gershberg and Winkler 2004), devolving responsibilities to the most appropriate level of implementation, though not to the degree that classroom innovations will not have any impact on the system as a whole. In national systems, the general control over the curriculum may remain at the level of the Ministry but care is taken to preserve linkages between curriculum advisers and teachers to ensure a genuine process of feedback between teachers and designers from pre-formulation of plans to implementation and evaluation. The curriculum is designed around the local needs and wants of teachers and learners. Deconcentration is an attractive concept but not easy to implement, especially in highly centralised systems, as it demands capacities, expertise and resources that may not be located in educational institutions faced with an innovation.

There have, however, been successes, one being the Brazilian ESP Project, which was based on a form of deconcentration. The project began in 1980 and is now embedded in the Brazilian higher education system (Holmes and Celani, 2006). The problems of tertiary-level students requiring English in their studies were initially identified by the teachers and the project never lost this sense of local ownership. Support from the Ministry and from participating universities was crucial, although the development of the curriculum and associated professional activities were never under their control. These were the responsibility of the project advisers, the coordinators and the teachers themselves. A centralising force operated at the level of the local project director and the UK specialists funded by the British Government, but was never coercive. There was a strong professional development strand to the project to ensure that individual capacities were developed to respond to the deconcentration of project roles.

A related view of an ecological model uses a systems approach to innovation (Pascale 1990; Checkland 1999; Senge 2006). Such an approach accepts that change is complex and operates within systems and sub-systems of inter-related components which cannot be isolated. It is a synthetic rather than an analytic approach. Systems theory tells us that change is dynamic, non-linear, develops over time and can be chaotic and unpredictable. Small changes may have unexpected effects throughout the system. Systems are open and self-organising with patterns emerging as components interact and receive feedback. Senge (2006) sees a systems approach as being essential in developing a learning organisation, one which can adapt and change as the environment changes, but four additional dimensions are necessary – ongoing staff learning, commitment, shared understanding of processes and team learning.

Larsen-Freeman and Cameron (2008) have applied the principles of a systems approach to language education. Descriptions of its relevance to general English classrooms can be found in Kindt (2004) and van Lier (2004), and to teacher development in Tajino and Smith (2005), though its use in educational innovation has been limited, perhaps because its meta-processes and meta-language are not easy to grasp and are also somewhat similar to more familiar ethnographic approaches (Holliday 1990).

In many ways, the ecological model is the most complex to apply, especially at national levels of change, compared to mechanistic and individual models, yet it may be the most fruitful since, as a model, it approaches the reality of change more closely than the other models, though it still remains an abstraction.

Case study

The case study deals with an ESP Project carried out in the 1980s in Tunisia, from which we can still learn today as it highlights a number of the issues raised in my account of the three models of change. The description below draws on Kennedy (1987), Daoud (2007) and Labissi (2010), and reflects my two years with the project as the ESP Adviser (other advisers joined during the twelve-year life of the project).

Background

The Tunisian ESP Project, funded by a British aid agency (then the Overseas Development Agency), managed by the British Council and led by a KELT (Key English Language Teaching) officer recruited from UK, was planned to last for four years (subsequently extended) after which it would be managed and developed locally with Tunisian staffing and funding. Its objectives were the establishment of a national ESP Resources and Advisory Centre based at the Institut Bourguiba des Langues Vivantes (IBLV) in Tunis. The Centre would provide assistance on ESP methodology and materials design, and promote ESP training and development in the Tunisian ESP 'sections' or units, around 30 at the time, based in higher education institutes and faculties throughout the country, which serviced the English language needs of students in social sciences, engineering, sciences and medicine.

The context

At the time, Arabic was spreading into more domains of use in Tunisia (and continues to do so today), and English was gaining importance as an international language, with French remaining a major language for both internal and external purposes.

The educational system was highly centralised with top-down planning being the norm. A number of constraints were created as a result of educational policies which had to be accepted as there were no means by which they could be changed during the life of the project. Undergraduate students in higher education did not need English, except in a legal sense, to complete a degree. Needs were therefore deferred, and motivation as a consequence was not high. The ESP units suffered from low status and the teachers had little teacher training, no ESP training and a lack of ESP resources. ESP teachers were seconded from secondary schools. If they did gain further qualifications, they generally joined university English departments rather than remaining as ESP teachers, so there was no professional cadre of ESP teachers nor a career structure. Most teachers worked part time and needed to have more than one teaching post for financial reasons, and many were female with social and domestic demands on their time.

The Resources Centre was a national centre but located in a higher education institution in Tunis (the IBLV), while most ESP units were distributed around the country. Access to the Centre was therefore difficult for many ESP teachers and the psychological perception that the Resources Centre 'belonged' to one institution rather than to all ESP teachers was difficult to dislodge. Even this brief description reveals the number of interconnecting components and the value of using a systems approach to appreciate the complexity of the context.

Implementation

Although the Ministry did not play a direct role in the management of the project, a strategy was adopted to brief Ministry officials and university Deans through personal visits and short reports. Positive support from superiors was important. A note from the Minister of Higher Education recommending the project in the first edition of the Tunisian ESP (TESP) Newsletter (see below) increased teachers' willingness to take part in the project, confirming the importance of Ajzen's social norms (1991), and showing how in systems theory effects can be achieved out of proportion to a cause.

Aspects of the project adopted a rational approach to change, using devices such as the creation of the TESP Newsletter to raise awareness and increase knowledge of the project nationally, and to create an ESP teacher identity. Regular seminars were held throughout the country with topics generated by participants as part of this rational approach to change. Visits to ESP units explaining the project were made and further meetings took place at the request of teachers who also decided the purpose and format of the visit: to create a sense of ownership and ensure that advice and assistance with materials and methodology responded to local needs identified by local participants. The emphasis was on problem-solving and collaborative work with the external adviser acting as a facilitator.

One particular group of teachers declared an interest in more than periodic advice and assistance. The ESP unit concerned was based in a business institute in Tunis, and the head of the unit had identified a need for English language materials development, an EAP situation, with second year undergraduate business students. She wanted an alternative approach to the current 'explication de texte', which was product-based and reliant on vocabulary explanation and practice, and which gave no training to the students in the reading strategies needed for their present or postgraduate studies or their future professional careers. Meetings were held regularly with the group of teachers responsible for the second year teaching and interested in developing new materials, though attendance was not always regular because of the constraints on teacher time mentioned above.

Two objectives emerged at this point. The first was the immediate need for the teachers to produce materials; the second was a project objective to develop the teachers and expose them to alternative ESP and EAP approaches. The intention was to develop the second general objective through the first specific one. A cognitive problem-solving approach was taken using action learning with practice driving the need for theory. Gaps in knowledge were filled by discussion and readings in the relevant area provided by the adviser until a decision was made to proceed. For example, the decision to implement a discourse approach to reading generated the need to develop skills in text analysis. This in turn prompted discussions on the applications of text analysis to materials design, leading to experimentation with different types of materials and exercises which were then piloted, evaluated and revised. Theory and practice were not tackled in linear fashion and theory was only introduced when the results of practice demanded it.

Decisions were never imposed but were reached as a result of negotiation. There was considerable discussion among the teachers of their current beliefs and attitudes (see the Didactic column in Table 2.2) and the contrast with different ideas on learning and teaching that were being presented, but not imposed, by the adviser (operating in the Authentic framework in Table 2.2). The process was one of collaboration and learning to produce the best solution for the teachers and the students in the local context. A course was finally produced and taught, and later, two of the teachers approached a publisher who agreed to publish the materials.

Reflection

Using a rational approach providing information to teachers through regular visits, the newsletter, seminars and the Resources Centre was successful, though how the information was used was not investigated. In terms of sustainability, this aspect of the project worked well since the Resources Centre still exists as part of a university department in Tunis, with 600 members (Daoud 2000).

The Business English materials project was successful as a local innovation and the materials were eventually published. As a teacher development programme in the particular institution, the project worked well. Its success, using Ajzen's model (1991) must be accounted for partly through the use of a cognitive approach which changed teachers' attitudes to current practice and created positive beliefs about the new approaches. These positive beliefs and attitudes were strong enough to overcome problems of time and external commitments (potential negative behavioural control). The opportunities the teachers had to trial and adapt the new materials also overcame behavioural control perceptions including concerns that students would reject the new approach, which in fact they welcomed. Care had been taken to involve students closely in the innovation from its inception, collecting feedback from them and, crucially, acting on it. Social norms also operated positively. The Director gave his moral and political support and the head of the ESP unit showed considerable leadership of the teachers to encourage their support of the innovation.

With other groups, teachers' perceptions of behavioural control and their beliefs and attitudes about present and new approaches appeared to hinder their participation in materials developments. However, the ESP project, though national, was small-scale with limited resources. There was one UK adviser and no Tunisian local leadership till much later in the project and no doubt had it been scaled-up by providing more advisers, more could have been achieved.

The systemic constraints listed previously at the beginning of this case study section had a negative effect and, were these to change, the Tunisian ESP situation would be very different and a project such as that described here would be easier to implement. Such changes, however, cannot be implemented successfully without taking account of effects on other parts of the system. As an example, in 1996, the Tunisian Ministry mandated that all students in higher education should take English, a large expansion in ESP provision. In principle, this could be seen as a positive move for the development of ESP in Tunisia, but, in order to resource the development, the Ministry advised that existing ESP teachers should increase their teaching load by 50 per cent and that Deans should hire more part-time teachers (Daoud 2000), effectively neutralising any potential benefits of the new policy for the local ESP community.

Conclusion

The case study has demonstrated that change takes place within a complex system and that a mix of mechanistic and individual change, an ecological approach, is generally preferable. Such an approach has similar characteristics to those described by Parker and Parker (2007). It is person-centred, considers users' needs, identifies problems rather than rushing to solutions, and does not rely on top-down mechanistic models but is a process that works towards interaction between participants at all levels.

Key readings

Hargreaves, A. and M. Fullan (eds) (2008). *Change Wars*. Bloomington: Solution Tree. This is a collection of essays from experts in educational innovation, covering systems, organisational change, school management, teacher professionalism and leadership.

Tribble, C. (ed.) (2012). *Managing Change in English Language Teaching*. London: British Council. Four overview essays on issues in ELT change management are provided in this collection together with summaries of 21 projects from 18 countries, dealing with policy and design, implementation, evaluation and dissemination.

References

Ajzen, I. (1991). *Attitudes, Personality and Behaviour*. Milton Keynes: Open University Press.

Allwright, D. (2005). Developing principles for practitioner research: the case of exploratory practice. *Modern Language Journal* 89: 355–366.

Aubusson, P., R. Ewing and G. Hoban. (2009). *Action Learning in Schools*. London: Routledge.

Buchanan, D. and D. Boddy. (1992). *The Expertise of the Change Agent*. Hemel Hempstead: Prentice Hall.

Budge, M., C. Deahl, M. Dewhurst, S. Donajgrodzki and F. Wood. (2009). *Communications and Behaviour Change*. London: Central Office of Information.

Bullock, D. (2011). Learner self-assessment. *English Language Teaching Journal* 65(2): 114–125.

Burns, A. (2010). *Doing Action Research in English Language Teaching: A Guide for Practitioners*. New York: Routledge.

Chang, K. (2007). Innovation in primary English language teaching and management of change. *Primary Innovations Regional Seminar*. Hanoi: British Council: 61–66.

Checkland, P. (1999). *Systems Thinking, Systems Practice*. Chichester: Wiley.

Daoud, M. (2000). LSP in North Africa. *Annual Review of Applied Linguistics* 20: 77–96.

Daoud, M. (2007). The language situation in Tunisia. In R. Kaplan and R Baldauf (eds) *Language Planning and Policy in Africa*. Bristol: Multilingual Matters 2, 256–302.

Gershberg, A. and D. Winkler. (2004). Education decentralisation in Africa. In B. Levy and S. Kpundeh (eds) *Building State Capacity in Africa* Washington: World Bank Institute, 325–356.

Havelock, R. (1971). *Planning Innovation through Dissemination and Utilisation of Knowledge*. Ann Arbor: University of Michigan.

Hayes, D. (2010). Duty and service: life and career of a Tamil teacher of English in Sri Lanka. *TESOL Quarterly* 44(1): 58–83.

Holliday, A. (1990). A role for soft systems methodology in ELT projects. *System* 18(1): 77–84.

Holmes, J. and M. Celani. (2006). Sustainability and local knowledge: the case of the Brazilian ESP Project 1980–2005. *English for Specific Purposes* 25(1): 109–122.

Hord, S., W. Rutherford, L. Huling and G. Hall. (2004). *Taking Charge of Change.* Austin, Texas: SEDL.

Hu, G. (2005). Contextual influences on instructional practices. *TESOL Quarterly* 39(4): 635–661.

Kalaja, P., V. Menezes and A. Barcelos (eds) (2008). *Narratives of Learning and Teaching EFL.* London: Palgrave Macmillan.

Kalantzis, M. and B. Cope (2008). *New Learning.* Cambridge: Cambridge University Press.

Kennedy, C. (1987). Innovating for a change – teacher development and innovation. *English Language Teaching Journal* 41(3): 163–170.

Kennedy, C. (1996). Teacher roles in curriculum reform. *ELTED Journal* 2(1): 77–89.

Kennedy, C. (2011). Challenges for language policy, language and development. In H.Coleman (ed.), *Dreams and Realities; Developing Countries and the English Language.* London: British Council, 24–38.

Kennedy, C. and J. Kennedy. (1996). Teacher attitudes and change implementation. *System* 24(3): 351–360.

Kennedy, D. (1999). The foreign trainer as change agent and implications for teacher education programmes in China. In C. Kennedy, P. Doyle and C. Goh (eds) *Exploring Change in ELT.* Oxford: Macmillan Heinemann, 29–37.

Kiernan, P. (2010). *Narrative Identity in ELT.* London: Palgrave Macmillan.

Kindt, D. (2004). *An Emergent View of Course Design.* PhD thesis, University of Birmingham, UK.

Labassi, T. (2010). Two ESP projects under the test of time: the case of Brazil and Tunisia. *English for Specific Purposes* 29: 19–29.

Larsen-Freeman, D. and L. Cameron. (2008). *Complex Systems and Applied Linguistics.* Oxford: Oxford University Press.

Mourshed, M., C. Chijioke and M. Barber (2010). *How the World's Most Improved School Systems Keep Getting Better.* London: McKinsey.

OECD. (2010). *Teaching and Learning International Survey.* Paris: OECD.

Parker, S. and S. Parker (eds) (2007). *Unlocking Innovation.* London: Demos.

Pascale, R. (1990). *Managing on the Edge.* London: Penguin Books.

Prapaisit de Segovia, L. and D. Hardison. (2009). Implementing education reform: EFL teachers' perspectives. *ELT Journal* 63(2): 154–162.

Rogers, E. (1995). *Diffusion of Innovations.* New York: Free Press.

Senge, P. (2006). *The Fifth Discipline.* London: Random House.

Slater, D. (1985). The management of change. In M. Hughes, P. Ribbins and H. Thomas (eds) *Managing Education.* London: Cassell, 445–468.

Tajino, A. and C. Smith. (2005). Exploratory practice and soft systems methodology. *Language Teaching Research* 9(4): 448–469.

Tsui, A. (2007). Complexities of identity formation: a narrative inquiry of an EFL teacher. *TESOL Quarterly* 41(4): 657–680.

Turner, M. (2002). Whatever happened to deconcentration? Recent initiatives in Cambodia. *Public Administration and Development* 22(4): 353–364.

van Lier, L. (2004). *The Ecology and Semiotics of Language Learning: A Sociocultural Perspective.* Boston: Kluwer.

World Bank. (2008). *The Road Not Travelled; Education Reform in the Middle East and Africa.* Washington:World Bank.

3

CONTEXTS OF CHANGE

Numa Markee

Introduction

When the editors of this volume contacted potential contributors, they asked us to document, if at all possible, an example of a successful innovation. Given what we know about how difficult it is to make change happen (see Waters, 2009), I am loath to make any overblown claims of success with respect to the innovation I analyze in this chapter (an ESP course on energy systems for Italian undergraduate engineering students that I designed and (co)taught at an American university from 2006 to 2008). However, based on the results of three evaluations over three years of students that indicate high levels of satisfaction with the course, I pronounce this innovation to have been successful, at least for the moment. This tactic is actually an artful ploy for subsequently problematizing this claim in the Reflections and Conclusions section of this chapter.

Contexts of change

I now continue with some brief pre-analytic reflections on *context*, which constitutes one of the key words of my title. Within the innovation literature in TESOL, the idea that *context* is a multi-layered phenomenon is particularly widespread. For example, C. Kennedy (1988) has proposed a model of context in which he asserts that (in descending order of importance) cultural, political, administrative, educational and institutional factors all affect the possibility of classroom innovation. More specifically, Kennedy argues that cultural factors are the most important drivers of change, and thus strongly influence the hierarchically lower levels of political and administrative factors. In turn, these factors shape educational and institutional factors, which finally *determine* what may or may not licitly happen in individual classrooms.

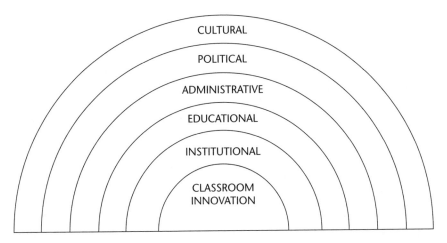

FIGURE 3.1 The hierarchy of interrelating subsystems in which an innovation has to operate

This model has been extremely influential. For example, it provides the analytic framework for answering the 'Where' question in my own 'Who adopts what, where, when, why and how?' model of curricular innovation (Markee, 1997), and, 12 years later, it still figures prominently in the state of the art review article on managing innovation in TESOL by Waters (2009). However, like all good models, Kennedy's model has been subject to criticism. For example, in Markee (1997), I pointed out that the model was surely incomplete, as it says nothing about either economic or demographic factors. At the time, the thrust of this criticism was to encourage researchers and practitioners to develop more complete models of context. In other words, I was arguing we needed *more* layers of context. Now, however, in light of my current work in conversation analysis (CA: see Markee, 2000), I prefer to ask two rather different questions about such models, *including* the one that I used in my 1997 book. First, what *empirical* evidence is there to support the *theoretical* claim that culture is the most important layer of context to consider as we try to effect change? Note that in order to demonstrate this hypothesis, we would need to use an experimental research paradigm, which is a rare bird indeed in the TESOL innovation literature (but see Stoller, 1994). Second, even if we ever agreed on a complete, hierarchically organized list of contextual layers (which I rather doubt will ever happen), how can we show *empirically* that participants are actually paying attention to *any, some,* or *all* of these different layers of context in the (usually unnoticed) micro-details of everyday talk-in-interaction? Notice, in contrast, that this kind of question requires the use of a qualitative approach to research.

Waters (2009) quite rightly points out that Kennedy's original model has changed in a number of ways (see, for example, C. Kennedy & J. Kennedy,

1996, and J. Kennedy & C. Kennedy, 1998). For present purposes, the call in the second publication just cited for an *emic* (that is, participant-relevant) approach that complements the more traditionally *etic* (that is, researcher-centric) perspectives that underlie C. Kennedy's initial model are particularly welcome. The ethnographic work of Holliday (1994) and, more recently, the ethnographies of change provided by some of the contributors to the special issue edited by Adams and Newton (2009) attest to the value of adopting such a perspective on curricular change. Furthermore, J. Kennedy and C. Kennedy (1998) make two intriguing, but fleeting, references to *ethnomethodology*, which is also firmly entrenched in the emic ontological and epistemological camp (Markee and Kasper, 2004). I therefore propose to show in this chapter what the adoption of an ethnomethodological approach to analyzing curricular innovation looks like. In so doing, I will invoke a radical respecification of context, which even ethnographically trained readers may well find strange, not to say downright disconcerting. I address these issues in the next section.

Contextualising context

As I have already hinted in the previous section, defining what context means is a controversial undertaking. It may even be an unattainable goal (Goodwin and Duranti, 1992). Here, I largely limit myself to discussing how context has been understood within ethnomethodology. As I note in Markee (2011:603–604; see also Roger & Bull, 1988:3), ethnomethodology (EM) is a radical form of sociology founded by Garfinkel (1967). EM seeks to develop member-relevant (i.e., emic) analyses of how people engaged in everyday actions co-construct common-sense understandings of what it is that they are doing at any particular moment in time, and how they incorporate these analyses into observable courses of action such as announcing, complaining or requesting, etc. The most well-known offshoot of EM is CA, which analyzes how members orient to the turn-taking, repair and sequence organization practices that constitute the underlying 'machinery' that organizes real-time talk-in-interaction (a notion which subsumes both ordinary conversation and institutional talk: see Schegloff, 1987). Thus, whereas for ethnographers and anthropologists context is typically a broad construct (Gumperz, 1992; Gumperz & Hymes, 1972; Hymes, 1974; Schiefffelin & Ochs, 1986; Watson-Gegeo, 1988, 2004), for conversation analysts, context is a narrow, technically specified practice. More specifically, the context of talk is talk itself.

Following Heritage (1988), talk in-interaction is both *context shaped* and *context renewing*. That is, talk-in-interaction is context shaped in the sense that the meaning of a current speaker's turn is understandable only by referring to what the previous speaker has just said in previous turn and in terms of the work that the speakers are currently doing to achieve a particular course of action, such as doing an invitation sequence. At the same time, talk is context renewing, in that a speaker's current turn also provides a relevant context for the next speaker's interpretation of what action is relevantly due in next turn. In other words, 'modes of interactional organization [i.e., turn-taking, repair, and sequence organization] might themselves be treated as contexts' (Schegloff, 1987: 221; clarification in square brackets provided by the author).

Not surprisingly, this very local version of context has been subjected to intense criticism (see, for example, Cicourel, 1992, Moerman, 1988, and Young, 2009, among others). However, apart from the minor accommodation suggested by Schegloff (1992), who argues that appealing to exogenous (that is, talk-external) context is analytically permissible only when *speakers themselves* observably invoke other layers of context to display to each other (and thus to analysts) what they understand to be happening at a given moment in a given conversation, conversation analysts who work with ordinary conversation have by and large stuck to their methodological guns on this issue on strictly empirical grounds (see, for example Schegloff, 1987, 1991, 1992). Maynard (2003) suggests that the analysis of institutional talk (such as classroom interaction) may benefit from a brief ethnographic introduction that sets the general stage for the main CA event (see for example Heritage & Sefi, 1992). But as Maynard goes on to say, the fundamental question that ethnographic approaches to formulating context have so far been unable to answer is 'why that now?' (Schegloff & Sacks, 1973). So, for example, the question that I asked earlier concerning C. Kennedy's (1988) model of context—namely, 'how can we show *empirically* that participants are actually paying attention to *any*, *some*, or *all* of these different layers of context in the (usually unnoticed) micro-details of everyday talk-in-interaction?—is a prototypical example of how context is formulated in ethnomethodological CA. Let us now see how these ideas actually work.

Data used in the case study

The data I analyze in the next section consist of the first task from a unit on fossil energy, which forms part of an ESP course that provided academic and language support for an engineering course on energy systems that I designed and co-taught in 2006 (i.e., the 'successful' innovative project on iterative curriculum design, implementation, and evaluation that I mentioned in the Introduction to this chapter). Each of the first three units was based on the following template of tasks: Prediction; Reading and Evaluating Source Content; and Discussion and Assessment. The readings for the materials were taken from the engineering course and were delivered online (see Figure 3.2).

After Unit 1 had been taught, it became clear to the instructor and me that the students did not understand the purpose of the prediction task shown above. They always tried to find the answers to the questions above by reading the hyperlinked materials first, which was only supposed to happen during

Unit 3
Fossil Energy

[Oil, Coal and Gas]
[Advanced Coal Technologies]
[Advanced Oil Technologies]
[Coal Gasification and Liquefaction]

Prediction

1. Group work

• Using your own knowledge, how would you answer the following
three questions:

i. What are fossil fuels?
ii. How are they extracted?
iii. How are they refined?

1. Summarize your discussions on the Discussion Board.

FIGURE 3.2 Prediction task from Unit 3 of NPRE 201 English support course

the Reading and Evaluating Source Content phase of the unit. The following
Learning Hint was therefore added to Unit 2:

> Learning Hint: Prediction tasks are useful because they get you to think
> about what you already know about a topic. So when you read or listen
> to information on this topic, you will already be primed to read or listen
> for certain types of information in the text. This not only makes
> *processing* the information easier, it also provides you with a means of
> subsequently *evaluating* what you *already knew* and what you *have
> learned* from the text after you have read it. You will be asked to evaluate
> your predictions in R and E 2.

So far, I have documented how the prediction task changed over two weeks
at the level of materials design. However, despite these changes, it became
clear from videotaped interactions between the instructor and the students
(not shown here) that occurred during the implementation of Unit 2 that the
majority of students were still not doing the prediction task well, if at all.
Thus, when I taught Unit 3, I was particularly concerned to find out how the
students accomplished this task. I therefore decided to use CA to analyze
how participants interpreted the written versions of tasks-as-work-plans
shown above and transformed them into tasks-as-social-activity (Coughlan &
Duff, 1994). In other words, I decided to discover *empirically* whether, and
if so how, participants were actually paying attention to *any, some,* or *all* of
these changes at the level of materials design in the micro-details of their talk.

Finally, let me say a brief word about the three fragments of talk that I
analyze below. Fragment 1 exhibits the instructions that the instructor (that

is, me) gave to the whole class before they began to do Unit 3. As we will see shortly, these instructions focus on how to do the prediction task. In Fragments 2 and 3, we can observe the extent to which the students in Group 2 actually fulfill the instructor's expectations, and also the extent to which they pay attention to the instructor's injunction not to use Italian. This group has been selected for analysis because it splits into two dyads. The observational evidence available suggests that this split occurred because, just as the task was about to start, one of the students had to reboot her computer. At that moment, the instructor told the group to divide into two pairs, perhaps in an effort to minimize the delay that the rebooting process would have caused to the entire group. In any case, this happenstance sets up two naturally occurring, simultaneous conversational contexts, which allow us to observe how these two pairs achieve the same task-as-work-plan as thematically related, but nonetheless observably different, social activity.

Analysis of transcripts as micro contexts of change

In Fragment 1 below, the instructor is giving oral instructions to the whole class about how he expects the students to work through Unit 3. The unit is being projected onto the screen at the front of the classroom, and many of the students have the same material up on the screens of their own computers. All the participants are therefore clearly orienting to these talk-external cultural artifacts (that is, the materials design layer of contextually situated change), which gives the analyst the kind of empirical warrant that is needed to include the task-as-work-plan in the analysis that now follows.

Fragment 1: Teacher's instructions

```
429 Numa(T):   ok. (.) so:, we're going to be
430            <using, (.) the same:, (0.4) .hh
431            sequence of (.) ta:sks.> (.)
432            ok?=we are going to start off,
433  →         (0.3) by, (0.2) making some
434  →         predictions:? (0.2) .hhh you're
435            ↑then going to:, (.) read some:
436            (0.4) some materials, that (.)
437            that (.) u:hm (0.5) uh ↓will (.)
438  →         ↑amplify what your predictions
439  →         ↑are.=we- (0.2) we com↑PA:re
440  →         (0.2) what you: (0.2) ↓predicted
441            and what (0.2) is (.) in: (0.2)
442            the materials, (0.3) same as
443            before. (0.2) ok? .hhh so:,
444            (0.2) u:hm (0.2) if you can::,
```

```
445 →          (2.2) start off:, (2.5) with the
446 →          prediction? (0.3) ok? (0.3) a:nd,
447 →          (0.3) ↑this=is what i want you
448 →          to: (0.2) to predict. (0.7) ok?
449 →          (0.4) how (.) how they are going
450 →          to:: (.) define these, (0.4)
451 →          these things. (0.9) alright? .hhh
452            so::, (.) can we:: (.) ↑do
453            ↓that,=in about (0.3) ↑five (.)
454            ↓minutes:.
```

We can see that the way in which these instructions are produced is highly organized. For example, the mode of delivery throughout this fragment is generally slow and deliberate (the entire fragment lasts for 59 seconds). Furthermore, this spate of talk is punctuated throughout with many pauses, sound stretches, cut offs and exaggeratedly high or low patterns of intonations. All these repair tokens, which break down the flow of speech, are typical of teacher talk. In terms of context, note also how the instructor explains to the students how to do prediction by emphasizing twice that they have had previous experience of doing the same kind of task before, in Units 1 and 2 (see lines 429–431 and 442–443). Furthermore, in the arrowed turns in lines 433–434, 438–440, and 445–451, the instructor tells the students to predict the content of the reading on the basis of whatever *technical knowledge about fossil fuels* that the students already possess. He achieves this action by using the pronouns '↑this' in line 447 and 'these, (0.4) these things.' in lines 450 and 451, which deictically refer to the three written prediction questions in the materials.

Let us now analyze how Pair 1 and Pair 2 set about following these and other instructions. I begin with Pair 1's talk, which is exhibited in Fragment 2 below.

Fragment 2: Pair 1

```
1               (1.6)((Numa approaches Pair 1))
2     NUMA(T):  °ok. (0.4) try-° (0.2) try and
3               do this in english and no
4               (italian.) (0.3) ok? (0.7) speak
5               as much english as you can. (0.3)
6               alright?
7               (0.7)
8     GIANNI:   (of course.) (0.6) i don't know:,
9               (0.7)
10              it's (better) probably if we:
11              (0.2) ((unintelligible)) (↓them
```

12		↑a::ll,)
13		(0.8)
14		(how) (0.3) (are) fossil fuels
15		formed,
16		(2.0)
17		°ok.°
18		(0.4)
19		coal,
20		(0.5)
21	ANNA:	co[al,]
22	GIANNI:	[oil,]
23		(0.3)
24	GIANNI:	[°and gas.°]
25	ANNA:	[oil,] (.) a:nd (.)
26		(g[as?)]
27	GIANNI:	[(oil] and gas.)/[(all] i guess.)
28		(1.1)
29	GIANNI:	°ok.° (0.2) u::[::h,]
30	ANNA:	[how are] they
31		ex↑trac↓ted.
32		(3.4 + [-----)]
33		[(((Gianni points at Anna)]
34	ANNA:	>°i don't know.°<
35		(1.4)
36	GIANNI:	how are they extracted.
37		(9.3)
38	ANNA:	↑coal=u::h, (0.8) *miniera,*
39		(1.5)
40	GIANNI:	°mine.° (0.9) *miniera è* <u>mine</u>.
41		(0.8)
42	ANNA:	°mine?°
43		(0.5)
44	GIANNI:	coal? (0.2) from mines.
45		(0.2)
46	ANNA:	a-↑ha.
47		(0.3)
48	GIANNI:	uhm. (.) (right.)
49		(0.2)
50	ANNA:	i think,
51		(0.6)
52	GIANNI:	°of course.°
53		(0.4)
54	GIANNI:	you're <u>right</u>.
55		(0.3)

```
56   GIANNI:   right. .hhh (0.5) u:hm,=
57   ANNA:     =o:il=[ u::]:h,
58   GIANNI:          [oil?]
59             (3.7)
60   GIANNI:   from the:: (1.1) i'd say (.) from
61             the:: (0.7) ((unintelligible))
62             (0.8) ((unintelligible))=
63   ANNA:     =ok.
64             (0.2)
65   GIANNI:   °i don't know.° (1.0) a:nd=u:h
66             (.) [in the ↑SEa] ↓o:r,
67   ANNA:         [natural  ]
68             (1.0)
69   GIANNI:   from below the ↑se[a, ]
70   ANNA:                       [sì.]
71             (1.1)
72   GIANNI:   o:r (0.5) (or) (.) othe:r, (0.8)
73             (place.)
74             (1.7)
75   ANNA:     and natural ↑gas=u::h,=
76   GIANNI:   =natural gas, (0.4) u:hm,
77             (4.3)
78   GIANNI:   °i don't know. (.) i don't know
79             anything about [(na]tural)° ↑gas.
80   ANNA:                    [eh.]
81             (1.0)
82   GIANNI:   u::h,
83             (0.4)
84   ANNA:     eh. (.) me [too.               ]
85                        [(((Anna points at Gianni))]
86             (2.6)
87   ANNA:     e:: (.) how are they, (0.2)
88             °refined?°
89   GIANNI:   how are they refined.
90             (0.7)
91   ANNA:     refined?
92   GIANNI:   raffinati.
```

More specifically, in lines 2–6 of Fragment 2, we can see that the instructor tells the students in Pair 1 to use English as much as possible. The video and transcript show that Gianni and Anna (the names of the students in both pairs are pseudonyms) try to conduct their prediction talk in English, despite the fact that Anna has demonstrably limited proficiency in English. More specifically, Anna never utters more than a few words or vocalizations in

English at a time. Furthermore, in lines 38–46 and 89–92, we can see that the two participants co-construct a translation methodology on the English words 'mine' and 'refined', respectively.

Note particularly, in line 38, Anna produces the turn '↑coal=u::h, (0.8) *miniera,*'. Notice that both the English and Italian words are produced with rising intonation. Furthermore, the rush through and the 0.8 second pause in this turn indicate that a first position repair is underway. After a silence of 1.5 seconds in line 39, Gianni interprets this talk as a translation request, which he honors in line 40 by saying '°mine.° (0.9) *miniera è* mine.' After a pause of 0.8 seconds in line 41, Anna repeats the word '°mine?°' with reduced volume and high rising intonation. Another pause of 0.5 seconds ensues in line 43, and in line 44 Gianni then repeats the link between 'coal' and 'mines' that Anna had first raised in line 38. Finally, after a shorter pause of 0.2 seconds in line 45, Anna makes a claim of understanding in line 46 by saying 'a-↑ha.' Similarly, in line 89, Gianni quotes the prediction question 'how are they refined.' After a pause of 0.7 seconds in line 90, Anna initiates a second position repair in line 91 by saying '*raffinati?*' with high rising intonation, which Gianni then immediately translates into Italian by saying 'refined?' in line 92. Consequently, Gianni has to carry most of the load of the prediction work exhibited in this fragment (see, for example, lines 8–20). However, this does not mean that Anna does not contribute to the prediction work, or that she gets nothing out of the interaction. For example, in lines 30–31, she reads out loud the second prediction question 'how are they ex↑trac↓ted.' Similarly, in lines 87–88, she reads out the third question 'e:: (.) how are they, (0.2) °refined?°' These two turns have the effect of moving the conversation forward.

In terms of our ongoing discussion of context, it is empirically noticeable that these two participants do not try to read the source readings prematurely. Furthermore, it is methodologically important to note that, from a CA perspective, the fact that Anna and Gianni both speak Italian only becomes procedurally relevant to the analysis I have just outlined when they engage in the two translation sequences I have just analyzed above. The fact that they share the same language is not relevant a priori to this analysis, as it would be in many ethnographic analyses of such data.

Let us now see how Pair 2 fares in Fragment 3, which, as I have already noted, occurs simultaneously with Pair 1's oral activity in Fragment 2.

Fragment 3: Pair 2

```
01    GIADA:    (what ↑are) (0.2) fossil fuels? ((reading))
02              (0.8)
03    MARIA:    fossil ↑fu↓els (.) a::re, (1.0)
04              fuels that ↑co:me, (0.2)
05              ↓fro::m:, (0.4)
```

```
06                    transfor↑ma↓tio:n:, (0.7)
07                    ↑chemi↓ca::l,
08    GIADA?:         yeah.
09    MARIA:          transformation,=that occu:rs
10                    undernea:th the ↑ground. (0.6) in
11                    hundreds and hundreds of ↑years.
12    GIADA:          hh hu hu. (0.6) wow! hh
13                    (0.7)
14    MARIA:          yeah. .hhh (0.4) (eh=a=u:::h)
15                    (0.5) and they ↑a:re,
16                    (0.2)
17    GIADA:          (right.)=
18    MARIA:          =but ↑oil
19    GIADA:          oil, (0.4) coal,
20                    (0.5)
21    MARIA:          coal,
22                    (1.0)
23    MARIA:          u:::h, (0.7) ↑torba,=hh he he
24    GIADA:          tor(h) hh hu
25                    (2.8)
26    MARIA:          ↑i don't ↓know (like.)=we can
27                    ↓try (.) ↑u:hm.
28                    (0.4)
29    ?              (       là.)
30                    (.)
31    MARIA:          [ah! wikipedia.                        ]
32                    [((Maria points toward Giada's screen))]
33                    (0.3)
34    ?              mh.
35    GIADA:          yeah.=
36    MARIA:          =AH! hydrocarbons. (i)t's right.
37                    (0.4) °hydrocarbons.°
38                    (1.2)
39    MARIA:          ↑formed from (.) the re↑mains ↓of
40                    dead plants and animals. (0.8)
41                    yeah. (2.4) these are sometimes
42                    ↑known instead as ↓mineral
43                    [fuels.                       ] ((reading))
44    NUMA(T):        [((Numa clears his throat)) ok.] (.)
45                    remember you're pre↑dicting.=so:
46                    i don't want you to read
47                    sources.=
48    GIADA:          =i'm sorry.
49    NUMA(T):        ok?
```

```
50                (0.8)
51    GIADA:      because (.) i don't know (.)
52                anything (.) about this.

.

.

.

74    MARIA:      we dig. (0.4) we dig mines, (0.2)
75                °yeah.° (0.4) dig.=
76    GIADA:      =°dig?°
77    MARIA:      dig means (.) [fu fu (0.2)fu          ]
78                [Maria makes a digging]
79                [motion with her hands]
80                [fu  ]
81    GIADA:      [AH!] hu hu hu scaↄvare,
82                (0.3)
83    MARIA:      sca↗vare.=
84    GIADA:      =i under↑stand.
85                (0.5)
86    GIADA:      it's clear.
87    MARIA:      ok.
88    GIADA:?     hhhu hu hu
89    MARIA:      A::nd,
90                (1.1)
91    MARIA:      how are [they (re)f]ined?=u:h,
92    GIADA:              [°ho:w,°  ]
93    MARIA:      refined?=u:h,
94                (0.3)
95    MARIA:      ah. (.) raffinati.
96                (0.2)
97    GIADA:      eh.=
98    MARIA:      =o:h!
99    GIADA:      u-h[u. ]
100   MARIA:         [oh.] EAsy.=
101   GIADA:      =hhh oh. (0.3) hu hu °yeah.° (.)
```

In line 01, Giada reads the first question of the materials, to which Maria develops a seemingly well-informed answer in lines 03–17 on the basis of her pre-existing knowledge about fossil fuels. In lines 18–19, Maria then moves on to the more specific topics of coal and gas. At first blush, this talk seems to be consistent with the teacher's instructions in Fragment 1 on how to do prediction tasks. However, visual evidence from the video shows that, as Maria's computer was booting up prior to the start of Fragment 3, Giada had filled the long silence that had ensued by surfing the Web. It turns out that the page that Giada had up on her screen before she and

Maria started talking was a Wikipedia page on hydrocarbons. After an (incorrect) translation sequence in lines 19–24 (one of three that occur in this fragment, which I analyze later) fails to resolve the meaning of an English vocabulary item, Maria notices in line 31 that Giada has the same Wikipedia page on her screen (see the gloss in line 32 concerning this visual information). Thus, in lines 39–43, Maria is reading information from this online cultural artifact.

To return to the theme of what these multi-layered, but nonetheless demonstrably locally occasioned sources of context demonstrate, we can make a good case that, whereas Giada (after three weeks of participation in a five week course) has manifestly still not understood how and why she is supposed to do prediction tasks, Maria has a better understanding of what is required. However, Maria is *contingently* 'led astray' by the availability of Giada's illicit Wikipedia page on her monitor. The fact that this cultural artifact cannot be used *at this particular moment* of the lesson is confirmed by the evidence in lines 44–49. More specifically the instructor, who happens to be physically close to Maria and Giada at this moment, notices that Giada has the Wikipedia page displayed on her screen and comments negatively on this infraction. This sanction causes Giada to close the Wikipedia page, to apologize in line 48, and to offer the rationalization in lines 51–52 that she does not know anything about the topic.

I now comment on the three translation sequences that occur in Fragment 3 ('coal' → 'torba', lines 21–28; 'dig' → 'scavare', lines 74–88; and 'refined' → 'raffinati', lines 93–101). Briefly, all these translation sequences are also prohibited courses of action in terms of the local speech exchange rules that the instructor has laid out in lines 2–6 of Fragment 2. Furthermore, as in Fragment 2, all three sequences in Fragment 3 are achieved as repairs. The first sequence ('coal' → 'torba') happens to be incorrect, since 'torba' means 'peat', not 'coal.' The remaining sequences are all correct. But from a CA perspective on context, the most interesting of these three spates of talk is the 'dig' → 'scavare' sequence. This sequence contains another instance of *locally occasioned, visual and kinesic context* (specifically, see the gloss in lines 78–79; see also Goodwin, 2000a, 2000b, 2003a, 2003b for a discussion) that complements the verbal analysis of talk-in-interaction. More specifically, Maria's digging hand gestures that accompany the onomatopoeic sounds of dirt flying in lines 77 and 80 are the visual clues that lead Giada to understand the meaning of 'to dig.'

Finally, in terms of evaluating whether the desired changes in prediction behavior and micro-level language policy have been successfully implemented, notice that the concurrent nature of Fragments 2 and 3 also allows us to make comparisons between the interactional work done by two pairs in the same group, and potentially with the simultaneous interactional behaviors of all the other groups in the class. These data therefore provide a powerful illustration of CA's ability to problematize *how and when interactional, visual, kinesic, and, under specific conditions, exogenous layers of context* may legitimately be invoked in real time accounts of curricular change.

Reflections and conclusions

In this chapter, I have sought to develop local, interactionally based understandings of context and change that, to my knowledge, have little currency in the current TESOL innovation literature. Let me now return to the question of whether the ESP course that I described at the beginning of this chapter was in fact an example of successful curricular innovation. On the basis of these ethnographic self-report documents, I suggested that these evaluations provided tentative support for the conclusion that the course had been successful. In the quantitative part of the surveys, students generally reported high levels of satisfaction with both the materials and the instruction they received. In the qualitative section on Suggestions for Improvement, traces of classic diffusion of innovation-related concerns clearly surface in this document: see, for example, the comment 'I could say that should be useful some teaching of basic grammar aspects that should make the course more completely than it is.' This feedback refers to the fact that the course did not present traditional (i.e., decontextualized) grammar exercises but relied on students getting grammar through (in cognitive SLA terms) a methodological focus on form (Doughty & Williams, 1998). Other concerns that emerged include a lack of time to complete tasks, a wish for more interaction with American students, and the students' inability to comply with the English only policy of the class.

Now, all of these comments led to substantial revisions in the course. However, I would like to point out that the feedback on the English only policy of the class ('More English during presentation making – professor tryed to tell you 'speek in english' but sometimes we didn't understand') says nothing about how this policy was interactionally achieved in real time. Furthermore, not a single student talked about any difficulties that they may have experienced with respect to doing the prediction tasks that were part of Units 1–4. Of course, evaluation protocols that invoke more or less macro notions of context are rarely comprehensive. But a good case can be made that the reason why students did not mention this issue as something that needed improvement in future iterations of the course (which in fact included a brand new, separate 'learning how to learn' unit on reading strategies) has to do with the fact that the micro-details of talk-in-interaction with which I have been concerned in this chapter are so routine, ordinary, and small, that few, if any people (unless they have professional training in CA) are likely to notice them. I therefore urge students of context and curricular innovation minimally to consider including small notions of context in our methodological armories. By doing so, we may get a more fine-grained sense of how successful our efforts to implement pedagogical change *in real time* actually are.

Key readings

Kennedy, C., Doyle, P. and Goh, C. M. (1999). *Exploring change in English language teaching.* Oxford: MacMillan Heinemann. This edited collection consists of three main sections: 1) National change; 2) Changes in institutions; and 3) Classroom change. Contributors (who are mostly practitioners or language specialists) use their considerable range of experience in Malaysia, Hong Kong, China, Singapore, Finland, the United Kingdom, Saudi Arabia, and Chile to provide teacher-friendly accounts of change in action.

Lamie, J. M. (2005). *Evaluating change in English language teaching.* New York: Palgrave MacMillan. This monograph has three sections: 1) Defining change; 2) Implementing change; and 3) Measuring change. It provides a useful theoretical and practical update on the management of curricular innovation first developed in the 1980s and 1990s that graduate students and researchers interested in this area of applied linguistics will find quite useful.

Murray, D. (2008). *Planning change, changing plans.* Ann Arbor, MI: The University of Michigan Press. This edited collection is the most recent of the three publications included in this annotated bibliography. It is divided into two parts: 1) Changing curriculum; and 2) Changing teachers. The first section focuses on top-down curricular reforms in various countries, while the second documents how teachers are impacted by innovations such as national assessment initiatives and teacher development programs, and also by teachers' individual expectations, beliefs and culture. This makes for a teacher-friendly account of change in action.

References

Adams, R. and Newton, J. (2009). TBLT in Asia: Constraints and opportunities. *Asian Journal of English Language Teaching* 19: 1–17.

Cicourel, A. (1992). The interpenetration of communicative contexts: Examples from medical encounters. In A. Duranti and C. Goodwin (Eds.), *Rethinking context* (pp. 291–310). Cambridge: Cambridge University Press.

Coughlan, P. and Duff, P. (1994). Same task, different activities: Analysis of SLA task from an activity perspective. In J. P. Lantolf and G. Appel (Eds.), *Vygotskyan approaches to second language research* (pp. 173–193). Westport, CT: Ablex.

Doughty, C. and Williams, J. (1998). *Focus on form in classroom second language acquisition.* Cambridge: Cambridge University Press.

Garfinkel, H. (1967). *Studies in ethnomethodology.* Englewood Cliffs: Prentice Hall.

Goodwin, C. (2000a). Action and embodiment within situated human interaction. *Journal of Pragmatics* 32: 1489–1522.

Goodwin, C. (2000b). Practices of seeing: Visual analysis: An ethnomethdological approach. In T. van Leeuwen and C. Jewitt (Eds.), *Handbook of visual analysis* (pp.157–182). London: Sage.

Goodwin, C. (2003a). Pointing as situated practice. In S. Kita (Ed.), *Pointing: Where language, culture and cognition meet* (pp. 217–241). Mahwah, N. J.: Lawrence Erlbaum Associates.

Goodwin, C. (2003b). The body in action. In J. Coupland, and R. Gwyn (Eds.), *Discourse, the body, and identity* (pp. 19–42). Mahwah, N. J.: Lawrence Erlbaum.

Goodwin, C., and Duranti, A. (1992). Rethinking context: An introduction. In A. Duranti and C. Goodwin (Eds.), *Rethinking context* (pp. 1–42). Cambridge: Cambridge University Press.

Gumperz, J. J. (1992). Contexualization and understanding. In A. Duranti and C. Goodwin (Eds.), *Rethinking context* (pp. 229–252). Cambridge: Cambridge University Press.

Gumperz, J. J. and Hymes, D. (1972). *Directions in sociolinguistics: The ethnography of communication.* New York: Holt, Rhinehart and Winston.

Heritage, J. (1988). Current developments in conversation analysis. In D. Roger and P. Bull (Eds.). *Conversation* (pp. 21–47). Clevedon: Multilingual Matters.

Heritage, J. and Sefi, S. (1992). Dilemmas of advice: Aspects of the delivery and reception of advice between health visitors and first time mothers. In P. Drew and J. Heritage, (Eds.), *Talk at work* (pp. 359–417). Cambridge: Cambridge University Press.

Holliday, A. (1994). *Appropriate methodology and social context.* Cambridge: Cambridge University Press.

Hymes, D. (1974). *Foundations in sociolinguistics: An ethnographic approach.* Philadelphia: University of Pennsylvania Press.

Kennedy, C. (1988). Evaluation of the management of change in ELT projects. *Applied Linguistics* 9: 329–342.

Kennedy, C. and Kennedy, J. (1996). Teacher attitudes and change implementation. *System* 24: 351–360.

Kennedy, J. and Kennedy, C. (1998). Levels, linkages, and networks in cross-cultural innovation. *System* 26: 455–469.

Markee, N. (1997). *Managing curricular innovation.* New York: Cambridge University Press.

Markee, N. (2000). *Conversation analysis.* Mahwah, NJ: Lawrence Erlbaum Associates.

Markee, N. (2011). Doing, and justifying doing, avoidance. *Journal of Pragmatics* 43: 602–615.

Markee, N. and Kasper, G. (2004). Classroom talks: An introduction. *Modern Language Journal* 88: 491–500.

Maynard, D. (2003). *Bad news, good news: Conversational order in everyday talk and clinical settings.* Chicago, IL: Chicago University Press.

Moerman, M. (1988). *Talking culture: Ethnography and conversation analysis.* University of Pennsylvania Press.

Roger, D. and Bull, P. (1988). Section 1: Concepts of interpersonal communication. In D. Roger and P. Bull (Eds.), *Conversation* (pp. 1–8). Clevedon: Multilingual Matters.

Schegloff, E. A. (1987). Between macro and micro: Contexts and other connections. In J. Alexander, B. Giesen, R. Munch, and N. Smelser (Eds.), *The micro-macro link* (pp. 207–234). Berkeley: University of California Press.

Schegloff, E. A. (1991). Reflections on talk and social culture. In D. Boden and D. Zimmerman (Eds.), *Talk and social structure* (pp. 44–70). Cambridge: Polity Press.

Schegloff, E. A. (1992). In another context. In A. Duranti and C. Goodwin (Eds.), *Rethinking context* (pp. 191–227). Cambridge: Cambridge University Press.

Schegloff, E. A. and Sacks, H. (1973). Opening up closings. *Semiotica* VIII: 289–327.

Schiefffelin, B. B. and Ochs, E. (1986). *Language socialization across cultures.* Cambridge: Cambridge University Press.

Stoller, F. (1994). The diffusion of innovations in intensive ESL programs. *Applied Linguistics* 15: 300–327.

Waters, A. (2009). Managing innovation in English language education. *Language Teaching* 42: 421–458.

Watson-Gegeo, K. A. (1988). Ethnography in ESL: Defining the essentials. *TESOL Quarterly* 22: 575–592.

Watson-Gegeo, K. A. (2004). Mind, language, and epistemology: Toward a language socialization paradigm for SLA. *The Modern Language Journal* 88: 331–350.

Young, R. F. (2009). *Discursive practice in language learning and teaching.* Malden, MA: Wiley-Blackwell.

4

CULTURES OF CHANGE: APPROPRIATE CULTURAL CONTENT IN CHINESE SCHOOL TEXTBOOKS

Yafu Gong and Adrian Holliday

Key ideas and concepts

The innovation described in this chapter is an ongoing, large project, which is still very much at the research stage. It concerns revising the cultural content of Chinese secondary school textbooks and research to establish what might be meaningful and authentic innovation for students. Based on interviews with students, we argue that a long established 'native speaker' model of ELT and an equally long-standing view of culture, both as curriculum content and as a construction of language learners, have influenced the secondary school curriculum in such a way that it has been taken away from the 'real worlds' of Chinese students, and that an innovative approach to culture and the curriculum is required to address this.

The chapter is set within the broader context of a developing understanding that what is meaningful to English language students, especially in state educational settings, has continued to remain hidden beneath the paraphernalia of ELT professionalism, and has often been expressed in the non-formal aspects of classroom life (e.g. Canagarajah, 1999; Holliday, 2005). This lack of recognition of English language student experience has been linked to the politics of how perceptions of culture have been falsely constructed within the academy and in everyday life to marginalize non-Western realities (Kumaravadivelu, 2007). This lack of recognition has resulted in a false impression that East Asian students are not able to be self-directed, critical or creative because these attributes are not encouraged by collectivist cultures. There is a growing body of research which counters this 'collectivism' theory and indicates that East Asian students have no problem being as independent in their views and actions as anyone else given the opportunity (Cheng, 2000; Clark & Gieve, 2006; Grimshaw, 2007; Kubota, 1999; Ryan & Louie, 2007;

Tran, 2009). Where they appear otherwise, it is more because of the strictures of particular educational or classroom regimes, including the high scrutiny and management of talk found in Western classrooms, than with an underlying cultural deficiency (Holliday, 2005: 63–84, 94).

The critique of the way in which the culture of students has been mis-constructed also connects with a broader movement towards a critical cosmopolitan view of culture which refutes national cultural profiling (Holliday, 2011). Indeed, this chapter demonstrates that the students interviewed are way ahead of established simplistic views of culture as surface artefact and tradition. *Even* if they come from what might be considered limited rural experience, they possess a highly sophisticated cosmopolitanism which demands a greater complexity of cultural content in their textbooks and classrooms. As promised by Stuart Hall (1991a: 34), they speak from the margins and claim the world.

Case study

Background and context

China has started to implement its new 2010–2020 *National Mid-&-Long Term Educational Reform and Development Plan*. The strategic goal is to develop each student as a 'whole healthy person' with mental, physical and social well-being, with an emphasis on values, attitudes, ideology, cognitive, affective and interpersonal skills. The students' critical thinking skills and creativity are also described as one of the strategic goals.

Within primary and secondary ELT, meeting these humanistic goals has been a real challenge. Dramatic changes in materials and methods in the last decade to meet the 2001 National English Curriculum (NEC) have been led by new authorised textbooks which advocate Task-Based communicative teaching (TBLT). The books have been criticized (Zhang, 2007), particularly with regard to the cultural awareness component.

The ideology which is widely accepted among the Chinese schoolteachers is that teaching culture means developing students' awareness of the English native speakers' cultural norm. In the 2011 version of the NEC, 'culture' is defined as 'the target language countries' history and geography, local people's features, natural conditions and social customs, living habits, behaviour norms, arts and literature as well as values and ideology' (p.23). Most of the tasks, therefore, concern Western urban life, with the assumption that most Chinese students will sooner or later go to English-speaking countries to live or study. In recent years, some Chinese elements have also been added, such as Chinese traditional festivals and typical Chinese food. It is believed we think mistakenly that this is intercultural communication.

In order to assess the appeal and appropriate content of such textbooks (which are mainly published by international publishers in English-speaking countries and adapted by Chinese publishers), a study was conducted in big cities, small towns and rural areas in ten provinces in China from 2007–2010. This involved classroom observations and 20 unstructured interviews with teachers and students from junior and senior high schools which might be considered 'in the middle' and did not include key schools in urban areas or the most undeveloped areas. Students aged 14 to 17 were randomly selected with an almost equal number of males and females, and interviewed in focus groups of seven to nine. Some students had started to learn English from age nine and some from twelve.

The interviews revealed a wide variety of opinions about learning culture and the value of English education. One of the problems both teachers and students reported was the thematic content which in turn reflects how ELT professionals perceive cultural awareness in China and its influence on English education. The following are some findings from the study.

Problematic native speaker topics in rural areas

One set of interviews was conducted in a school in the suburbs of Zhuhai, which is only 25 kilometres from the downtown area. (Zhuhai is close to Macao and is one of the most developed areas in South China.) The teachers explained that some of the topics in the textbook were very unfamiliar to the students, such as touring other countries, fast food, and cooking – for example, 'how do you make a banana milk shake', 'the brand I like'. They said the students therefore have nothing to talk about in class. They explained that most of the students are from local farmers' families and have never been to other places in China, and even have no ideas where the Great Wall is. They painted a picture of parents in the villages who have sold their land, become rich overnight, and do nothing but gamble with cards and other traditional games, of families who seldom use computers or read magazines and newspapers, and of children who believe they can live a good life without going to school. They said that both students and their parents needed to be educated about the values of life.

Students, especially those from rural areas (more than 65 percent of the student population), said they had no experience of cities and found it difficult to engage with urban life topics such as 'asking the way' and 'planning a trip to Europe', or concepts like 'turn left at the third block' and 'two traffic lights'. A senior high school girl from a Zhejiang mountain school asked: 'Are these textbooks written for us?' Then, she answered the question herself: 'Not'. The small village she lived in had no restaurant, no traffic light, only a muddy road.

This supports McKay's (2003: 10) observation that 'whereas it is possible that target cultural content is motivating to some students, it is also quite possible that such content may be largely irrelevant, uninteresting, or even confusing for students'. One of the tasks in the textbooks asks students to talk about their weekend activities, with the examples: 'go to see a movie, go to an art museum, or go to piano lessons in a coaching school'. However, our interviews revealed that students at a countryside school in Jiangxi, a central province in China, go to pick bamboo shoots, mushrooms in the mountains or go fishing for food during the weekend. They have to cook for themselves as their parents have left home to get money in more developed areas. There is no cinema in the town, which is 30 kilometres away from the village. Another task in a primary textbook is to teach ten-year-old kids to order pizza in a fast-food restaurant. A visit to a school in Yunan revealed that there was only one dish of boiled cabbage in a big pot in the school kitchen, but the textbooks introduce all kinds of food and ask students to role-play what they prefer to eat in the school canteen. This has some negative impact on the students as they think that society is unfair and complain about being born in poor families.

Devaluing the home culture

Students do learn the differences between the cultures of Chinese and English speaking countries from the textbooks. When students from a national poverty county in Jiangxi province were asked what else they learned from English classes besides the language itself (grammar, vocabulary, etc.), they answered 'culture'. When asked for detailed examples, they said: 'People in foreign countries do not ask people's age. When you praise someone they say thank you instead of saying something modest'. 'Not like Chinese, foreigners do not ask about your private things'. When asked which way they preferred, they said (in a low voice), 'English culture'.

Students from Beijing seemed to enjoy the stories in the textbook. Observation of a primary school class in downtown Beijing revealed that the students could express themselves clearly and fluently in English. The reading passage was about a girl from a poor Cuban family; she lived in a shabby house and did not have enough food to eat. After immigrating to the US, she became a famous singer star and a very rich lady. The teacher asked what students wanted to do in the future. One boy said: 'When I grow up, I do not want to go to university but to make big money in the future'. Another boy said: 'I think going to school is boring and I want to go to work as soon as possible'. We do not suggest that these lessons have a direct influence on students' thinking, but as one of the observers commented afterwards, the reading passage was 'propaganda'. This may relate to what Ellis (2003: 332) refers to as 'the hidden socio-political messages' in the tasks.

Also, some teachers only seemed to ask students to accept the culture norm introduced in the textbooks. One male junior high student from Taiyuan, the capital city of Shanxi, in North China, said: 'We are students and we can only accept the reality and the ideas as we are not mature enough to challenge the ideas in the textbook, so we had better just follow what is written in the textbook'. English teaching may also have an impact on student identity choice. He concluded: 'When we learn English, it is a totally different culture. Since we learn English and use it in the future, the ultimate goal is to change ourselves into another person and behave like English speaking people'.

What are students interested or not interested in?

The teaching of intercultural communication embeds in functional dialogues some popular culture, such as going shopping, talking about the weather, introducing people, ordering food, and table manners. However, most of the students interviewed expressed their dissatisfaction with these functional conversations. Students in Taiyuan and Kunming, the capital city of Yunan in the Southwest, rated as second grade in economic development, both said that interpersonal communication topics simply involve dialogues with fixed expressions and recycle the same things with different grammar structures. They said nobody would use them in everyday life and repeat the same things. They thus found them very boring.

When asked why they did not want to speak English, some students expressed their frustration. Students from Guilin, a tourist city of Guangxi, a western province considered as less developed, said: 'We can only use a few daily conversations, such as greetings and asking about the weather. We soon lose interest since there is nothing new for us to express ourselves. What we do want to say are not in the textbooks'. One of their teachers said: 'There are few topics that the students really enjoy reading. The texts do not seem to touch the hearts of the students'.

Some students from Beijing laughed at the topics about weekends because most students attend coaching school on weekends and they have as heavy a workload as they do during week days. The reality of Chinese education is still under the pressure of test-driven instruction and students do not have much time to enjoy weekends. It is reported that 85–90 percent of the urban students go to tutorial classes in their spare time, where they are taught more adult material so that they can take the tests to prove their level of English and be enrolled into better schools.

The need for guidance in life and 'real-world' meaningfulness: love, politics and life skills

What do students want to talk about? Some students in different places expressed their ideas about this. They said that they liked something meaningful for their lives, including stories that may give them guidance for their futures. They also enjoyed songs and sports, movies and literature. Students in Yunnan reported that they liked to talk about movies, food, things they want to do in the future, politics, comments about China by people from other countries. They preferred topics on friendship, love and life skills. Some students liked to listen to the BBC news about China. They also liked popular music, and sports.

The teachers from Shanxi reported that students had strong pressure from their families and liked classroom topics that helped them to deal with and talk about this pressure. They liked topics such as violence, because lots of students had experienced robbery out of school. When the teacher taught a love poem, they were surprised how much the students simply loved to read it. The students were mature enough to think about their life and the future and wanted to share their ideas and feelings, and talk about it in class. One student from Hongsibao, a small town in Ningxia, a Hui minority Autonomous Region in North China, said:

> I want to read something deeper, underlying the surface of life, sophisticated with philosophy. Even some fables could give me enlightening in life. For example, if I go out and meet up some problems, how can I solve these problems? I do not like to read something that just describes a 'beautiful life' and recites it, which is far away from our own reality.

A teacher from Beijing also mentioned that she gave students some supplementary reading materials and one of them was on school bullying. She thought this topic might be too serious for students. But the students simply enjoyed reading it and had a good discussion. A female student from a senior high school in Suzhou, in central China and considered one of the most developed cities, said: 'I like to read articles about other countries on how their people solve certain problems, about their worries and concerns, their way of life, such as the ones in *Reader*' (a very popular Chinese magazine which carries some articles about the life of famous heroes, touching stories, mottos and jokes).

Students from a senior high school in Kunming, Yunnan, complained that they did not have time to read enough to acquire new knowledge, and were therefore not so interested in everyday domestic things:

> We can't talk about anything, even in Chinese. We need something more complicated, new things happening in the world, things to keep us up with current society, new things we need to be exposed to.

When they were asked if they had chances to speak to English speaking people, one student said: 'Yes, once I just came up and said 'hi' to them. But I couldn't express more complicated ideas when the talk continued'. A girl from a Jiangxi rural area school said: 'I want to exchange ideas on how to deal with our parents and teachers on the phone with my classmates in English, so my parents won't understand what we talk about'.

The above interviews provide evidence that students like to learn about social and personal issues rather than simply about topics concerning English speaking countries. Richards (2001) cited Morris (1995) about a curriculum perspective which develops 'knowledge, skills, and attitudes which would create a world where people care about each other, the environment, and the distribution of wealth, tolerance, the acceptance of diversity and peace' and 'social injustices and inequality would be central issues in the curriculum' (2001: 118). Thus, communication is only one goal of learning English and the development of students' awareness of their own personalities and social roles, responsibilities, sense of self-confidence and self-realizations should also be pursued (Candlin, 1987).

The innovation: to set up socio-cultural goals in the curriculum

The interviews shed much light for our rethinking of the goals of ELT in the Chinese context. The authors believe there is a need to reconceptualize the purpose and content of culture teaching in the curriculum. First, we need to rethink the purpose of English education for schools. We propose to teach socio-culture, cognitive and thinking skills through the learning of English, rather than 'culture'. Social-cultural goals include interpersonal relationships, ways of thinking, lifestyles, attitudes toward life, society, politics and economics. Students in classrooms need to exchange ideas about these topics (Cook, 2007) so that 'the linguistic components lose their predominant position' (Yalden, 1984: 18).

Thus, English education will set up three independent and integrated goals. We may call this 'a multi-goal approach'. A multi-goal approach is to develop new perceptions of reality in Chinese society and the rest of the world, so that students may experience cognitive and affective changes in their world view, and have a better idea of what their goal is in the future and behave differently in light of such perceptions. They may learn to develop a critical eye and different perspectives for seeing the world, and adapt new cultural norms and personalities. More familiar topics which are relevant to their life should be included in their textbooks, so that the students in both rural and urban areas have something to talk about, and textbook writers will have to think what should be selected as appropriate content in terms of tasks (Breen, 2001; Candlin, 2001).

The culture component in the curriculum may be replaced with social-cultural thematic content which is not limited to popular culture, but can also include ideology, world views, values, beliefs and socialization. Intercultural communication should not be perceived as a way of imposing 'native speaker' cultural norms or of forcing students to accept and imitate 'native speaker' normality, but instead as a means for learning how to become a multicultural person. Thus, students would not necessarily take in the cultural norms of the English speaking West, but learn how to be tolerant, learn other cultural perspectives and express their own or develop 'a third culture' (Kramsch, 2009). Curriculum designers need to take the values of ELT, the Chinese reality, educational goals, teaching and learning environments, and students' future needs into consideration in designing the ELT curriculum for Chinese schools.

Reflection: understanding and combating the influence of native-speakerism on ELT

It seems that from the curriculum to classroom reality, the ideology of English education in China is influenced by 'native-speakerism' (Holliday, 2005), which believes that the ultimate goal of English language education is to help students to communicate with 'native speakers' of English and that the culture of English-speaking countries should be the norm for ELT. Within this ideology, the purpose of teaching is to help cope with the problems of a so-called 'real world' which is perceived mistakenly to be the context in English-speaking countries. The 'native speaker' language is considered as the only model. Most of the task content reflects daily life, beliefs, values and attitudes of Western countries and intercommunication is to help learners to understand target language speakers' way of thinking.

This native-speakerism does not only appear in the curriculum and the textbooks, but also in language teaching research and journal articles. According to a survey by the National Association of Foreign Language Education, Chinese Educational Society (Gong, 2011), between 2005 and 2010, 95 percent of journals published in the Chinese mainland for school teachers on the teaching of culture refer to 'intercultural communication' as introducing the cultural norms of English-speaking countries. Only one article compares Chinese culture with Western culture, but each comparison concludes with comments on the inappropriateness of Chinese culture.

Such ideas about English language teaching and cultural norms are challenged within the notion of English as an international language (EIL) from political, cultural, local appropriateness, and economical perspectives (Pennycook, 1989; Phillipson, 1992; Holliday, 2005; Kumaravadivelu, 2003; Rajagopalan, 2004; Cummins & Davison, 2007). The increasing growth in multicultural and multidimensional communication is challenging traditional single-culture values (Kramsch & Whiteside, 2008) and some recent mainstream SLA research is criticized as being unable to capture the complexity of language, the language learner, the processes of language learning, and learners' multiple identities from socio-cultural or socio-historical perspectives (Okazaki, 2005). Others also challenge the ideology of native-speakerism for imposing Western culture and values onto other countries, under the heading of 'linguistic imperialism' (e.g. Phillipson, 1992). Kumaravadivelu (2003) also points out that the special purpose of developing learners' ability for 'native speakers' of English may result in the individual voice and the cultural identity of the second language learner becoming hopelessly marginalized. This leads us to rethink the purpose of ELT and the objectives in the curriculum.

The interviews also help us to understand why some students seem very passive and keep silent in the English classroom. The students may want to express themselves in the classroom, but simply have nothing to say because the content is not what they are familiar with or not what they are really interested in. This is an example, to some extent, of 'hidden realities' (Holliday, 2005: 85ff), where:

> while it is certainly the case that when going into classrooms in many parts of the world, students will *appear* to be lacking in autonomy, it is false logic to assume that their outward behaviour in these particular institutional settings reflects their internalized perceptions and abilities. (Holliday, 2005: 86, original emphasis)

We need to redefine some of the popular terms which have been interpreted in different ways, such as 'real world', 'appropriate language use', 'authenticity' and 'negotiation of meaning'. What are the 'real-world tasks' for Chinese high school English learners? Apparently, some of the tasks for students are far away from students' real world. Distinguishing the difference between 'competence' and 'capacity', Widdowson suggests that the communicative language teaching is not defined, 'as it usually is, in reference to native speaker norms of knowledge and behaviour. The contexts which make instances of the possible appropriate as communication do not have to be replications of native speaker realities' (2007: 218).

The appropriate purpose of ELT as a school subject

Moving away from the desire to assimilate English learners within a native-speakerist ideal requires a rethinking of the appropriate purpose of ELT as a school subject, especially in those countries in Asian areas where most learners seldom have chances to use English for interpersonal communication in their daily life. In a discussion of task-based language teaching, Candlin points out that:

> Targets for language learning are all too frequently set up externally to learners with little reference to the value of such targets in the general educational development of the learner. Because we are concerned with *language* learning, it is very easy to forget that we should be equally if not more concerned with the developing personalities of our *learners*. (Candlin, 1987: 16–17, original emphasis)

According to Cook (2007), the goals of ELT can be divided into two categories: external goals and internal goals. External goals refer to actual language use outside the schools and internal goals relate to the educational aims for the schools itself. The former focuses on how students benefit from language teaching in terms of language knowledge and skills; and the latter emphasizes students' overall mental development as a qualified citizen, for example, their personality, way of thinking and tolerance of other cultural experience.

The English education program as a school subject should give emphasis to students' cognitive development and critical thinking skills so as to educate a generation with both international and national visions. They are multicultural citizens who are not only able to communicate with people about their own and other cultural realities but also able to express their own views and opinions (Alptekin, 2010). Besides, they can think and reflect critically from both their own perspective and other perspectives and can even effectively solve problems such as misunderstandings and conflicts in communication (Álvarez, 2007).

Nunan (1999) points out the need for language education to develop generalized capacities in learners and points out the possible problems of teaching English as a foreign language, 'not because there is any likelihood that they (learners) will actually use the language, but because it will foster the development of cognitive, affective, interpersonal, and intercultural skills, knowledge, and attitudes' (p.155). We believe these are the key values of English language education for schools in which English is a school subject.

It is true that each year, many Chinese school students go abroad to study and the number has increased dramatically in the last ten years. For such students, interpersonal communication skills are very important as they may have to assimilate into the society they live in, which is their reality and their 'real world'. However, the number of students going abroad to study only comprises a small proportion of the student population. The situations presented in textbooks are not the 'real world' of most students, especially those students in rural areas. The students' 'real world' is their inner-world, their knowledge world and their future world.

Rethinking 'intercultural communication' teaching

In recent years, much has been published on the study of intercultural communication and it is time to abandon the traditional concept of 'culture' teaching in foreign language education. First, culture does not only refer to the popular culture of eating habits, food, clothing, or festivals. Indeed, reducing cultural identity to such things is considered by many to be essentialist, demeaning and patronizing (Hall, 1991b: 55–56; Holliday, 2011: 82; Kumaravadivelu, 2007: 109). Neither is it something which is fixed inside national cultural boundaries.

Following Max Weber's social action view of society, culture can be described in terms of:

> Categories of cultural action: global position and politics (how people position themselves with regard to foreign others within a global order), statements about culture (what people say about their culture), cultural resources (what people draw on, in particular situations, from national or other cultural realities), and underlying universal cultural processes (cultural strategies shared by everybody). (Holliday, 2011: 24)

These categories embody a strong sense of personal cultural trajectories within which individuals form their cultural realities through the particular histories they develop through life (Holliday, 2011: 49ff). There is some relationship here with Scollon and Scollon's cultural categories of ideology (history and world view, e.g., beliefs, values, and religion), socialization (e.g., education, enculturation, acculturation), forms of discourse (e.g., functions of language, non-verbal communication), and face system (social organization, e.g., the concept of the self, ingroup–outgroup relationship) (2001: 138). Obviously, culture takes in many concepts of values, world views, ideology, social relationships and organizations, self-identity and popular culture. It is essential to foster students' ability to be tolerant, open-minded and to learn positive concepts of social values rather than being narrow-minded or subservient to foreigners, to worship foreignness blindly and to be deprived of national dignity.

Sticking with an emphasis on cultural differences may not only bring some negative perception about students' own culture and develop essentialist stereotypes, but it may result in frustrations and even insult. Once, one of the authors was visiting an American testing company and an American lady wanted to meet him at the company's café at 5 o'clock; but she did not show up until almost one hour later. When asked why she was so late, she said: 'Isn't it you Chinese who are usually late for a meeting?' When asked who told her this, she said her husband is a Chinese man from Taiwan!

Also, Chinese society is changing quickly; the current culture in the urban areas is quite different from what it was 30 years ago. 'Chinese culture' has changed dramatically in the last 30 years in terms of living and eating habits, daily greetings, communication, transportation, clothing, ways of thinking, perception of values and even language. If one goes to the department stores in the regional capital cities in China, one will find there is no big difference from cities in most industrialized European countries. Perhaps it is true to say that there is much greater cultural difference between urban and rural areas within China than between Beijing, Shanghai and other big cities in other countries. In China, Chinese scholars frequently engage in controversial debate about the core feature of 'traditional Chinese culture'. Thus, it is not necessary to differentiate 'cultural differences'. Second, the current practice of ELT in Chinese schools does not seem to meet the goal of education, in that the students, despite their critical tone during the interviews, tend to behave as passive receivers of the facts and repeat the formulaic expressions. From the interviews, one may find what Clark described is true:

Reconstructionist approaches all seem to imply that learners have to learn to recreate the exact speech pattern of the target language community. Learners tend to be asked to learn stereotypical language. They act out particular roles, but do not seem to create what they say and do. In real life, however, the roles that we adopt are functions of the interactions we engage in, rather than static possessions. The language we use originates from deep roots in our personality, rather than from predetermined scripts. If we do not have practice at making the necessary links between the deeper processes of our cognitive and affective make-up and whatever language tokens are available to us, we may never learn how to mould the foreign language to our own ends. (Clark 1987: 38)

However, we are not suggesting that there should not be an introduction to and discussion of values, ideology or history and geography. What we suggest is an abandonment of the traditional ideology of intercultural communication which comprises a one-way information transfer and emphasises cultural differences. There are commonly accepted values, such as honesty, responsibility, social justice, peace and human rights which are also stated as requirements in the Chinese educational plan, though different people may have a different understanding of what these concepts really mean. However, this gives the student the opportunities to develop 'critical culture' ability and to become a 'multicultural person' (Alptekin, 2010). This is more likely to realize the goal of development of 'a whole person' perused in the Chinese educational reform and development plan.

Conclusion

The research reported in this chapter reveals the often unappreciated worlds of primary and secondary students in China. The innovation implicit in any textbook reform must therefore address how sophisticated and cosmopolitan these young people are, how, despite the massive pressures placed upon them, they have genuine interests in exploring the world. This understanding opens up exciting challenges for making the English curriculum more adult and authentic. It also requires us to shake established views about culture in ELT, and confirm recently expressed theories about culture as a moving, creative force which can be shared and owned in a multiplicity of ways.

Key readings

Holliday, A. R. (2005). *The struggle to teach English as an international language.* Oxford: Oxford University Press. This text explores the impact of native-speakerism on the professional discourses of ELT and argues that they Other and hide the cultural abilities and complexities of so-called 'non-native speaker' students and teachers.

Holliday, A. R. (2011). *Intercultural communication and ideology*. London: Sage. This text examines why Western images of culture fail to appreciate the immense complexity and proficiency of non-Western cultural realities, which often have the potential to be shared by everybody and to enable transcultural travel and innovation.

Kumaravadivelu, B. (2007). *Cultural globalization and language education*. Yale: Yale University Press. This text applies a cosmopolitan view of culture to English language education and examines how culture in the classroom must embrace the hitherto unrecognised cultural complexity of students.

References

Alptekin, C. (2010). Redefining multicompetence for bilingualism and ELF. *International Journal of Applied Linguistics*, 20(1), 95–110.

Álvarez, I. (2007). Foreign language education at the crossroads: Whose model of competence? *Language, Culture and Curriculum*, 20(2), 126–139.

Breen, M. (2001). Syllabus design. In R. Carter & D. Nunan (Eds.), *The Cambridge guide to speakers of other languages* (pp. 87–99). Cambridge: Cambridge University Press.

Canagarajah, A. S. (1999). *Resisting linguistic imperialism*. Oxford: Oxford University Press.

Candlin, C. N. (1987). Towards task-based language learning. In C. N. Candlin & D. F. Murphy (Eds.), *Language learning tasks* (pp. 5–22). Englewood Cliffs, NJ: Prentice-Hall International (UK) Ltd and Lancaster University.

Candlin, C. N. (2001). Afterword: Taking the curriculum to task. In M. Bygate, P. Skehan & M. Swain (Eds.), *Researching pedagogical tasks: Second language learning, teaching and testing* (pp. 229–243). Harlow, England: Pearson Education.

Cheng, X. (2000). Asian students' reticence revisited. *System*, 28(3), 435–446.

Clark, J. (1987). *Curriculum renewal in school foreign language learning*. Oxford: Oxford University Press.

Clark, R., & Gieve, S. N. (2006). On the discursive construction of 'the Chinese Learner'. *Language, Culture and Curriculum*, 19(1), 54–73.

Cook, V. (2007). The goal of ELT: Reproducing native-speakers or promoting multicompetence among second language users? In J. Cummins & C. Davison (Eds.), *International handbook of English language teaching* (pp. 237–248). New York: Springer.

Cummins, J., & Davison, C. (2007).The global scope and policies of ELT: Critiquing current policies and programs. In J. Cummins & C. Davison (Eds.), *International handbook of English language teaching*. Vol. 1 (pp. 237–248). New York: Springer.

Ellis, R. (2003). *Task-based language learning and teaching*. Oxford: Oxford University Press.

Gong, Y. (2011). A third approach to communicative language teaching: General English education approach for schools. *Foreign Languages in China*, 43(5), 70–77.

Grimshaw, T. (2007). Problematizing the construct of 'the Chinese learner': Insights from ethnographic research. *Educational Studies*, 33, 299–311.

Hall, S. (1991a). The local and the global: Globalization and ethnicity. In A. D. King (Ed.), *Culture, globalization and the world-system* (pp. 19–39). New York: Palgrave.

Hall, S. (1991b). Old and new identities, old and new ethnicities. In A. D. King (Ed.), *Culture, globalization and the world-system* (pp. 40–68). New York: Palgrave.

Holliday, A. (2005). *The struggle to teach English as an international language*. Oxford: Oxford University Press.

Holliday, A. (2011). *Intercultural communication and ideology*. London: Sage.

Kramsch, C. & Whiteside, A. (2008). Language ecology in multilingual settings, towards a theory of symbolic competence. *Applied Linguistics*, 29(4), 645–671.

Kramsch, C. (2009). Third culture and language education. In V. Cook & W. Li (Eds.), *Contemporary applied linguistics.* Vol. 1 (pp. 233–254). London: Continuum.

Kubota, R. (1999). Japanese culture constructed by discourses: Implications for applied linguistics research and ELT. *TESOL Quarterly,* 33(1), 9–35.

Kumaravadivelu, B. (2003).Critical language pedagogy: A postmethod perspective on English language teaching. *World Englishes,* 22(4), 539–550.

Kumaravadivelu, B. (2007). *Cultural globalization and language education.* Yale: Yale University Press.

McKay, S. L. (2003). Toward an appropriate EIL pedagogy: Re-examining common ELT assumptions. *International Journal of Applied Linguistics,* 13(1), 1–21.

National English curriculum standards for compulsory education (2011). Beijing Normal University Press.

Nunan, D. (1999). *Second language teaching & learning.* Heinel & Heinel Publishers.

Okazaki, T. (2005). Critical consciousness and critical language teaching. *Second Language Studies,* 23(2), 174–202.

Pennycook, A. (1989). The concept of method, interested knowledge, and the politics of language teaching. *TESOL Quarterly,* 23 (4), 589–618.

Phillipson, R. (1992). *Linguistic imperialism.* Oxford: Oxford University Press.

Rajagopalan, K. (2004). The concept of 'World English and its implications for ELT. *ELT Journal,* 58 (2), 111–117.

Richards, J. C. (2001). *Curriculum development in language teaching.* Cambridge: Cambridge University Press.

Ryan, J., & Louie, K. (2007). False dichotomy? 'Western' and 'Confucian' concepts of scholarship and learning. *Educational Philosophy and Theory,* 39(4), 404–417.

Scollon, R., & Scollon, S. W. (2001). *Intercultural communication: A discourse approach* (second ed.). Oxford: Blackwell Publishers.

Tran, L. T. (2009). Making visible 'hidden' intentions and potential choices: International students in intercultural communication. *Language and Intercultural Communication,* 9(4), 271–284.

Widdowson, H. (2007). Un-applied linguistics and communicative language teaching: A reaction to Keith Johnson's review of notional syllabuses. *International Journal of Applied Linguistics* 17 (2), 214–220.

Yalden, J. (1984). Syllabus design in general English education: Options for ELT. In C. J. Brumfit (Ed.), *General English syllabus design: Curriculum and syllabus design for the general English classroom* (pp. 13–22). Pergamon Press Ltd. and British Council.

Zhang, Z. (2007). Four problems in English education in China. *Foreign Language Teaching and Research in Basic Eeducation.* No.1.

5

THE MANAGEMENT OF CHANGE

Alan Waters and Maria Luz C. Vilches

Introduction

On the face of it, the *management* of change is something of an oxymoron. As the three preceding chapters have indicated, change in English language education is typically multifaceted, occurs in particular contexts and cultures, and is perceived and experienced in different ways by the different parties involved. The number of variables, and the number of ways in which they can interact, are therefore potentially vast. As a result of this complexity, planned approaches to educational change can and do frequently go awry (Murray 2008).

At the same time, however, there is an expectation attached to most educational change proposals that, in due course, outcomes will emerge which approximate reasonably closely to those envisaged at the outset. As Fullan (2007: 117) says, 'Recognizing the limitations of planning is not the same thing as concluding that effective change is unattainable'. The management of change projects therefore also needs to be grounded in an awareness of this perspective as well.

In what follows, a number of concepts from the literature on the management of change which attempt to take this duality of views into account are first of all discussed. They have also been selected because they are regarded as being among those which are most central to the kinds of management dilemmas that the literature on English language education change projects (see, e.g., the 'Recommended reading' items below) indicates they are prone to. This is followed by a description and evaluation of the use of these ideas within the context of one such change initiative, the Philippines English Language Teaching (PELT) Project (1995–2000), in order to illustrate both their potential for facilitating purposeful change and the effects on their operation of the exigencies of the innovation situation. Some of the lessons that might be learned for the management of other, similar change projects, are also identified.

Basic concepts

'Public performance' vs. 'backstaging'

However well-planned and systematically worked through a proposed change may be, it is unusual for a widespread consensus in favour of it to already exist. To have to engender support for the change will therefore often be the first main change management task. The question then arises of how this can best be achieved.

In their study of expertise in change management, Buchanan and Boddy (1992) identified two main management 'activities' that were used by their research participants in order to gather support for their change projects, namely i) 'public performance' and ii) 'backstaging'.[1] 'Public performance' is the projection of a project management style which can be viewed as promoting 'rationally considered and logically phased and visibly participative change' (*ibid*: 27). This is necessary in order to conform to 'common sense' expectations about how the change management process should be seen to proceed. To support the presentation of such an approach, however, the research participants regarded it as also essential for the change manager to participate in extensive '"backstage activity" in the recruitment and maintenance of support and in seeking and blocking resistance' (*ibid*).

As Buchanan and Boddy (1992: 29) go on to say (cf. Alderson 2009), the latter kind of activity is needed, and is in a mutually supportive relationship with the former, because:

> The logic of problem solving must be seen, in most organizations, to unfold in the expected and acceptable manner. However, this public performance must be supported by *backstaging* – the politicking, the wheeler-dealing, the fixing and negotiating, the coalition building and trade-offs – which typically cannot be openly discussed in the organization without damaging individual credibility or the legitimacy of the change attempt.

In other words, while it is important in the development of support for a project for its public appearance to convey the impression of carefully thought-through, rational planning, the key to establishing this perception is for the change manager to succeed in convincing each of the various constituencies involved that their 'stake' in its construction has been properly considered and valued, and this can involve discussion of matters which are too sensitive to be debated more publicly. As a result, rather than only 'centre stage', the work of establishing initial project 'ownership' has to be done as much or more 'behind the scenes'.

The overall concept here can also be understood in terms of the distinction made in Fullan (2007: Ch. 2) between the 'objective' and 'subjective' meanings of change. The former is the change as expressed in the form of, e.g., a curriculum development document, a new set of teaching materials, and so on, i.e., from the point of view of the proponent of the change. The latter are the personal interpretations of the proposed change as perceived by the individuals and/or groups who will be affected by it. For a variety of reasons, it is typical for these two sets of perceptions to differ markedly. At one level, to garner support, the innovation project needs to have a well-established 'objective' meaning. However, this can only be accepted as such if it is seen, however paradoxically, to arise out of and to have been satisfactorily reconciled with its range of potential subjective meanings. The backstage management of meaning is therefore crucial for satisfactory public performance in change management, and thereby, for the development of the necessary level of support for the change.

Horizontal and vertical integration

The concept just discussed can be seen as part of what is involved in achieving the initial impetus for change. The one to be described next can be regarded as concerned with maintaining subsequent momentum by attempting to ensure that sufficient integration occurs between existing innovation situation pedagogical 'constructs' and educational 'structures' and the change project. It is based on an amalgam of insights found in several parts of the change management literature, and involves creating adequate project 'grounding', on the one hand, and giving it sufficient 'reach', on the other. As Wedell (2003: 447–448) puts it:

> to support teachers through the TESOL curriculum change process planners need to explicitly consider the implications of their plans from two interdependent points of view. Firstly they need to try and identify the degree of cultural shift that the practices implied by the proposed changes will represent for most teachers, and so what sort of support will be needed by whom for how long, to help teachers make the transition. Secondly, they need to consider what imbalances the proposed curriculum changes may introduce among other influential components of the language education system, and so what adjustments will be required, when [sic], to restore balance and so support the introduction of new practices.

The first of the points made here is the need to ensure that 'the degree of cultural shift' involved in the change is a manageable one. As Rogers (2003: 240) indicates, on the basis of his study of a wide range of innovations (cf. Markee 1997: Ch. 2), potential for adoption correlates strongly with 'the degree to which an innovation is perceived as consistent with the existing values, past experiences, and needs of potential adopters' – its so-called 'compatibility' characteristic. Research in Stoller (1994) likewise shows that English language education innovations that involve a 'Zone of Innovation' (ZoI) that adheres to the 'Goldilocks Principle' – i.e., one which is neither too big nor too small – are more likely to be successful. In other words, it is vital for the change being proposed to be seen to sufficiently build on rather than contradict existing traditions (cf. Kelly 1980; Marris 1986; Fullan 2007: Ch. 2), i.e., to be adequately 'grounded' within the innovation context.

The second of the main points in the quotation from Wedell concerns the need to also ensure that the change management strategy takes into account the way that introducing an innovation in one part of the educational 'ecology' of the innovation situation, will have a 'ripple' or 'knock-on' effect on the remainder of it, requiring consultation with and the involvement of all the parties thereby affected, and the consequences arising incorporated into the management plan. A well-known expression of this concept is in Bowers (1983: 101), where the main elements in an education system (e.g., 'materials', 'teacher trainers', etc.) are displayed in the form of a 'spider's web' diagram. Movement in any one part of this structure will, of course, affect all the other parts, in the way that, for example, the introduction of a new teaching approach will have implications for teacher training, which will, in turn, entail consequences elsewhere in the system in terms of time and money, and so on.

A related concept in this area is that of 'secondary' innovations (Markee 1997: 172ff). These are innovations, such as teacher training programmes, which are created in order to support the implementation of a 'primary' innovation (e.g., a new set of teaching materials). Thus, for example, Markee shows how the introduction of a redeveloped materials design training programme was crucial in increasing the levels of understanding and ownership of teachers in his 'CATI' curriculum development project. The overall point here is that the project change management strategy needs to be sufficiently thought through so that the wider 'ripple' effects of the primary innovation are also taken properly into account, including, as necessary, via the creation of additional, secondary innovations.

These two main forms of 'embedding' or 'integration' of the innovation within the innovation situation can be thought of, as in Waters and Vilches (2001), as involving a consideration by the change agent of, respectively, both the 'vertical' and 'horizontal' dimensions of innovation management needs. The result is the creation of a change management 'map' based on attempting to systematically build on and build in the perceptions and structures which already exist in the innovation situation (cf. Wedell 2009: 47–53).

Delegation

The third (and final) concept to be discussed is concerned with how appropriate change project outcomes can be achieved in tandem with (*inter alia*) the application of the two previous concepts. It relates to the importance of basing the management of change on what 'management', in its essence, can be understood to involve. Blanchard, Oncken, and Burrows (2004) provide a convenient 'Occam's razor' for distinguishing management (whether of change or any other kind) from other forms of activity when they characterise it as 'getting things done *through others*' (ibid: 98 – our emphasis), i.e., ultimately, it is concerned with attempting to achieve effective (supervised) *delegation*. In other words, all other matters being equal, the measure of successful management is not so much what managers themselves do, but, rather, what they enable *others* to do.

This overall conceptualisation of what (change) management involves is particularly important to take into account within the context of change projects, since it is also motivated separately but equally crucially by a number of aspects of innovation theory. First, as pointed out in Rogers (2003: 180–188), 're-invention', i.e., 'the degree to which an innovation is changed or modified by a user in the process of its adoption and implementation' (p.180), is a widespread feature of innovation dissemination, especially in educational contexts, and there is evidence that 'a higher degree of re-invention leads to a faster rate of adoption …[and] a higher degree of sustainability of an innovation' (p.183). This occurs because:

> The general picture that emerges from studies of re-invention is that innovation is not a fixed entity. Instead, people who use an innovation shape it by giving it meaning as they learn by using the new idea (pp.187–188).

It therefore appears highly desirable for change management to be of a sufficiently 'delegated' nature to allow for and foster reinvention activity in positive ways.

Other concepts from innovation theory that are also of relevance to the overall area under focus here include:

- the 'normative re-educative change strategy' (Chin & Benne 1970; Kennedy 1987), which is based on the view that meaningful change management can only occur if those involved are given sufficient opportunity to explore and work out for themselves what the change involves;
- 'the transition curve' (Waters 2009: 444–445; also see, e.g., Bridges & Mitchell 2000), where the process of innovation implementation and 'institutionalisation' is conceptualised as involving a number of stages during which the potential adopter of the change is gradually encouraged to take increasing responsibility for working with and exploring its potential until personal 'ownership' is achieved;
- similarly, in Hall and Hord (2001: Chs. 4 & 5), the innovation adoption process is modelled as typically comprising a series of steps which

manifest themselves as 'levels of use' and 'stages of concern' in innovation implementation: both 'scales' view adoption as successful only when relatively autonomous identification with and 'mastery' of the change occurs.

In summary, it can be seen that, from the perspectives of both management and innovation theory, the effective management of change must involve creating opportunities for the degree of individual and independent action and reflection needed to develop the potential for those on the receiving end of the innovation to eventually be willing to adopt it.

Case study: the PELT Project

Let us now turn to a 'worked example' of the application of each of these principles, as they occurred in the PELT Project. The overall aim of this project was to improve the teaching methods of teachers of English working in state-sector secondary schools in around half of the educational administrative regions of the Philippines. The project was jointly sponsored by the UK and Philippines governments. (The first author of this chapter was the principal project consultant, and the second was the project co-ordinator.)

Establishing 'ownership' and 'legitimacy': the use of 'backstaging'

'Backstaging' was a crucial part of the overall PELT Project change management strategy. Although the project, as already mentioned, was aimed at state-sector teachers, i.e., those working within schools funded by what was then known as the Philippines Department of Education, Culture and Sports (DECS) (now the Department for Education, or 'DepEd'), a decision was made before its inception that it would be co-ordinated by the Ateneo de Manila Center for ELT (ACELT), rather than by DECS. ACELT was (and remains) an organisation with a long history of involvement in a variety of similar projects in close co-operation with DECS/DepEd, but an 'outsider' in terms of the state-sector school system, being an 'arm' of one of the leading private universities in the Philippines. The initial planning also made provision for a UK institution to provide training and consultancy services, and the Institute for English Language Education at Lancaster University was selected for this role. This meant that, in this respect as well, project activity was 'out-sourced', in this case to an overseas organisation with, albeit some prior experience of providing teacher training within the Philippines and for Philippines' students in the UK, was, like ACELT, an outsider in terms of the administrative structures of DECS.

The significance of these arrangements, from a change management point of view, was that the most important initial task for the project management team (the authors) was to attempt to establish the levels of confidence, trust and co-operation with DECS essential for the smooth unfolding of the project.

This was seen as far more than a matter of establishing logistical procedures for identifying training venues, budgets, recruiting training 'seminar' participants and all the rest, vital though these concerns also were. Rather, it was viewed as primarily finding a solution to the problem of proper 'ownership' of the project by DECS, given the risk of perceived 'slight' and lack of information and communication about the project goals, and so on, occasioned by the decision to locate the management of the project outside DECS. In other words, it was necessary to undertake a good deal of 'backstaging' in order for the public presentation of the project to be perceived to have the necessary 'legitimacy'.

The first main part of the strategy for achieving this aim was to work towards securing the agreement of a key official within DECS – the national head of its secondary school division – to become the third member, along with the authors, of the 'project management team', thereby creating a dual, 'insider–outsider' project management structure. This process was begun by formal meetings in Manila between the authors and the official in question, but was cemented by several visits the latter and some of his colleagues undertook to the UK, in which there were extensive, open-ended opportunities not only to discuss details of project planning, but to also interact more informally, establish positive interpersonal as well as working relations, and so on. Indeed, it was during the first such visit that the initiative was taken by the DECS secondary school division head to suggest that he should become the third member of the project management team.

These visits were also important in terms of familiarising DECS colleagues with the physical as well as the 'psycho-social' environment of the UK training venue, once again helping to build up a more 'visceral' understanding of this wing of the project operation. These occasions were also invaluable for increasing the authors' understanding of DECS' procedures, viewpoints, the personalities of the various individuals involved, and so on. A logistically more constrained but similar approach was subsequently applied with respect to others in the '(ELT) managers' category of DECS personnel, i.e, regional level directors and ELT advisors, division-level superintendents and ELT supervisors, school principals and ELT heads of department (also see below). In short, a good deal of time and energy was spent in these ways on a process of mutual acculturation, so that, as far as possible, the 'soft' understandings (Holliday 1990) were created that were seen as essential for underpinning the public presentation of the project for it to be seen to have the necessary degree of 'ownership' and 'legitimacy' on the part of key personnel within DECS.

Creating a project development matrix

We come next to an illustration of how the PELT Project attempted to make use of the second of the main concepts introduced earlier, i.e. the achievement of first 'vertical' and second 'horizontal' coherence between the project and the innovation situation.

The vertical dimension

At the outset of the PELT Project, although it was clear from the original log-frame that the main outcome expected was that 'Capability of secondary EL teachers [would be] improved', this left open, of course, the question of in exactly what respects this might occur. Fortunately, there were opportunities before the design of the project training programme for the authors to conduct a series of 'field visits' to a representative cross-section of regional DECS centres and secondary schools, in order to gather views from a variety of personnel about training priorities and, in particular, to observe teaching, with a view to trying to determine an appropriate 'ZoI' (Stoller 1994) for the training.

Thus, and in keeping with the concept outlined above (the need for 'vertical' coherence), it was felt important in formulating the training focus: i) to first of all acknowledge what was of value in the prevailing teaching approach, and ii) to seek to identify ways in which it might be further strengthened and built on. In this way, it was hoped that Stoller's 'Goldilocks' principle could be observed, i.e., a ZoI devised that was neither too big nor too small.

In a nutshell, our field visits led us to conclude that the teaching approach observed tended to make use of a number of important techniques for encouraging learning, such as the 'presentation' and 'practice' phases of grammar teaching, but, on the other hand, used others, such as the grammar 'production' stage, much less frequently, if at all. Similarly, although whole-class work was used extensively and often successfully, there was very little use of related, more autonomous work involving small groups or pairs of students. Most questions asked were 'within the information given', thereby building up a firm basis for comprehension, but few opportunities were subsequently provided to also deepen understanding via the use of questions that went 'beyond the information given'; and so on. We therefore concluded that the project training should focus on helping the teachers to see how their existing approach might be built on and extended by more frequent use of 'complementary' techniques of the kind indicated, ones that we felt there was a well-established consensus for regarding their importance in facilitating learning.[2]

How well, however, did this approach work out in practice, particularly in terms of evidence of trainees' take up and use of the project teaching ideas? Evaluation data in Waters (2002: Chs. 7 & 8; 2006: 40–43) indicate that, while there was a good deal of interest in and, with respect to some of them, reasonably widespread use of the teaching techniques focused on in the training, impact was constrained by two main factors. These were, first, the relatively limited amount of course-based training that could be provided (seven days, on a 'one-off' basis). Many trainees indicated that a longer introduction to the ideas was needed at this stage. The second main constraint was the conditions prevailing in many schools, especially with respect to factors such as the students' low level of English, large class size, and lack of resources/teaching materials: many of the trainees indicated that they would have used all of the project teaching ideas a lot more frequently if these problems had not existed.

What can be concluded, therefore, is that while it makes sense, in terms of the theoretical perspectives discussed earlier, to attempt to bring about change in teaching methods by building on existing practice, rather than in a more 'top-down' manner, there will nevertheless be an irreducible amount of training needed to introduce teachers to new teaching ideas, however rooted they may be in existing practices. The ZoI, in other words, needs to be of an appropriate size quantitatively as much as qualitatively.

Equally, it also needs to be borne in mind by the change manager that the reason teachers tend not to use certain teaching techniques, and to favour other ones, is likely to have as much or more to do with the everyday realities of their teaching situations as, e.g., their lack of knowledge or motivation. In other words, it also needs to be ascertained in the first instance whether, within any given school system, the capacity for meaningful innovation exists, or whether, for this to occur, additional 'secondary innovations' (ones which, in this case, unfortunately, were beyond the capability of the project to effect, e.g., sufficient teaching materials) must first be introduced. As a corollary, despite the observations of and discussions with teachers that accompanied decision-making about the PELT project training focus, a more 'insider-oriented' perspective (e.g., by the inclusion of one or more practising secondary school teachers in the project management team – an arrangement which was logistically impossible to achieve at the time, however) might have helped to increase the compatibility of the training ideas further.

The horizontal dimension

In terms of attempting to also achieve 'horizontal' coherence in the PELT project, the proposed changes in teaching methods just described were regarded by the management team as creating related sets of teacher, trainer and 'ELT manager' needs, all of which also had to be properly catered for, in order to create the potential for the initial change to succeed. In what follows, because of the space available, the main focus is on only the last of these sets of needs, but further details of this aspect of project management as a whole are discussed in Waters and Vilches (2001).

Although the trainees were obviously those most immediately affected by the changes in teaching methods introduced by the PELT project, they were operating, of course, like all teachers, within the educational management structures of their school, itself part of the wider educational administration system. Numerous studies show that, as a consequence, for successful change to occur in teachers' teaching methods, school- and system-wide collaboration and co-operation is essential (see, e.g., Hopkins 2001; Adey 2004; Fullan 2007; also cf. Richards & Pennington 1998). Although no provision was made in the initial PELT project log-frame for activity aimed at attempting to establish links of this kind between the project and the 'host' systems, it was felt essential by the management team to attempt to do so, and so an 'ELT Managers Orientation Programme' (EMOP) was developed accordingly, partly as a formalisation of the process of initial familiarisation and consensus-building described above.

This programme took the form of a series of meetings, in each of the DECS educational administrative regions, with the regional and division-level ELT advisors, ELT heads of department, and so on, i.e., those with the most direct responsibility for monitoring and supporting the efforts of the trainees to implement the PELT project teaching ideas. Initially, these meetings were mainly of an information and discussion nature, i.e., concerned with trying to ensure that there was basic understanding of the project teaching ideas and their rationale[3] and of the proposed roles and responsibilities of project trainers and ELT managers in helping them to be implemented by the trainees (also see below). Subsequent meetings were mainly concerned with reviewing and fine-tuning these understandings and arrangements, in light of ongoing field experiences.

How effective was this part of the project change management strategy in practice, however? In a nutshell, data in Waters (2002: 353–354; 2006: 43–47) indicate that, while the concept of the programme was warmly welcomed by the ELT managers, since they, too, regarded the potential for success of the project training effort as hinging crucially on the close mutual collaboration between the project 'training system' and themselves, many of them also felt it should have been a good deal more extensive in terms of providing them with the necessary level of understanding about both i) the project teaching ideas, and ii) the operation of the training seminar school-based follow-up system (see below). These limitations were, however, a product of the original project conceptualisation, as already explained, which did not include provision for an element of this kind, and it was therefore always recognised by the project management team that the resources for mounting it would therefore, unfortunately, be a good deal more limited than should have been the case. It nevertheless seems clear that such a component should be a *sine qua non* for the development of an effective educational change management strategy.

The 'School-based Follow-up Development Activity' (SFDA)

The final practical illustration of the ideas mentioned above concerns its third part, i.e., the importance of an overall 'delegation'-oriented change management strategy. The primary way in which this was attempted in the PELT project was through its 'School-based Follow-up Development Activity' (SFDA) element. In addition to the motivations already discussed for wishing to encourage as much delegation of innovation development as possible to potential adopters, there is a considerable body of evidence (see, e.g., Adey 2004) that the learning of new teaching ideas by teachers is rarely possible on the basis of course-based teacher learning only; rather, in addition, a lengthy period of structured school-based experimentation is also required. It was, therefore, for this reason, as well as for the others already discussed, that the PELT project teacher training vehicle consisted both of a period of course-based ('seminar') study of the teaching ideas being proposed *and* a related 'SFDA', i.e., a sequence of activities planned by the teachers during the seminar to guide their attempts, after the end of the seminar, to put one of its teaching ideas into practice in their home teaching situations, in collaboration with their ELT managers.

In this way it was intended that the training seminar, rather than being a one-way, mainly input-oriented 'end in itself', would instead become a starting point for encouraging a process of relatively autonomous experimentation with the seminar teaching ideas – 'delegated learning' – on the part of the trainees and their ELT managers. The project EMOP, as already explained, was intended to provide a measure of 'after-care' for this process, a 'light-touch' trouble-shooting service to ensure that any unforeseen problems were solved and the system fine-tuned as necessary. However, in overall terms the main responsibility for take-up of the training ideas was devolved in this way by the project SFDA to the school system. As a result, it was assumed, the potential for creative reinvention of the teaching ideas would be maximised, and thereby also their potential for ownership and long-term 'institutionalisation'.

Space prevents further discussion of the operational details of the SFDA, but additional information is available in, e.g., Waters and Vilches (2000). What is essential to consider here, however, is the extent to which there is evidence that the overall purpose of this part of the project was achieved. Research data in Waters (2002: Chs. 7–10; 2006: 39–46) show firstly that, from the perspective of many of the trainees, although the SFDA was perceived positively, in terms of the opportunities it provided for attempting to transfer and tailor the training ideas to the home teaching situation, the amounts of 'seminar' training provided – with respect to both the new teaching ideas (which, of course, acted as 'input' to the SFDA), as well as in relation to the procedures for implementing the SFDA itself – were frequently regarded as insufficient. Problems in obtaining the necessary co-operation and support from school authorities in executing the SFDA were also frequently reported. Secondly, although ELT managers were likewise well-disposed towards the basic concept of the SFDA, there was also a perception by a significant number of them (as already mentioned in the previous section) that insufficient information and guidance had been provided about certain aspects of both the project teaching ideas and the operation of the SFDA.[4]

These were limitations which the authors were painfully aware of during the unfolding of the project: however, the SFDA element, like the EMOP, had not been envisaged in the original project framework, and was therefore similarly difficult to resource adequately. Nevertheless, the overall lesson to be drawn is that the SFDA itself was perceived as a welcome and important element in the project change management strategy, by both teachers and ELT managers, and that change initiatives such as the PELT project need to be designed from the outset so that the appropriate level of resources for facilitating effective partnership and delegation in the development of the change is provided.

Reflection and conclusion

As has been seen, despite the application to it of the change management concepts described above, the level of change that the PELT project was able to achieve was, in certain respects, less than intended. However, as has also been shown, this was mainly due to a lack, in the initial planning and resourcing of the project, of the level of provision needed for more fully incorporating a number of the elements essential for the effective management of change. One of the main lessons of the PELT experience, thus, is the need for greater understanding on the part of project planners of what the management of change involves, and for this to be properly allowed for in the initial project design.

At the same time, there are clear signs that the change management concepts that were used in the PELT project were successful in many ways. The focus on extensive 'backstaging' paid extensive dividends in terms of establishing good-will, trust and commitment on the part of DECS towards the project, despite the inauspicious circumstances surrounding the original management arrangements. The 'incremental' approach to establishing the focus of the teacher training meant that a more relevant set of teaching ideas were identified than would have otherwise been the case. Also, the EMOP and SFDA were both widely appreciated as providing the right kind of change management structure, in terms of the opportunities for collaboration and independence they provided for both teachers and ELT managers. It is therefore hoped that the examples of the theory and practice of managing change in English language education that this chapter has been concerned with will be of use to others working on similar change initiatives elsewhere.

Notes

1 The research subjects were change project managers working in a range of manufacturing and services industries. None of them was involved in education. This difference in background obviously needs to be borne in mind, but the central management issue – of establishing support for a change initiative within an organisation – is clearly a generic one.

2 The resulting project teacher training topics were 'Levels of Thinking', 'Small-group Work', 'Facilitating Learner Involvement', 'Integrating Language Work' and 'Making Grammar Work More Creative'.

3   To the same end, ELT managers were also encouraged to attend the project teacher training seminars as 'auditors'.
4   It can also be concluded that this was one of the reasons for the perception by some teachers of a lack of responsiveness in this area by their school authorities.

Key readings

Kennedy, C., Doyle, P., & Goh, C. C. M. (Eds.). (1999). *Exploring Change in English Language Teaching*. Oxford: Macmillan. Contains a wide-ranging set of articles covering change management projects at the national, institutional and classroom levels, all well supported in terms of theoretical background and 'practitioner-friendly' detail.
Markee, N. (1997). *Managing curricular innovation*. Cambridge: Cambridge University Press. Provides an analysis of a number of major recent innovations in English language education, a summary of many important aspects of innovation theory, a case study of one of the author's own major curriculum innovation projects, and a discussion of the overall implications for the management of change.
Wedell, M. (2009). *Planning for Educational Change – Putting People and Their Contexts first*. London: Continuum. On the basis of a survey of a number of aspects of innovation theory, this book provides an overall algorithm for thinking through the management of change in English language education projects, and then illustrates its application in the evaluation and design of a series of large-scale, public-sector change projects in a range of different areas.

References

Adey, P. (2004). *The Professional Development of Teachers: Practice and Theory*. Dordretch, The Netherlands: Kluwer Academic Publishers.
Alderson, J. C. (2009). Setting the scene. In J. C. Alderson (Ed.), *The Politics of Language Education* (pp. 8–44). Bristol, UK: Multilingual Matters.
Blanchard, K. H., Oncken, W., & Burrows, H. (2004). *The One Minute Manager Meets the Monkey*. London: Harper Collins.
Bowers, R. (1983). Project planning and performance. In C. J. Brumfit (Ed.), *ELT Documents 116: Language Teaching Projects for the Third World* (pp. 99–120). Oxford: Pergamon Press/The British Council.
Bridges, W., & Mitchell, S. (2000). Leading transitions: a new model for change. *Leader To Leader Journal* (Vol. 16). New York: Leader to Leader Institute.
Buchanan, D. A., & Boddy, D. (1992). *The Expertise of the Change Agent: Public Performance and Backstage Activity*. New York: Prentice Hall.
Chin, R., & Benne, K. (1970). General strategies for effecting changes in human systems. In W. Bennis, K. Benne, & R. Chin (Eds.), *The Planning of Change* (pp. 32–59). London: Holt, Rinehart, and Winston.
Fullan, M. (2007). *The New Meaning of Educational Change* (4th edn). Abingdon, Oxon: Routledge.
Hall, G. E., & Hord, S. M. (2001). *Implementing Change: Patterns, Principles, and Potholes*. Boston: Allyn and Bacon.
Holliday, A. (1990). A role for soft systems methodology in ELT projects. *System*, 18(1), 77–84.
Hopkins, D. (2001). *School Improvement for Real*. London; New York: Routledge.
Kelly, P. (1980). From innovation to adaptability: the changing perspective of curriculum development. In M. Galton (Ed.), *Curriculum Change: The Lessons of a Decade* (pp. 65–80). Leicester: Leicester University Press.
Kennedy, C. (1987). Innovating for a change. *ELT Journal*, 41(3), 163–170.

Markee, N. (1997). *Managing Curricular Innovation*. Cambridge: Cambridge University Press.

Marris, P. (1986). *Loss and Change* (rev. edn). London: Routledge & Kegan Paul.

Murray, D. E. (2008). Learning to anticipate the unforeseeable. In D. E. Murray (Ed.), *Planning Change, Changing Plans* (pp. 5–10). Ann Arbor: The University of Michigan Press.

Richards, J. C., & Pennington, M. (1998). The first year of teaching. In *Beyond Training* (pp. 173–190). Cambridge: Cambridge University Press.

Rogers, E. M. (2003). *Diffusion of Innovations* (5th edn). New York: Free Press.

Stoller, F. L. (1994). The diffusion of innovations in intensive ESL programs. *Applied Linguistics*, 15(3), 300–327.

Waters, A. (2002). *In-service Teacher Learning in ELT Projects and Programmes: An Integrated Approach*. Unpublished Ph.D. thesis Lancaster University, UK, Lancaster.

Waters, A. (2006). Facilitating follow-up in ELT INSET. *Language Teaching Research*, 10(1), 32–52.

Waters, A. (2009). Managing innovation in English language education: state-of-the-art review. *Language Teaching*, 42(4), 421–458.

Waters, A., & Vilches, M. L. C. (2000). Integrating teacher learning: the school-based follow-up development activity. *ELT Journal*, 54(2), 126–134.

Waters, A., & Vilches, M. L. C. (2001). Implementing ELT innovations: a needs analysis framework. *ELT Journal*, 55(2), 133–141.

Wedell, M. (2003). Giving TESOL change a chance: supporting key players in the curriculum change process. *System*, 31(4), 439–456.

Wedell, M. (2009). *Planning for Educational Change – Putting People and Their Contexts First*. London: Continuum.

SECTION 2

Innovation and change in teacher education

6

INNOVATION THROUGH TEACHER EDUCATION PROGRAMS

Karen E. Johnson

The emergence of what has been coined the 'sociocultural turn' in the disciplines of Second Language Acquisition (Block, 2003), Second Language Teacher Education (SLTE) (Johnson, 2006; 2009), and more generally in Applied Linguistics (MLJ Focus Issue, 2007) has led to an understanding of human cognition and cognitive development (learning) as originating in and fundamentally shaped by engagement in social activities (Vygotsky, 1978; 1986). From this epistemological perspective, cognitive development cannot be removed from activity since it originates in and is framed by the very nature of that activity. Thus, it follows that *what* is learned will be fundamentally shaped by *how* it is learned. Taken up within the context of SLTE, it can be assumed that what teachers learn about L2 learning and teaching will be shaped by how they learn it. In other words, while novice teachers will most certainly learn about language, language learning and language teaching in their SLTE programs, *what* they learn will be fundamentally shaped by the quality and character of the activities they engage in within their SLTE programs.

More than three decades of research on teacher cognition (see Borg, 2006; Freeman, 2002) has documented the fact that teachers typically ground their understandings of teaching and learning as well as their notions about how to teach in their own instructional histories as learners (Lortie, 1975). However, when novice teachers enter SLTE programs, they are exposed to the latest theory and research that reflects the profession's current stance on what constitutes theoretically and pedagogically sound L2 instruction. This disjuncture, between teachers' *everyday concepts* (Karpov, 2003) about language, language learning and language teaching gleaned from their instructional histories and the *scientific concepts* (Karpov, 2003) they are exposed to in their SLTE programs, epitomizes the persistent theory/practice divide that remains a major challenge for SLTE programs today. When addressing this divide from a sociocultural theoretical perspective, it becomes the responsibility of SLTE programs to present relevant scientific concepts to teachers, but to do so in ways that bring these concepts to bear on concrete practical activity, connecting them to their everyday concepts and the goal-directed activities of actual teaching.

SLTE programs attempting to embrace a sociocultural theoretical perspective on teacher learning (Johnson, 2009) must take stock of how they are expecting teachers to develop teaching expertise by asking: What is the nature of the activities embedded in our teacher education programs? What are we collectively attempting to accomplish in these activities? What sort of assistance are we providing for teachers as they engage in these activities? And how does participation in these activities support and enhance the development of teaching expertise? This chapter addresses these questions by looking at the social practices and situated contexts through which teachers are expected to engage in the activities embedded in SLTE programs. In particular, it traces the implementation of a restructured microteaching simulation in a TESL methodology course in order to demonstrate how this innovation creates spaces for strategic mediation in teacher learning, as well as opportunities for novice teachers to materialize their emerging understandings of both pedagogical and subject matter concepts within the authentic activities of L2 teaching.

Linking theory/practice: the microteaching simulation

The microteaching simulation, in which novice teachers plan and teach 'mini-lessons' in front of their peers as a component of a methodology course, has been a common practice for bridging the theory/practice divide in teacher education programs. In its initial iterations, the microteaching simulation was framed from a positivist epistemological perspective in which teaching was conceptualized as a set of discrete behaviors that could be broken down into smaller behavioral components that could be studied, practiced, and mastered through imitation and repetition (Politzer, 1969). Thus, novice teachers were asked to move through a cycle of plan-teach-observe-critique until a particular instructional behavior was mastered. As more interpretive epistemological perspectives began to influence how teaching was conceptualized, a reflective component was added to the microteaching simulation in which participants were asked to engage in careful self-examination and critical self-reflection on the broader social and institutional contexts in which teaching takes place (Richards & Farrell, 2005; Wallace, 1996). Despite claims that the microteaching simulation provides novice teachers with a taste of 'real' teaching where they feel supported and receive useful feedback (Farrell, 2008), the fact remains that the learners aren't real, the subject matter isn't real, and the context in which the microteaching is carried out isn't real. In this sense, the microteaching simulation does not simulate 'real' teaching, largely because the social, cultural, and institutional factors that are endemic to 'real' teaching are simply not present.

The innovation: the extended team teaching project

Within the context of an introductory TESL methodology course, the microteaching simulation was re-conceptualized based on a sociocultural theoretical perspective on teacher learning (Johnson & Arshavskaya, 2011). The goal of the project was to create multiple opportunities for novice teachers to participate in a range of authentic activities associated with language teaching, to create multiple opportunities for strategic mediation (Wertsch, 1985) from peers and the TESL course instructor throughout the various activities embedded in the project, and to support novice teachers through multiple attempts at materializing and enacting their teaching practices, all with the ultimate goal of moving them toward greater self-regulation of theoretically and pedagogically sound instructional practices.

The extended team teaching project required teams (three to four) of novice teachers enrolled in a 15-week TESL methodology course to teach a 75-minute lesson in an actual ESL course. The project was designed to move team members through the following chronology of activities:

a) *Classroom Observation* – In order to establish a better sense of the situated context in which the team would eventually teach, each team member individually observed at least one session (most observed two) of their assigned ESL course. The observations enabled the team to gain a greater sense of the ESL students' goals, motivation, and L2 proficiency, the particulars of this instructional setting, including the curricular materials and required assessments, and the local settings that the ESL students would be expected to function in once they completed the ESL course. The observations also created opportunities for team members to observe the instructor's teaching and speak informally with the ESL students and course instructor before and after the class and to gather course syllabi and other relevant instructional materials.

b) *Tutoring Assignment* – Each team member participated in six one-hour tutoring sessions with a student enrolled in his/her assigned ESL course. This activity created an opportunity for extensive informal tutor/tutee interaction in which the novice teachers provided assistance on relevant course assignments and/or other L2 learning priorities identified by three to four ESL students. A final reflective paper was required in which novice teachers reflected on what they had learned about L2 learners, L2 learning, and L2 tutoring, based on this experience. The tutoring experience proved to be critical in both planning and teaching the eventual lesson because team members gained invaluable information about the ESL course from their interactions with their tutees and they were assured of at least one familiar face in the ESL course they would eventually teach.

c) *Collaborative Lesson Planning: Pre-Practice Teach* – Based on content provided by the ESL course instructor, team members collaboratively constructed a lesson plan for the lesson they were assigned to teach. They were encouraged to supplement the required curriculum, however their lesson needed to meet the instructional objectives articulated in the course syllabi. Through both face-to-face and virtual meetings, the teams created a lesson plan that included instructional objectives, how they had conceptualized the content, the organization of the lesson, strategies for supporting student learning, and an assessment plan.

d) *Practice Team Teach* – Each team completed a one-hour 'practice teach' in front of their peers and the TESL course instructor. During the practice teach, instruction was halted at numerous points to allow peers and the course instructor to ask questions, provide feedback, and/or make suggestions. Such intermittent probing, commentary, and suggestions proved to be a critical form of strategic mediation as the team members attempted to reconcile what they had planned for the lesson with how it was being experienced by their peers, and how the lesson might be re-conceptualized to better meet the instructional needs of the ESL students. This activity also created an opportunity for the teachers to materialize their lesson, both in concrete artifacts, such as handouts and PowerPoint presentations, but also in the ways in which they organized student participation in the activities they were attempting to enact in the lesson. The entire 'practice teach' session lasted one hour and was video recorded.

e) *Collaborative Lesson Planning: Post-Practice Teach* – Based on feedback during the 'practice teach' each team revised their original lesson plan. Some teams met face-to-face with the instructor, while others met virtually and then submitted their final lesson plan for feedback prior to the 'actual teach'. This activity created an opportunity for the teams to rematerialize their lesson plans with an eye for how it might be experienced by their ESL students, to reorient the sequencing of activities, and for some teams, to restructure or supplement the content to be covered in order to better achieve the goals of the lesson.

f) *Actual Team Teach* – Each team then taught the redesigned lesson to their assigned ESL course. The TESL methods course instructor attended the session but did not intervene. This activity prompted the team to make many in-flight decisions as it became clear that in the activity of actual teaching, they needed to alter or adjust their plans depending on how the ESL students responded to teacher-initiated questions and/or engaged in certain instructional activities. In addition, team members supported each other, for example, if one member struggled to explain an activity or failed to understand an ESL student's question/comment. The 'actual teach' session lasted 75 minutes and was video recorded.

g) *Team Stimulated Recall Session* – Within 48 hours, the team watched their video recorded 'actual teach' with the TESL methods course instructor. They were allowed to stop the recording at any point to comment on what they were doing, what they were thinking, or how they were feeling. They were encouraged to externalize their thinking and consider alternative instructional strategies that might have been appropriate in the lesson. This activity created an opportunity for the teachers to externalize their thoughts while at the same time receiving strategic mediation from their fellow team members and the TESL course instructor. The 'stimulated recall session' lasted 75 minutes and was audio recorded.

h) *Team Teaching Individual Reflection Paper* – Each team member was given a digital copy of the 'practice teach', the 'actual teach', and the 'stimulated recall session' and then asked to write a five to seven page reflection paper in which they focused primarily on what they learned about themselves as teachers, about the activity of L2 teaching, and about their learning-to-teach experiences throughout the entire extended team teaching project. This activity created a final opportunity for team members to externalize their understandings of themselves as teachers and the activity of L2 teaching based on their experiences in the extended team teaching project.

Table 6.1 shows the timeline for the extended team teaching project.

A case study: tracing teacher learning

A team of four novice teachers, two undergraduate and two graduate students, were assigned to teach a lesson on the concept of nominalization in academic writing in a university-level ESL freshman composition course. The instructor

TABLE 6.1 Timeline for the extended team teaching project

Week 5	Weeks 5–9	Weeks 9–13	Weeks 9–13	Weeks 9–13	Week 15
Observation of ESL course	Weekly 1-hour tutoring sessions with student from the ESL course	'Practice team teach' in TESL methodology course	1-week following the 'practice team teach' – 'actual team teach' in the ESL course	24–48 hours after the 'actual team teach' – stimulated recall session with teacher educator and team	5–7 page reflection papers due

of the ESL course provided the team with a handout entitled 'useful and useless nominalizations' around which they structured their initial lesson plan. In fact, one teacher mentioned that the team felt constrained by the handout, stating in her reflection paper:

> We felt constrained by the materials that had been provided to us by the teacher of the class. We felt as if we had to integrate his materials into our lesson and organized our lesson in a way that was based strongly on the organization of his materials. (Reflection Paper T2).

As is typical of novice teachers, the team's initial conceptualization of nominalization was 'object-regulated' based on the materials given to them by the ESL course instructor. Thus, their initial materialization of the lesson focused first on the grammatical structure of nominalization, in other words, 'turning a verb or adjective into a noun, i.e., *discover* became *discovery*, *move* became *movement*, *react* became *reaction* etc.' (Nominalization Handout 1). They planned to accomplish this with a 'matching activity' in which students matched slips of paper containing a verb or adjective with its nominalized form. During the 'practice team teach', however, the matching activity failed to orient their peers to the purpose of the lesson which was brought to the team's attention (T1-4) first by a peer (S1) and later by the TESL course instructor (I).

Practice team teach. Excerpt 1: strategic mediation – re-conceptualizing the pedagogical concept of orienting

S1: I think it might be better to... like I understand that you were, like, ah, introducing the concept and then explaining it but it might be better to explain it and then do *this* activity.

T1: (Yes).

S1: Because I just. I mean. I <u>speak</u> English so I just matched them together so that it makes sense. But if they do need help with English and doing things like this they might not be able to match them up, that well. You know what I mean? **But if they understand the <u>purpose</u> of what they are doing, it might help them to be able to figure out some of these match-ups.**

T1: so explain more?

S1: I don't know

T4: The activity is more of atten- attention-grabber so just the beginning of this.

I: Right. And I I get that strategy and I really like that strategy a lot and because what you wanna do is to bring them right into the language but I I <u>knew</u> what you guys were doing today and I looked at this and I was like 'what are we doing?' And then [S6] of course told me what we were supposed to do and so I figured that out. **But remember when I was** talking last week to you about orienting ((in a slowed tempo)) your students? One thing you could say is that this whole activity was orienting, right? You were trying to orient them to it. But orienting in what way? Like, for me, as a <u>learner</u> what I wanted to know is. Why do I care about nominalization? Why is it an important thing? How does it fit in into any kind of context? (00:21:30–00:23:46)

In excerpt 1, the 'practice team teach' not only created a public space for the team to receive feedback on how their peers were experiencing this opening activity, but it also gave the TESL course instructor an opportunity to remind the team of the pedagogical concept of *orienting* (Gal'perin, 1989), defined as:

> Orienting – situate the concept, skill, or content you are teaching in such a way as to make all of its features salient and relevant to the students; help them relate to it in some concrete or personally relevant way … this will help them see the 'big picture' and relate what they already know to what you are going to teach them. (TESL Course Handout #1)

Despite the fact that the TESL course instructor had defined, modeled, and emphasized the instructional value of *orienting* during the TESL methods course, the comment made by a team member (T4) that 'The activity is more of atten- attention-grabber so just the beginning of this' suggests that, at least initially, the team had not conceptualized this opening activity as a way of *orienting* the students to the concept of nominalization but instead as an 'attention grabber'. Thus, the 'practice team teach' created a mediational space where once the team's intentions behind the matching activity became public, their thinking became open to social mediation and restructuring by the TESL course instructor who explicitly inserted the pedagogical concept of *orienting* into the ongoing flow of the team's teaching activity while simultaneously reminding the team of its pedagogical value in L2 instruction.

Later in the 'practice team teach' (Excerpt 2), the pedagogical concept of *orienting* emerged again, initiated by a peer (S7) who indicates that he 'missed a big part of it' [the purpose of the lesson] because the team had failed to orient them to the concept of nominalization. This again created an opportunity for the TESL course instructor to remind the team of the pedagogical concept of *orienting* and reiterate its instructional value for their lesson.

Practice team teach. Excerpt 2: strategic mediation – re-conceptualizing the pedagogical concept of orienting

S7: another problem is too that when it's done presentation style (as was done in the beginning) it kinda goes over your head, which by the final activity you don't get those first parts, then they'd get to see (early on) because they didn't do any activities **because they'd miss a big part of it** ( )

I: **That's that's what I mean by orienting. When you want to** <u>orient</u> **your students you want to give them a** <u>big picture.</u> **You wanna give them some contextualized big thing that they can say – oh I get it! Now let's dissect it, and pull it apart, and figure out how these thing work and play with it, and do different things, but without that sort of** <u>big picture</u> **I'm kinda left wandering around, I'm not really sure.** And hopefully, you know you can get it this way, but you can also get it right in the beginning by getting it by a sort of big picture when you have those two examples that you can look at. **Now let's start looking about the different ways that we nominalize, what effect does that have, let's try doing it, that kind of thing.** (1:04:38–1:05:41)

When it came time for the 'actual team teach', the team rematerialized their opening activity as a question–answer exchange which served to orient the ESL students to the notion that 'nominalization is a tool that can make academic writing clear and concise' (Team 1 Actual Team Teach). In Excerpt 3, one team member (T2) walks the ESL students through an introductory question-and-answer exchange in which he attempts to situate the concept of nominalization, moving from broad generalizations about genres of writing to the role of nominalization in academic writing.

Actual team teach. Excerpt 3: re-materialization of the lesson – orienting the students to the concept of nominalization

T2: Can people list for me anything you use writing for?
Students offer suggestions, teacher writes them on the board

T2 … and for every different type of writing the purpose is different, the characteristics you associate it with are different, ah the audience you are trying to write for is different

T2 … so, what are the characteristics of academic writing? How would you describe academic writing? *Students offer suggestions, teacher writes them on the board*

T2 … and in <u>this</u> class we are going to try to improve word choice in writing and to improve conciseness in writing using nominalization (0:01:15–0:06:43)

Thus, we see evidence that the team took up the mediation provided during the 'practice team teach' and attempted to orient the ESL students to the concept of nominalization. Their efforts were subsequently reinforced during the 'stimulated recall session' when the TESL course instructor stopped the video recording of the 'actual team teach' and named their introductory question/answer exchange as successfully *orienting* the ESL students to the concept of nominalization.

Stimulated recall. Excerpt 4: naming activity – emerging understanding of the pedagogical concept of orienting

T2's introduction to the class is being watched.

I: **So I would call that an orienting activity.** I don't know if you guys thought of that in that way but basically you are saying you got academic writing has (sort of) certain characteristics to it, what we're gonna do today is X, and and er it's clear and concise, one way we can (do it) clear and concise is nominalization. **Just orients them to (why are we talking about nominalization) what that has to do with- and I like the way you did that.** Sort of like open up here and finally get down to what the thing we are gonna do today. I think this kind of orientation is is (helpful for them to understand) why they are bothering to do this. OK.

Video is being watched.

I: So for your part, how did you feel about that?

T2: Ah. I didn't have to change it much from before which we sort of just switched around it as we discussed when we practiced in class. How, the, **the matching activity was kinda confusing because you didn't know what you were doing-**

I: Right- **there was no orienting to it**

T2: **so to give them the idea of what we are trying to do and in the context of their class**—(0:10:27–0:12:10)

In excerpt 4, team member T2 admits that their original matching activity had failed to orient their peers to the concept of nominalization and thus the question/answer activity enabled them to orient the ESL students to the purpose of their lesson within the context of their composition course.

Further evidence of the team's emerging understanding of the pedagogical concept of *orienting* was also found in their final reflection papers. Team member T3 appropriates the conceptualization emphasized by the TESL course instructor.

> One of the key factors I learned about teaching was that it is very important to orient your students before you get into the lesson. This is essential because it gives students a sense of the subject of the lesson, where it is going, and what is expected from them. A good way to orient students is to provide examples that illustrate the point of the lesson in a contextual way. (Reflection Paper T3)

She followed this comment with reference to the pedagogical value of *orienting* during the portion of the lesson she was responsible for.

> With regards to my part of the lesson, I hope it helped the students to be able to orient themselves as to what nominalization can do to their writing and how to avoid it … how nominalization works, how to avoid

over using it, and how to identify too much nominalization in their own writing. (Reflection Paper T3)

T2 also appropriates the TESL course instructor's conceptualization of orienting, along with several others, as 'important teaching strategies that can be applied to any lesson' (Reflection Paper T2):

> Another strategy we discussed was making instruction predictable. This can be done by orienting the lesson and letting the students know what we are going to be doing and what the expectations of them are going to be. This aids in the process of engineering participation and making the students comfortable in the learning environment. (Reflection Paper T2)

The other two novice teachers in the team explicitly framed the 'practice teach' experience as enabling them to see their instruction from the students' perspective. T4 indicates that the failure of the matching activity to successfully orient her peers pushed the team to re-order their lesson plan.

> Practice teaching our lesson plan in APLNG 493 was not what we expected, and, consequently, a major learning experience. Our idea to begin with showing, rather than introducing, failed as an attention grabber and succeeded only in confusing all of our practice students. If our class couldn't follow us, how would the ESL students from 004? (Reflection Paper T4)

Similarly the novice teacher T1 who led the matching activity, mentioned the value of seeing her teaching from the students' perspective and recognized the value of modeling as a way to orient students to the activity at hand.

> During the practice, our classmates became our students and helped us a lot to rearrange the lesson plans more from the students' perspective. Usually, it's easy for teachers to think from their own perspective that their students might know something. For example, I thought students could know how to match the verbs/adjectives with the proper suffix right when getting the pieces of papers right away, so I don't have to spend so much time explaining how to play the game or modeling for them. Without practicing this, I may never find that modeling is necessary for the students. (Reflection Paper T1)

As the team's understanding of the pedagogical concept of orienting emerged, so too did their understanding of the subject matter concept they were expected to teach; namely, nominalization. While their initial materialization of the lesson focused on 'word-structure' (i.e., react -> reaction) and 'types' (i.e., useful/useless nominalizations), overuse of nominalization (contrasting sentences/paragraphs) and de-nominalization (making sentences 'sound' better), during the 'practice team teach' there are multiple instances of strategic mediation where the TESL course instructor attempts to re-orient the team's conceptualization of nominalization. For example, in excerpt 5, the TESL course instructor emphasizes the rhetorical effects of nominalization and suggests that the team try to contextualize their examples as a way to highlight the various types of nominalizations.

Practice team teach. Excerpt 5: strategic mediation – re-conceptualizing the subject matter concept of nominalization

I: OK. So. Because what I was thinking was em if we could <u>see</u> just two texts which were just short paragraphs and one had virtually no nominalization in it at all and then the other had all the different types you are gonna now present to us=

T2: =Right

I: And then **if we looked at them as whole pieces we kinda get the <u>effect</u> of what nominalization does to the reader and <u>then</u> you break out the examples and put them in so so this particular example of nominalization shows how you can refer to a previous subject and this type of nominalization is how you go from a verb to a noun, or whatever.** (00:30:47–00:31:32)

In excerpt 6, team member T2 questions the value of his own explanations of 'useful and useless nominalizations' to which the TESL course instructor tries again to move the team away from presenting nominalization as a list of different 'types' to making the rhetorical effects of nominalization more salient to the ESL students.

Practice team teach excerpt 6: strategic mediation – re-conceptualizing the subject matter concept of nominalization

T2: I'm not sure how important these explanations, of what it is,

I: a:hu

T2: are. You could just give the examples and,

I: That's what I'm thinking.

T2: then it's more clear

I: That's what I'm thinking. Because otherwise it seems that there are ten different ways to nominalize and here are the ten different ways and I have to memorize them. **But it's not really what is important. It's really the rhetorical <u>effect</u> of the writing on the <u>reader</u>. So maybe you can sorta <u>get rid of</u> different types and just present some examples and have them sort of talk about it. What's the <u>effect</u> of that? Why is that clearer or not clearer?** (00:43:02–00:43:33)

When comparing the team's 'practice team teach' to their 'actual team teach' the essential difference in their re-materialization of the lesson was not so much in *what* they did, but *how* they did it. In other words, while their instructional activities were essentially the same, the way they verbally framed each activity placed a much greater emphasis on the salient features of nominalization; highlighting both its effect on readers and appropriate usage. For example, during the 'practice team teach', T3 only mentioned the rhetorical effects of nominalization once, as a concluding remark at the very end of the lesson.

T3: So, hopefully through this exercise you can see how **using too much nominalization, especially in academic writing, can confuse the meaning that you are trying to get across, um, to your reader.** (Practice Team Teach 00:52:23–00:52:39)

However, during the 'actual team teach' she opened this activity by stating:

T3: So, now that [T2] and [T1] have kinda explained to you guys what nominalization is and how you create it, we're gonna take a look at **the effects it has on your writing and how it can change the meaning of it, so** (Actual Team Teach 00:17:08–00:17:20)

After the ESL students had analyzed two contrasting sentences for appropriate and inappropriate uses of nominalization, she concluded:

T3: … so basically there's an over usage of nominalization there, so you can see how, **if you use it too much, it can make your sentence difficult to understand** and then this one below, basically takes the same words and turns them into nouns or back to adjectives or adverbs and **its much more clear for the reader, so you can understand better the meaning of the sentence.** (Actual Team Teach 00:19:02–00:19:28)

And after they had discussed two contrasting paragraphs, she ended the activity with:

And so, even though this is not something you would find, academic writing, it's not a piece of academic writing, it kinda gives you an idea of what **over usage of nominalization can do to your writing, in general, and just how it can change the idea that you want it to express through your writing.** (Actual Team Teach 00:29:24–00:29:53)

Evidence from the team's final reflection papers supports a reorientation in their understanding of the concept of nominalization. For example, T4 admits that the team was initially unfamiliar with the concept of nominalization but eventually came to understand it more in terms of its use.

it took some time to familiarize ourselves with the concept. ... we understood that nominalization is the process of changing a verb or an adjective into a noun, but it was interesting to learn that there is an appropriate and an inappropriate time to do this. (Reflection Paper T4)

T3 emphasizes the importance of enabling ESL students to understand the meaning of nominalization in context rather than its formal definitions.

> I think it would have been more beneficial to the students if we began the lesson with examples of nominalization in context instead of just solitary sentences. It is more difficult to see the positive or negative effects of nominalization when it is used as part of an isolated sentence versus in a complete paragraph. I think this ... would have helped them to understand the meaning of nominalization better than simply providing the formal definitions of nominalization. (Reflective Paper T3)

While T2 refers to 'nominalization as a tool', in both the 'practice teach' and the 'actual teach', in his reflection paper he indicated that if the team were to teach the lesson again, they should place even greater emphasis on 'using nominalization as a tool'.

> Instead of focusing on nominalization we could focus on making writing more clear and concise using nominalization as a tool. (Reflective Paper T2)

T3 hints at her own struggle, as a native speaker, to simply understand the concept of nominalization no less to teach it without having the meta-language to do so.

> The biggest challenge of teaching is that the teacher must understand the materials well enough to explain it to someone else in a way that they will understand it ... for example, native speakers may experience difficulties teaching certain aspects of English because they were never explained to them in technical terms. (Reflective Paper T3)

Reflection: implications for teacher education programs

By design, the extended team teaching project detailed in this chapter represents an innovation that supports and enhances novice teachers' initial learning-to-teach experiences. It creates multiple opportunities for strategic mediation in teacher learning as well as opportunities for teachers to materialize their emerging understandings of both pedagogical and subject matter concepts within the authentic activities of L2 teaching. Data from the case study suggest that it was the simultaneous attention to content and pedagogy, multiple opportunities for strategic mediation, and multiple opportunities to externalize, materialize, and enact their emerging understandings of both pedagogical and subject matter concepts that worked in consort to push these novice teachers' emerging understanding of both what and how to teach.

By looking at the professional development activities embedded in our SLTE programs, we must ask the essential questions mentioned at the outset of this chapter: What is the nature of the activities embedded in our teacher education programs? What are we collectively attempting to accomplish in these activities? What sort of assistance are we providing for teachers as they engage in these activities? And how does participation in these activities support and enhance the development of teaching expertise? Innovations to SLTE programs in the future must not only ask these questions but attempt to structure their activities in ways that create opportunities for novice teachers to learn to teach by participating in the actual activities of teaching while also creating multiple opportunities for them to receive strategic mediation that supports and sustains productive teacher learning in SLTE programs.

Key readings

Johnson, K. E. & Golombek, P. R. (Eds.) (2011). *Research on second language teacher education: A sociocultural perspective on professional development*. New York: Routledge. Embracing a sociocultural perspective on human cognition and employing an array of methodological tools for data collection and analysis, this volume documents the complexities of second language teachers' professional development in diverse L2 teacher education programs around the world.

Burns, A., & Richards, J. C. (Eds.) (2009). *The Cambridge guide to second language teacher education*. New York: Cambridge University Press. This volume contains 30 state-of-the-art articles that cover the issues, debates, and approaches in contemporary second language teacher education and addresses the changing contexts of language teaching and teacher education.

References

Block, D. (2003). *The social turn in second language acquisition*. Washington, DC: Georgetown University Press.

Borg, S. (2006). *Teacher cognition and language education: Research and practice*. London: Continuum.

Farrell, T. (2008). Promoting reflective practice in initial English language teacher education: Reflective microteaching. *Asian Journal of English Language Teaching*, 18, 1–15.

Freeman, D. (2002). The hidden side of the work: Teacher knowledge and learning to teach. *Language Teaching, 35*, 1–13.

Gal'perin, P. I. (1989). Organization of mental activity and the effectiveness of learning. *Soviet Psychology, 27* (2), 65–82.

Johnson, K. E. (2006). The sociocultural turn and its challenges for second language teacher education. *TESOL Quarterly, 40* (1), 235–257.

Johnson, K. E. (2009). *Second language teacher education: A sociocultural perspective*. New York: Routledge.

Johnson, K. E. & Arshavskaya. E. (2011). Reconceptualizing the micro-teaching simulation in an MA TESL course. In K. E. Johnson & P. R. Golombek (Eds.) *Research on second language teacher education: A sociocultural perspective on professional development* (pp. 168–186). New York: Routledge.

Karpov, Y. V. (2003). Vygotsky's doctrine of scientific concepts. Its role in contemporary education. In A. Kozulin, B. Gindis, V. S. Ageyev, & S. M. Miller (Eds.) *Vygotsky's educational theory in cultural context* (pp. 65–82). Cambridge: Cambridge University Press.

Lortie, D. (1975). *Schoolteacher: A sociological study.* Chicago: University of Chicago Press.

Politzer, P. (1969). Microteaching: A new approach to teacher training and research. *Hispania, 52,* 244–248.

Richards, J. C., & Farrell, T. S. C. (2005). *Professional development for language teachers.* New York: Cambridge University Press.

The Modern Language Journal (2007) *Second language acquisition reconceptualized? The impact of Firth and Wagner (1997).* Volume 91, Focus Issue.

Wallace, M. (1996). Structured reflection: The role of the professional project in training ESL teachers. In D. Freeman & J. C. Richards (Eds.) *Teacher learning in language teaching* (pp. 281–294). New York: Cambridge University Press.

Wertsch, J. V. (1985). *Vygotsky and the social formation of mind.* Cambridge, MA: Harvard University Press.

Vygosky, L. S. (1978). *Mind in society.* Cambridge, MA: Harvard University Press.

Vygotsky, L. S. (1986). *Thought and language.* Cambridge, MA: MIT Press.

7

INNOVATION THROUGH ACTION RESEARCH AND TEACHER-INITIATED CHANGE

Anne Burns

Introduction

Action research (AR) is typically seen as 'empowering' teachers, enabling them to acquire deeper insights and understanding of their practices. At the heart of claims for AR is the notion of innovation and renewal through a systematic methodological approach that brings together classroom action, research, reflection and understanding. Some, however, contest the notion of AR (e.g. Allwright, 2005; Dörnyei, 2007; Allwright & Hanks, 2009) as being 'parasitic' (Allwright, 2005) on the professional lives and concerns of teachers, while others (e.g. Rainey, 2000; Borg, 2010) analyse the prevalence of teacher AR and point to the realities of the constraints and difficulties for many teachers.

This chapter takes a positive perspective on AR as a medium for professional innovation and investigation-based change and understanding. I first outline some central philosophies and describe the main steps. I then consider a key question related to the concept of innovation: *(How) does action research facilitate renewal in practice?* In response, the main part of the chapter describes a case study that explains how AR was introduced into a national educational sector as an innovation in teacher professional learning. The aim is to draw out key findings and understandings to explore how AR can be a catalyst for pedagogical innovation.

Key ideas and concepts

Essentially, AR combines two different but related forms of activity by participants operating in a particular social environment: 'action', in that participants enact plans embedded in their daily realities; and 'research', in that, simultaneously, they systematically investigate the impact and meanings of these plans.

I have discussed the epistemological origins, processes, and methods of AR extensively elsewhere (e.g. Burns, 1999, 2010); here I provide only the briefest definition:

> AR involves a self-reflective, systematic and critical approach to enquiry by participants who are at the same time members of the research community. The aim is to identify problematic situations or issues considered by participants to be worthy of investigation in order to bring about critically informed changes in practice. Action research is underpinned by democratic principles in that the ownership of change is invested in those who conduct the research. (Burns, cited in Cornwell, 1999, p.5)

I take 'problematic' in this definition to be, not recognising and solving problems as seems to be often portrayed in AR literature, but aligned with Freire's (1973, p. 154) concept of *problematization:*

> The process is basically someone's reflection on a content which results from an act, or reflection on the act itself in order *to act better together with others* within the framework of reality (my emphasis).

Most teachers are drawn to the idea of 'acting better' with their learners and colleagues, and Nolen and Vander Putten argue that AR is appealing as it provides 'a practical yet systematic research method' to investigate practices inside and outside the classroom (2007, p. 401).

Various discourses permeate the literature which make claims for the capacity of AR to motivate and mediate teacher-initiated change. These include:

1. *democratization* of research: effective change in theory and practice needs to be initiated by teachers; therefore a shift towards democratising research would include teacher practitioners.
2. *empowerment* of teachers: teachers are usually on the lowest rungs of educational power, and subject to top-down directives where rapid policy change must be enacted at the classroom level. AR is seen as giving teachers more power in understanding and managing top-down change.
3. *ownership*: through practical enquiry teachers gain greater agency in the enactment of syllabus/curriculum directives in the classroom.
4. *professionalization*: teachers gain skills through research that deepen understanding and improve practice.
5. *transformation*: transformative professional development in contrast to transmission-focused teacher training is enabled.
6. *change*: the basis is laid for teacher-driven change, as well as greater insights into the motivations for policy change.

This kind of rhetoric has, however, also tended to devalue AR as a serious investigative approach. Criticisms of AR include lack of: research training, rigour, established methods, forms of analysis, and robustness of the epistemological base (see Burns, 2011). However, it could equally be argued that more established forms of language teaching research, with their interest in stable, controlled pedagogical sites, place limitations on the kind of knowledge that is required if the field is to arrive at more profound theories of teaching and learning. These include knowledge about the shifting, dynamic and inherently unstable realities of language classrooms and their practices (see Burns & Knox, 2011). In this discussion, my aim is to illustrate through the case study that follows the potential of AR to contribute practical and theoretical insights into the inter-relationships between practitioner investigation and pedagogical innovation.

The case study

This initiative introduced a teacher research-based professional development opportunity into a large-scale national English language sector. My proposition is that the selection of practitioner AR as the medium for this opportunity offered a practicable and non-threatening institutional pathway into viewing research as a major contributor to enhancing quality in ELT education.

Background and context of the research

ELICOS (English Language Intensive Courses for Overseas Students) is one of Australia's major post-secondary English language teaching sectors. Despite recent declines in the influx of international students seeking preparation for study in Australia, which have emanated from a strong dollar, visa and resident changes in government policy, and overseas perceptions surrounding reputation, cost of living and security (e.g. Gallagher, 2011), ELICOS is one of Australia's major industries. In 2009, for example, 155,613 students studied here, with 60 percent of those enrolled on pathways to further study, bringing an income of AU$1.8 billion (approximately 1.3 billion Euros). The average course length was 12.6 weeks, taught by more than 2,500 ELICOS teachers based in 260 accredited vocational colleges or universities, or private language colleges, both independent and part of a college chain. The majority of students came from Asian countries (68 percent), while 13 percent were from Europe, 12 percent from the Americas, 6 percent from the Middle East and 1 percent from Africa.

English Australia (hence, EA) is the national peak body and professional association for ELICOS providers nationally (see http://www.englishaustralia.com.au). EA has over 100 member colleges and its focus is on supporting and enhancing the ELICOS sector through advocacy, professional development, and publication. A major theme in its mission and activities is to promote high quality English language educational provision, so that student satisfaction engenders increased income to the sector and thus to the country. Until recently, while EA's aim was to align with and project good practice and current developments in ELT internationally, and teachers in member colleges were required to undertake professional development, research, and more specifically teacher research, was not part of its activities.

From early 2009, as one of its strategic goals to 'raise levels of professional practice', EA decided to invest in a national program of teacher-initiated AR and partnered with Cambridge ESOL (hence, CE) in the UK to obtain funding. This decision was an innovation for both organizations. For EA, it was based on an assumption that AR would be a major route through which to enhance teaching quality and imbue a stronger culture of research, together with the concept of teachers acquiring research skills in the ELICOS sector. It constituted a bold step on the part of EA, as at the time of commencing the project, there was little evidence that teachers and Directors of Studies within the member colleges would embrace the concept of teacher research (Brandon, personal communication, 9 February, 2009). For CE, it was a step into the virtually unknown territory of professional development – in contrast to testing and assessment – in the Australian ELICOS system (Khalifa, personal communication, 31 March, 2009).

The innovation

Here, I outline the goals and plans that formed the core of the innovation and also the processes of implementation. In doing so, I also consider what affordances for development as teacher researchers the program offered participants during its implementation.

My role as a consultant/researcher within the program was to work with EA's Professional Support and Development Officer (PSDO) to initiate a pilot study in 2010 which would not only begin the facilitation of AR within the sector, but also investigate the potential and impact of the program, both at the piloting phase and for the future. From EA's perspective, there were two major strategic goals for the program:

a) to equip teachers with the skills to enable them to explore and address their own identified teaching challenges
b) to share the outcomes of this research.

In addition, EA anticipated four key outcomes that would build towards a major strategic goal to raise levels and quality of professional practice:

a) direct professional development of the teachers involved
b) development of teacher peer networks
c) increased teacher engagement with research and academic researchers
d) encouraging professional development by the teachers involved beyond the program itself.

In order to address these aspirations, we decided to call for expressions of interest (EOIs) from teachers around the country whose organisations would endorse their participation. There were two reasons for this decision: first, we wanted to make participation voluntary so that the initiative would not be perceived as 'top-down', or give the impression that AR was about to become compulsory for ELICOS teachers; second, we wished to establish the perception that this opportunity was open to all teachers who also had the support of their college administration. College support was viewed as a way of also placing the concept of teacher research on the agendas of the management, giving them close contact with pedagogical research and the processes involved, and encouraging them to see the benefits of research for quality curriculum development. The EOI call listed a range of possible topics giving teachers' ideas for 'priority areas' of ELICOS sector development (e.g. teaching the language skills, assessment, learning strategies, learner motivation). So that teachers could understand from the beginning what commitments were required, we outlined them in the EOI as follows:

- full participation in three workshop sessions (totaling three and a half days)
- conduct of the research between workshops for a period of six months, with ongoing support during this time
- interim and final written accounts of their research for eventual publication by CE
- a presentation of their research in a colloquium at the EA annual conference.

We believed that a key factor for success was that teachers should be fully aware of the time commitment before participating in the program and that all participation should implicate a sense of professional autonomy.

Program plan and structure

Our initial decisions for the framing and structuring of the project can best be described as 'fuzzy', since we were initiating a program with no precedents institutionally within the ELICOS sector. However, for many years I had conducted AR with teachers in Australia's Adult Migrant English Program (e.g. Burns, 1997; see also Roberts, 1998) and this experience provided a basis for planning, modifying and trialing possible procedures.

Because the intention was to offer equitable access to the program nationally, we set up a small Reference Group to monitor various decisions made during the program, such as selection of participants. We also decided that we needed to establish relatively clear timeframes to allow the program to be completed over the piloting period of one year. Moreover, because teacher-researchers were likely to come from different Australian states, we needed to find mechanisms to bring them together to work collaboratively as the research proceeded. My experience of conducting AR projects previously had convinced me that opportunities for teachers and facilitators to dialogue personally was a crucial aspect of building research skills, developing AR concepts, identifying issues and topics, and scaffolding the tasks and processes associated with the research, such as collecting and synthesising data and developing insights and understanding about the meaning of the research. We also wanted to ensure that understandings about the research was not confined to the group but disseminated widely to others in the ELICOS sector. At the same time, we needed to take into account the time and distance involved in attending research meetings, adequate periods of teaching for conducting the research given workplace requirements and opportunities for teachers' reflections on how the research was informing their practices.

Consequently, after much discussion between the facilitators and the reference group members, we decided to trial an approach involving:

- three face-to-face meetings for facilitators and teachers, two located in Sydney and one located at the Gold Coast the day before the EA annual conference (which the teachers would all attend)
- interim periods between meetings of putting the research into practice by the teachers
- email contact at regular intervals between teachers and facilitators to provide updates, exchange ideas, answer questions and comment on progress
- a series of short overviews at regular intervals written by the teachers in preparation for the individual papers that would eventually be published in the CE journal, *Research Notes*
- a colloquium presented by the teachers and facilitators at the EA Conference.

The eventual plan developed progressively and included several stages, outlined in the Appendix.

While some parts of this program structure became fairly clearly determined, other parts, especially those towards the end of the plan remained rather speculative. In this sense, throughout the program we knew we would be continuing to test out the viability of the framework against the unfolding processes and outcomes we could see emerging from the innovation.

Twelve applications were received for the pilot program of which six were selected by the Reference Group. The restriction to six participants was because the initiative was a pilot program with limited funding that was intended to explore the viability of AR for the sector. Three of the teacher-researchers were located in New South Wales, with two from the same institution, one in South Australia, one in Western Australia and one in Victoria. Location, however, was not one of the criteria for selection, which were related rather to the clarity of the application, the potential for focusing ideas for AR and the rationale the teacher gave for wanting to do workplace-based research. There was a range of experience and qualifications among the teachers, as shown in Table 7.1, which was felt by the Reference Group to be advantageous to the aims of equitable access, teacher networking, sharing of expertise and furthering of professional development across the sector.

The first one-and-a-half-day workshop introduced the teachers to the methodological parameters, major concepts, procedures, steps and methods of AR (see Burns, 2010), and the teachers were asked to outline their current ideas and plans for research in their chosen focus areas. We also used the workshop discussions to refine research plans collaboratively in order to reach a point where the teachers could go back to their classrooms with firmer ideas for initiating the research. The focus topics that emerged as a result of this workshop were:

- extensive reading programs, motivation and vocabulary development
- use of digital dictionaries
- learner responsibility in listening and speaking development
- extensive reading for beginner learners
- learner obligation and motivation
- progress, motivation and high-level learners.

To facilitate our goals for the program, we utilised the concept of dialogic exchange (Bakhtin, 1981; Wells, 1999) during the workshops, which involved both extensive and intensive peer interaction about ways to shape the research processes. Dialogic exchange supported participants to explain ideas, clarify thinking about research purposes, and make adjustments towards enquiry-based modes of conceiving of and characterising practice. My orientation in this process was not to project a naive role of teacher peer, and thus downplay my specialist knowledge (as is sometimes suggested for the role of academic facilitation in the AR literature), but to actively scaffold and orient emergent ideas about the nature of practitioner enquiry. An extract from the workshop illustrates the kind of dialogic exchange that occurred (AB = author, TR = teacher-researcher):

TR1: So they started off with a dictionary but now I'm getting them to add a video to that. Now I want to test whether my students are actually learning words and the only thing I can think of is giving them a comprehension test, where they put...

AB: Could you also interview them and ask them if they feel confident about using these words?

TR1: I don't know about a direct question like that... maybe an interview-*type* question

TR2: Maybe a way of demonstrating or explaining

TR1: One thing I have thought of is that there's a whole lot... I give them this program and they have to write a manual, so I was thinking maybe that would be a way to test

TR3: Yes, yeah

TABLE 7.1 Teacher participants' years of teaching experience

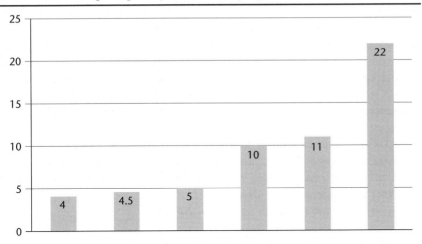

AB: Depending on what you want to test – their literacy skills or their spoken skills

TR1: Yeah they could explain it to us...because they do have to. So maybe if I can get them to explain...

AB: So what do they have to do for their courses – is it more verbally or in writing?

TR1: Well both, the lecturers are talking but also they have to write

The teachers' comments following the first workshop expressed increased knowledge, high motivation, and some trepidation about what their upcoming experiences of AR would mean in practice, for example: *What a steep learning curve!*; *A great insight into the research process. Very helpful insights from fellow participants.*

Any concerns we had previously harboured about ELICOS teachers' reactions to conducting AR were completely offset by responses to the question: *Are there any other points or comments you'd like to make?* Every comment reflected high motivation as well as appreciation of opportunities for self-initiated research:

- *Thank you so much for this amazing opportunity.*
- *Fantastic – every teacher should be involved in this type of group exploration.*
- *Just thank you.*
- *I loved this 2 day workshop.*
- *Really enjoyed the last couple of days feeling really positive about the project. Very invigorating!*
- *A great experience... It's really important to share ideas about classroom research with fellow teachers.*

The comments were written before the teachers began their research and when they were in the first flush of enthusiasm. The test of this enthusiasm would lie in the realities of initiating their plans. Responses to the second workshop suggest what developments in practice, thinking and skills had occurred in the interim period. These comments tended to be longer and more deeply reflective and raised issues the teachers were still working through. However, motivation to pursue their projects did not seem to have waned. These were some of the responses about gains from the second workshop:

- *One of the most important points for me was method of analyzing my data. Feedback from the participants helpful for further analysis of data.*
- *Workshop discussion helped to clarify direction of project – also provided clear structure for presentation/report.*
- *Affirmation that I was on the right track.*

The dialogic nature of workshop discussion seemed to prompt further reflection about the process, for example: *I didn't have it so clearly sorted in my head before today,* while motivation and enthusiasm for the program seemed undiminished:

- *I've learned a lot about myself as a teacher and researcher from Action Research and my students.*
- *Unwaning enthusiasm and motivation.*
- *Good to bounce ideas off each other and see where everyone is at. Very useful and, as last time, inspiring.*

The final workshop occurred the day before the teachers presented their research at the EA Conference. The purpose was to round off the studies and to provide an opportunity for the teachers to articulate their research processes and discoveries and, more importantly, their experiences of teacher-initiated research. The workshop was also an opportunity to finalise and rehearse individual presentations for the joint colloquium we would offer. As the initiators of the innovation, we also wanted to include open and frank discussion about the highs and lows of the teachers' experiences. It was important for us to encourage the teachers' honest responses to help us evaluate the program and prepare for further initiatives to promote teacher research as part of the sector culture. Below is an excerpt from the reflections the teachers shared:

TR4: It's been an awesome experience. My students have discovered that they really can set their own progress goals. It's brought home to me how important it is that the students decide. I honestly can't think of a negative comment – it was a really positive experience really worthwhile I'd recommend AR to anybody. It's been a little bit hectic, but no big deal. The one thing ... I think we didn't really communicate as much as we could have – I'd have loved to know more about what you guys were doing.

TR2: But we had a lot to do ... with motivation, to keep going. [Doing AR]'s awkward, lumpen and whatever ... like giving birth to a cow! It had to first come through me to go ... there. I want to share it now.

TR5: When I started I didn't think motivation was part of it. But the students brought it out ...

TR4: Are you going to continue with this ...?

TR2: Yes, It doesn't take time it takes thought. As for the project – the 'how are you feeling, how are you going'... if there's too much directive then ... too much to do and I felt I had to find my way. I didn't feel, I need to get involved in other's projects – I might have plagiarised! I've heard everyone else's ideas and there are definitely things I'll take back into my own teaching, especially going from technician to professional ... a reflective practitioner.

To implement their investigations between each workshop, the teachers carried out their AR in ways that best suited their personal styles of working, given the demands of their teaching contexts. Although it might have been possible to produce general guidelines and deadlines to structure the various phases of the AR cycle, as a group we decided against this approach. Instead support took the form of: i) personal copies of the author's book (Burns, 2010) which the teachers referred to at points of individual need, ii) regular group updates through email, iii) individual email messages sent to the group about challenges or problems and ways to address them as they arose in the research. Even though we made an attempt to set up a group blog, the teachers found that email contact proved easier and more immediate. Perhaps the greatest struggles with the AR process were where the teachers had initially been trained in subject areas based in more scientific–experimental paradigms, or were coming to the program with these presuppositions about research. It was sometimes more difficult for them to tolerate the ambiguity or apparent lack of certainty and experimental rigour in the AR process.

Because the initiative we introduced represented an innovation, not just for the individual teachers, but in the way it might be perceived in the broader ELICOS sector, we followed up this pilot program by asking the teachers' Directors of Studies (DOSs) to provide their reactions. The major themes from these responses suggest that the program had strengthened existing teaching initiatives; expanded personal and organisational professionalism; complemented institutional professional development plans; initiated other teachers into doing AR, increased general self-esteem; and given a sense of belonging to a TESOL community of practice. The comments provided further evidence that the program had the potential for a positive impact that could be felt in the ELICOS sector nationally.

Reflections

So far there have been few, if any, major challenges to the overarching concept that incorporating AR into professional development is a positive innovation in the ELICOS sector. The main tensions seem to be located in the surrounding political and economic climate where the recent downturn in international students to Australia may affect the willingness of colleges, especially those more distant from Sydney, to be involved. Colleges may find it increasingly difficult to release teachers and support their commitments to the program. However, the sustained professional support of the EA Board and the financial underpinning provided by CE are important balancing factors in persuading colleges of the value of teacher involvement.

There is ample evidence that the English Australia-Cambridge ESOL AR pilot program has had considerable impact on the ELICOS sector, and it is interesting to speculate why the program can be described as successful and what the key conditions surrounding that success might be. The impact is demonstrable at different levels of the sector: personal, organisational and systemic.

Personal level

Throughout the program, the teachers involved strongly and consistently expressed the view that they had gained valuable professional learning. The learning experience was not, however, isolated to these individuals. It appeared to have been more widely distributed through the teachers' personal interactions and initiatives. These included involving other 'like-minded' colleagues who collaborated as research partners or team members; providing regular updates at staff meetings; giving presentations as part of local professional development meetings; and demonstrating or sharing the teaching plans and activities they had investigated. One teacher went beyond her immediate college environment to give a presentation to the Masters' class in which she was enrolled, another teacher decided to enrol in a Diploma course to further her professional qualifications, while a third had an abstract accepted to present her research at an international conference.

Organisational level

Importantly, the impact at the personal level interacted with the impact at the organisational (college) level. Because colleges had committed support for individuals, they were open to capitalising on the teachers' experiences in order to strengthen their broader organisational curriculum and professional development plans. Participating colleges reported integrating the teachers' AR into their planning and making the research areas concerned a particular focus for curriculum development. They encouraged staff involvement beyond the participating teachers and provided time for the research to be highlighted at staff meetings. This positive attitude on the part of participating colleges and DOSs had a further 'ripple-effect' across the sector, which meant that non-participating colleges and their staff were influenced by, and informed about, the pilot program.

Sector level

At the sector level, EA as the national professional body provided various forms of capacity-building mechanisms to support the success of the project. Among these was the agreement with CE which provided a firm funding-base for the program. However, funding alone does not ensure success.

At each stage, the evolving program plans and goals were presented to and approved by the EA Board (as well as by CE), so that high-level imprimatur for the program characterised its implementation from the start. Members of the EA Board who had 'big picture' knowledge of the industry pressures, quality enhancement goals, and sector curriculum priorities, were involved in selecting participants. They were also key recipients of the interim and final teacher reports and took a major role in selecting the awardee for the program. These procedural and reporting strategies contributed to creating robust processes of accountability to the sector.

Important avenues for further dissemination, not only of the teachers' specific AR initiatives but also for the concept of practitioner research, also occurred at the sector level. In 2010, the first AR program colloquium at the annual EA conference took place, which has now been established as a yearly event, to publicise the research to other ELICOS teachers and to highlight the opportunities for their participation in future programs.

The factors and conditions operating in this pilot program overlap with many of those identified in the literature on innovation and change management in educational contexts and elsewhere (e.g. Senge, 1990; Kenny, 2002; Fullan, 2007). Fullan (2007: 71) notes that factors in innovation are constructed by a 'system of variables that interact to determine success or failure' and that cannot be isolated from each other. Paradoxically, he argues, success is mitigated by simultaneous and apparently conflicting tensions: simplicity–complexity; looseness–tightness; bottomupness–topdownness; fidelity–adaptivity; and evaluation–nonevaluation. These tensions make apparent the intuitively simple but socially complex nature of innovation and change.

The project reflected several of these elements: while the concept for the program (to introduce AR as a new form of professional development) was relatively simple, the enactment of the program was complex, with little initial evidence that it would succeed and decisions needing to be made constantly that would not alienate teacher or college participation. Looseness–tightness existed in the fact that EA was accountable to the funding body CE and to the Board of Directors and yet the specific details, features and plans for conduct of the program were never dictated. The program itself was planned along relatively flexible timescales with a loosely structured framework underpinning each workshop. This approach allowed for extensive input, dialectic discussion and program direction to come from the teacher-researchers concerned, who were also highly involved in creating the writing plans for their reports, and the format for their presentations at the final colloquium.

These aspects also ensured a combination of bottomupness–topdownness. The initial proposal for the program features, steps and timelines that was provided both to CE and EA created a framework for fidelity, within which adaptivity of timing, communications, contacts and processes eventuated dynamically during the program. Finally, throughout, the program was characterised by and founded on both evaluation and non-evaluation. The formal evaluation structures consisted of the reporting mechanisms to CE and EA, including: interim and final reports from the PSDO; monitoring of the proposed outcomes (by providing evidence and indicators of successful progress); interim and final papers from the teachers, which were edited for publication (Khalifa & Vidaković, 2011); and evaluation of the teachers' accounts of their research against specified criteria for the AR award presented by CE. In contrast to these formal processes of evaluation, as the data above show, while the teachers welcomed critical commentary on their research activities, they did not feel personally judged in the process. The program seemed to have enabled them to form strong professional bonds, despite geographical distance, which have continued into the present.

The impact of the program could be estimated, similarly, against success factors proposed by Kenny (2002). These include: sponsorship (clear support) by senior management; provision of adequate resources, including adequate time and staff with specialist skills as part of the project team; establishment of self-managed project teams with open communication processes; accountability processes, emphasising documentation of learning, iterative development, periodic reporting after each cycle, and dissemination to the organisation.

Conclusion

The program outlined here as an example of innovation through teacher-initiated research was in a position to be productive from its initiation. It contained conditions for success, which are not routinely found to be available in other educational contexts. Where policy makers and teaching institutions simply admonish teachers to undertake AR to improve their practices without providing the necessary implementation structures, they create a situation which is naive and bound to fail.

This program had secure funding and professional support from two powerful international and national organisations. Nonetheless, the essential lessons learned here in relation to the introduction and implementation of educational innovation and change would appear to hold true for innovations elsewhere. AR is now widely advocated as a means of teacher development and 'improvement'. However, without administrative, institutional and collegial support, AR carried out by individual teachers in the field of ELT is unlikely to have an impact of the kind that will lead to strengthening pedagogical knowledge, theory and practice more widely.

Acknowledgment

I wish to acknowledge Cambridge ESOL's sponsorship which allowed for the research to take place. Thanks also go to Sue Blundell, Katherine Brandon, Christine Bundesen, and Marian Star from English Australia, and to the ELICOS teachers, Dimitra Papadimitrou Aidinlis, Jock Boyd, Coral Campbell, Sylvia Cher, Kathryn Koromalis, and Laura McCrossan (the 2010 Action Research Award winner), who participated in the program.

Appendix: steps and timeframes for the pilot program

What	*How*	*Due*
Potential participants informed of project	PSDO prepares Expressions of Interest including project goals and milestones and participation and reporting requirements.	29 Jan
	PSDO sends email to members, EA conference database, website info.	15 Feb
	EOIs sent to PSDO. EOIs indicate areas of priority research preferred by participant; a recommendation and commitment to support from the Director of Studies.	13 March
Participants selected	6 participants – finalised by Reference Group	26 March
First workshop	One-and-a-half-day workshop in Sydney. Aims of meeting: • inform participants of project methodology • participants identify research question • complete administration • outline how to get research permission from organisations • distribute supporting resources • identify possible local coordinator.	End April/ beg May
Project, aims, focus and methods identified	Participants prepare project plans. Plans sent to EA PSDO.	One week following initial workshop

What	*How*	*Due*
Participant support	Email messages sent out requesting updates and any questions about project plans. Participants and facilitators share ideas by email. Useful existing research sources identified for participants.	Two weeks after first workshop
Implementation of projects	Participants implement plans, document findings and reflections and discuss with peers through email. (Projects may be in different stages.)	May – July
Second workshop	One-day workshop in Sydney with facilitators to ensure projects are on track. Participants present interim updates and reflections; group discusses findings, challenges and issues and identifies possible solutions. Next steps for research and deadlines for draft written reports decided. Reports to be considered in selection of AR awardee. Ongoing support provided through group email.	Late July
Third workshop	Pre-conference one-day workshop for project participants to discuss final outcomes and reflections, finalise conference presentation, discuss next steps for publication of final written accounts.	15 September
Dissemination of project and outcomes	Presentation at English Australia Conference. Program introduced and described by facilitators and individual project presentations by participants. Award for Outstanding Action Research presented.	16–18 September
	Publication of outcomes by University of Cambridge ESOL Examinations.	May 2011

Key readings

Borg, S. (2010). Language teacher research engagement. *Language Teaching*, 43(4), 1–39. A state-of-the-art discussion of how and why teachers engage in research, including the benefits, impediments, challenges and constraints that arise.

Burns, A. (1999). *Collaborative action research for English language teachers*. Cambridge: Cambrige University Press. The first book published in the English language teaching field to provide extended discussion of action research conducted collaboratively, drawing on the author's experience of collaborative action research in Australia.

Burns, A. (2010). *Doing action research in English language teaching: A guide for practitioners*. New York: Routledge. A hands-on, step-by-step overview, offering numerous examples of how to conduct action research, aimed at teachers new to doing practitioner research in their own teaching context.

References

Allwright, D. (2005). Developing principles for practitioner research: The case for exploratory practice. *The Modern Language Journal*, 89(3), 353–366.

Allwright, D., & Hanks, J. (2009). *The developing language learner.* Houndmills, Basingstoke: Palgrave Macmillan.

Bakhtin, M. (1981). *The dialogic imagination.* M. Holquist (Ed.), Austin, TX: University of Texas Press.

Borg, S. (2010). Language teacher research engagement. *Language Teaching*, 43(4), 1–39.

Burns, A. (1997). Action research, curriculum change and professional growth. In J. Field, A. Graham, E. Griffiths & K. Head (Eds.), *Teachers develop teachers research 2*, (pp. 94–112). Whitstable, Kent: IATEFL.

Burns, A. (1999). *Collaborative action research for English language teachers.* Cambridge: Cambridge University Press.

Burns, A. (2010). *Doing action research in English language teaching: A guide for practitioners.* New York: Routledge.

Burns, A. (2011). Action research in the field of second language teaching and learning. In E. Hinkel (Ed.), *Handbook of research in second languge teaching and learning.* Vol 2 (pp. 237–254). New York: Routledge.

Burns, A, & Knox, J. (2011). Classrooms as complex adaptive systems: A relational model. *TESL-EJ*, 15(1).

Cornwell, S. (1999). Interview with Anne Burns and Graham Crookes. *The Language Teacher*, 23(12), 5–10.

Dörnyei, Z. (2007). *Research methods in applied linguistics.* Oxford: Oxford University Press.

Fullan, M. (2007). *The new meaning of educational change.* 4th edn. Columbia: Teachers College Press.

Freire, P. (1973). *Education for critical consciousness.* New York: Continuum.

Gallagher, S. (2011). Standing can drive quality of students. *The Australian, Higher Education Review*, 10 August. Retrieved from http://www.theaustralian.com.au/higher-education/opinion/standing-can-drive-students/story-e6frgcko-1226111940071, 12 August 2011.

Kenny, J. (2002). Managing innovation in educational institutions. *Australian Journal of Educational Technology*, 18(3), 359–378. Retrieved from http://www.ascilite.org.au/ajet/ajet18/kenny.html, 12 August 2011.

Nolen, A. & Vander Putten, J. (2007) Action research in education: Addressing gaps in ethical principles and practices. *Educational Researcher*, 36(7), 401–407.

Rainey, I. (2000). Action research and the English as a foreign language practitioner: Time to take stock. *Educational Action Research*, 8(1), 65–91.

Roberts, J. (1998). *Language teacher education.* London: Hodder Education.

Senge, P.M. (1990). *The fifth discipline: The art and practice of the learning organisation.* Sydney: Random House.

Wells, G. (1999). *Dialogic inquiry: Towards a sociocultural practice and theory of education.* New York: Cambridge University Press.

8

REFLECTIVE TEACHING AS INNOVATION

Kathleen M. Bailey and Sarah E. Springer

This chapter focuses on reflective teaching as an example of an educational innovation. We take a historical view of teacher education practices, using Wallace's (1991) three models of teacher development and a model of reflective teaching from Zeichner and Liston (1996).

Key concepts

In this section, we first define some key constructs in reflective teaching and innovation. We then report on survey data in which language teachers described their efforts to engage in reflective teaching. There follows a brief case report which illustrates many of the processes documented in the survey. Finally, we connect these data about reflective teaching to some literature on educational innovation.

Reflective teaching

What is reflective teaching? Richards and Lockhart (1994: 1) define *reflective teaching* as a process in which 'teachers and student teachers collect data about teaching, examine their attitudes, beliefs, assumptions, and teaching practices, and use the information obtained as a basis for critical reflection about teaching.'

An important distinction was made by Schön (1983) between *reflection-on-action* (before or after our teaching) and *reflection-in-action* (during our teaching). Reflection-on-action, which includes planning, preparation and follow-up, 'refers to the ordered, deliberate, and systematic application of logic to a problem in order to resolve it' (Russell & Munby, 1991: 164). In contrast, reflection-in-action happens very quickly, during our lessons.

Simply thinking about teaching does not constitute reflective teaching: 'If a teacher never questions the goals and the values that guide his or her work, the context in which he or she teaches, or never examines his or her assumptions, then it is our belief that this individual is not engaged in reflective teaching' (Zeichner & Liston 1996: 1). In other words, simply planning our lessons or thoughtfully marking papers does not necessarily entail reflective teaching. By definition, this practice involves critical examination of our motivation, thinking, and practice. In Richards and Lockhart's (1994) definition, gathering data to promote such examination is also an essential component of reflective teaching.

These defining characteristics of reflective teaching are illustrated in this chapter through a case report of one teacher's professional development activities. Through a first-person narrative, the teacher relates how her assumptions and beliefs about both language learning and language teaching were challenged when she moved from a context in which grammar-based textbooks formed the basis of most syllabi, to one in which content- and project-based approaches were the norm. Using a variety of data collection practices interspersed with periods of critical reflection, she explores and documents her learning about what it meant to be a teacher in these two strikingly different contexts. She describes the importance of reflection as follows: 'With each phase came a growing recognition that I could not successfully adopt new curricular or pedagogical approaches without significant shifts in my thinking about macro-level topics such as the nature of language proficiency or the roles and responsibilities of teachers and learners in the learning process.' Thus, in order for this teacher to adopt some pedagogical innovations, reflection was necessary.

Innovation

In educational contexts, *innovation* has been defined as a 'qualitative change in pedagogical materials, approaches, and values that are perceived as new by individuals who comprise a formal (language) education system' (Markee, 1993: 231). Innovations spread through a population by two broad means. First, *dissemination* involves 'the strategies and activities by which it is intended that an innovation be passed on' (Kelly, 1980: 67). In contrast, *diffusion* refers to the spread of an innovation through a social system over time (Rogers, 1983). It includes both orderly and random activity, which can be social and/or personal. Thus, while dissemination is intentional, diffusion 'refers to what actually happens; to the interaction between dissemination and the complex of influences in the social context in which it occurs' (Kelly, 1980: 67).

Regarding innovation in general education, Kelly (1980) says that three conditions must be present for an innovation to be effective:

1. Feasibility: Can the innovation actually be implemented in the context?
2. Acceptability: Does the innovation match the teachers' style and philosophy?
3. Relevance: Does the innovation match the students' needs and improve their education?

An innovation is most likely to be implemented if there is a high degree of concordance on these criteria in the local context.

The advent of reflective teaching in language teaching

Reflective teaching exemplifies innovation in language teaching because, to quote Nicholls (1983: 4), it is 'a practice perceived as new ... which is intended to bring about improvement.' In this chapter, we will not treat reflective teaching as an innovation in one particular program, school system, province, or even a particular country. Instead, we consider it to be an innovation that has begun to influence the language teaching profession on a global scale.

One of the earliest treatments of reflective teaching in our field comes from Wallace (1991). He discusses three models of professional development that have been used in language teacher education over time. The first is the 'craft model' (p. 6), in which trainees are apprenticed with a 'master practitioner' (p. 6). After a period of time working under the supervision of the master, the trainee is deemed to be professionally competent. The second model is the applied science model (p. 9). In this view of teacher education, scientific knowledge is generated by experts. That knowledge is conveyed to the trainees, who are supposed to apply it to their practice, which is thought to result in professional competence. The third model is called the 'reflective practice model' (p. 49). It incorporates a cycle of practice and reflection, which generates experiential knowledge.

The reflective practice model incorporates the practice elements from the two earlier models, as well as the received knowledge component of the applied science model. But it also acknowledges that trainees enter teacher education programs with 'existing conceptual schemata or mental constructs' (p. 49). An additional element of the reflective model is experiential knowledge, which stems from both the trainees' experience as teachers and their experience as language learners. The multiple elements comprising this model – existing schemata, received and experiential knowledge, and cycles of practice and reflection – will be exemplified in more concrete terms in this chapter's case report (see also Figure 8.1).

The reflective teaching concept gradually made its way into language teaching from general education in the early 1990s. Along with Wallace (1991), the first published sources are Bartlett (1990), Ho and Richards (1993), Kwo (1994), Pennington (1992), Richards and Lockhart (1994), and Swan (1993). These authors in L2 education were influenced by key publications in first language education, particularly by Schön (1983).

More recently, the number of publications on reflective teaching has increased in the language teaching field. In fact, a reference list on reflective teaching in language education cites numerous items published since 1995 (please visit www.tirfonline.org/resources/references). Many authors have made strong claims about reflective teaching promoting professional development (see, e.g., Bailey et al., 2001; Farrell, 2008; Kamhi-Stein & Galvan, 1997; Murphy, 2001; and Wallace, 1996). All these publications are evidence of what Tremmel (1993: 434) called 'a growing interest in 'reflection' and 'reflective practice' in teacher education.' By the turn of the century, reflective teaching had gained enough momentum that Johnson (2000: 3) wrote, 'The notion of reflective teaching is not new to TESOL teacher education. In fact, during the 1990s, it has become the banner slogan of TESOL and general teacher education.'

Investigating reflective teaching as a grass roots innovation

Given the numerous publications about reflective teaching, we wanted to learn about the actual practices involved, so we conducted a survey of language teachers around the world regarding their reflective teaching activities. Our survey utilized a framework called the 'dimensions of reflection' (Zeichner & Liston, 1996), which built on the concepts of reflection-in-action and reflection-on-action.

The first two levels of the framework, which Zeichner and Liston (1996) call 'Rapid Reflection' and 'Repair,' are both types of reflection-in-action. The first level, *rapid reflection*, is part of our on-line decision-making while we teach. It happens very fast, almost constantly, and often privately, and can occur outside of a teacher's full awareness. The second dimension is called *repair*, but we shouldn't confuse it with *repair* in the sense of communication breakdowns or error treatment. Instead, repair happens while we teach and make decisions to alter our behavior in response to cues from students, such as questions or puzzled looks.

The third, fourth, and fifth dimensions are subtypes of reflection-on-action. They occur outside the boundaries of our actual teaching time. In *review*, the third dimension, teachers think about, discuss, or write about their teaching and/or the students' learning. Zeichner and Liston (1996: 46) say review 'is often interpersonal and collegial.' It can be a simple after-class conversation with a colleague, or it can be more systematic, such as writing a report on a student's progress. The fourth dimension is *research*, in which 'teachers' thinking and observation become more systematic and sharply focused around particular issues' (p. 46). This dimension entails a long-term process of collecting data over time. Conducting action research and keeping teaching journals – as well as using the kinds of surveys, interviews, and participant observations utilized in this chapter's case report – are examples of activities involving this level of reflection. The last dimension in this model is called *retheorizing and reformulating*. At this level, 'while teachers critically examine their practical theories, they also consider these theories in light of public academic theories' (p. 46). These are long-term processes which can continue for years and necessarily involve connections to the work of other professionals.

Carrying out these last three dimensions entails increasing time commitments because they involve ongoing processes of data collection and reflection. As a result, in our survey, we relied primarily on Richards and Lockhart's (1994) definition of reflective teaching, which included the three key components noted above: [1] 'teachers and student teachers collect data about teaching, [2] examine their attitudes, beliefs, assumptions, and teaching practices, and [3] use the information obtained as a basis for critical reflection about teaching' (p. 1). It is the data collection which places this definition squarely in the realm of reflection-on-action.

Survey instrument

As noted above, Zeichner and Liston's (1996) third, fourth, and fifth dimensions of reflection formed the basis of our questionnaire. We began by identifying eighteen practices that could be considered to be examples of reflective teaching in the categories of *review*, *research*, and *retheorizing and reformulating* (Zeichner & Liston, 1996): making notes on our lesson plans, getting feedback from students, discussing teaching with colleagues, observing other teachers' lessons, being observed by colleagues, audio-recording our lessons, video-recording our lessons, keeping a teaching journal, compiling a teaching portfolio, posting materials on a website, reading cases about teaching, writing cases about teaching, conducting action research, engaging in language learning experiences, team teaching, being mentored by other teachers, mentoring other teachers, and engaging in reciprocal coaching with other teachers.

The survey was drafted and then piloted with ten experienced ESL teachers. We revised the survey and distributed it via *SurveyMonkey* – an online program for constructing and distributing questionnaires, and retrieving the responses. The survey combined quantitative data (in which the respondents indicated the extent to which they agreed or disagreed with statements about reflective teaching practices) with qualitative data in the form of optional, open-ended comments. Richards and Lockhart's (1994) definition of reflective teaching was included in the body of the survey to insure the respondents would understand what we meant by the term. The statements were written to elicit information about the respondents' actual experience with the eighteen reflective practices listed above, as well as how appealing they found these practices to be.

The survey also asked for the respondents' ideas about getting started on reflective teaching. In addition, respondents rated their own knowledge about the target language(s) they teach, and their confidence using the target language(s). Finally, they were asked about their experience with and beliefs about administrators requiring and supporting reflective teaching.

We used a nine-point scale to allow the respondents sufficient room to make fine-grained distinctions in rating their attitudes and experiences. The respondents were asked to consider the points on the scale to be equidistant. Hatch and Lazaraton (1991: 179) note, 'If we believe the intervals are equal, we should be able to compute a mean and standard deviation for the responses.' These authors also state that longer scales become interval-like in nature. Likert scales are often represented as having just five points, which usually represent a continuum from 'strongly disagree' to 'strongly agree.' However, we used a nine-point scale because, as Busch (1993: 735) notes, '[F]rom a statistical viewpoint, longer scales of seven or more categories are more desirable because of the grain in score variability.'

Survey respondents

The respondents were self-selected but were initially identified through a variety of professional networks. They were contacted and invited to participate in the survey by email. Additionally, they were asked to share the survey's web address with any other practicing language teachers they knew. A total of 1,137 teachers responded to the online questionnaire from 60 different countries (48 percent North America, 18 percent Asia, 12 percent Middle East, 10 percent Latin America, and 5 percent or fewer from Oceana, Western Europe, Eastern Europe, and Africa).

The following background information was solicited from respondents: their current job responsibilities, their educational backgrounds, the ages of their students, their teaching situation (part-time vs. full-time), and their teaching experience. The picture that emerged shows that the vast majority of respondents (87 percent) work as classroom language teachers. Most have completed at least a four-year undergraduate college curriculum (80.6 percent) and 70 percent of the respondents have Masters degrees. The majority typically work with adult students from 18 to 22 years of age (85 percent) and/or 23 to 40 years of age (71.4 percent). Three-fifths of the respondents (61.7 percent) hold one full-time job. Half of the respondents have ten years or less of full-time experience, while half have more than ten years experience, and one-fifth have over 20 years of experience.

We also asked respondents to rate themselves on their knowledge about the target language and their confidence in using it. The results are summarized in Table 8.1.

TABLE 8.1 Respondents' self ratings regarding the target language

Language category	Mean	SD
Knowledge about the target language	7.95	1.19
Confidence in using the target language	8.21	1.09

These high mean scores and small standard deviations indicate that, in general, the respondents see themselves as knowledgeable about the target language(s) they teach. They are also confident in using the language(s).

In the next section, we report on the quantitative results and on some of the qualitative data from the survey. Because the quantitative data consist of Likert scale ratings, they are subject to the usual problems associated with self-selected, self-report survey data. For example, the respondents may not be representative of the wider population, and we have no way of verifying their ratings.

Experience and appeal ratings

The respondents rated both their experience with each of the eighteen reflective teaching procedures and the appeal of each procedure on the nine-point scale. In the experience ratings, '1' represented no experience and '9' represented substantial experience. In the appeal ratings, '1' meant that the procedure was not at all appealing and '9' meant the procedure was extremely appealing to the respondent. Using these data, we calculated the average ratings and the standard deviations for both experience with and appeal of the eighteen reflective teaching practices, as shown in Table 8.2.

One interesting pattern in these data is that in every case, the mean appeal ratings are higher than the mean experience ratings. This result suggests that, on average, the respondents find some procedures appealing that they have not yet experienced personally. This pattern indicates that many language teachers are open to the idea of trying some form of reflective teaching.

For the six procedures for which respondents reported having the greatest levels of prior personal experience, the difference between the experience and appeal means for each practice was relatively low (.86 points or less), while for the remaining items the appeal mean was between 1.67 and 2.73 points higher than the experience mean. It is possible that those items with the highest discrepancies between experience and appeal may indicate or help identify those approaches that would only be possible with additional support. For example, *Reciprocal coaching with other teachers* (2.73) and *Being mentored by other teachers* (2.37) both require formal coordination with colleagues (and possibly release time), while *Posting materials to a website* (2.24) and *Video-recording our lessons* (2.25) might involve additional training.

Recommended procedures for getting started

The respondents were asked to pick three different procedures from among the eighteen listed in the questionnaire that they would suggest for helping other language teachers get started on reflective teaching. The five most frequently suggested practices are listed in Table 8.3. (Percentages total more than 100 because respondents were asked to recommend *three* procedures.)

TABLE 8.2 Reflective teaching survey responses

Procedure	Experience			Appeal			
	Rank	Mean	SD	Rank	Mean	SD	Difference
Language learning experiences	1	7.04	2.19	1	7.86	1.65	.82
Discussing teaching with colleagues	2	6.87	1.91	2	7.69	1.62	.82
Getting feedback from our students	3	6.51	2.37	3	7.17	2.05	.66
Making notes on our lesson plans	4	6.11	2.24	6	6.96	2.14	.85
Reading cases about teaching	5	6.08	2.42	8	6.83	2.20	.75
Compiling a teaching portfolio	6	5.96	2.81	9	6.82	2.46	.86
Mentoring other teachers	7	5.39	2.87	5	7.06	2.10	1.67
Observing other teachers' lessons	8	5.04	2.38	4	7.10	2.04	2.06
Team teaching with a colleague	9	4.62	2.74	10	6.31	2.39	1.69
Being mentored by other teachers	10	4.55	2.64	7	6.92	2.23	2.37
Being observed by colleagues	11	4.07	2.36	11.5	5.97	2.38	1.90
Conducting action research	12	3.95	2.73	11.5	5.97	2.71	2.02
Making entries in a teaching journal	13	3.54	2.51	14	5.19	2.70	1.65
Reciprocal coaching with other teachers	14	3.09	2.73	13	5.82	2.65	2.73
Posting materials on a website	15	2.87	2.68	15	5.11	2.87	2.24
Video-recording our lessons	16	2.82	2.22	16	5.07	2.72	2.25
Writing cases about teaching	17	2.80	2.40	17	4.88	2.74	2.08
Audio-recording our lessons	18	2.35	2.08	18	4.40	2.71	2.05

TABLE 8.3 Frequently suggested practices for getting started on reflective teaching

Recommended reflective teaching practice	Percent of respondents recommending the practice
Discussing our teaching with colleagues	47.9 %
Observing other teachers' classes	45.4 %
Eliciting students' written feedback	42.0 %
Being observed by other teachers	32.8 %
Making notes on our lesson plans	31.4%

Respondents were invited to provide open-ended comments with suggestions for others who wished to get started on reflective teaching but found time constraints to be challenging. The main strategies suggested are listed below:

- Just do it. Make time. Use time management strategies. Set your priorities.
- Multi-task. Use time for travel or jogging. Talk with colleagues over lunch or a beverage.
- Start small. Set reasonable goals. Later develop more reflective teaching practices.
- Work with a colleague for accountability and support (team teaching, mentoring, peer observation, etc.).
- Choose a procedure that works for *you*.
- Record your thoughts as soon as possible after the teaching event.
- Self-assess regularly and honestly.
- Seek administrative support.

This last suggestion leads us to the final data set from the survey: the respondents' views about administrative support for reflective teaching.

Administrative requirements for and support of reflective teaching

The respondents were asked to indicate on the nine-point scale whether they agreed or disagreed with the following statements:

- Employers should require teachers to do some form of reflective teaching on a regular basis.
- One or more employers *have required* me to do … reflective teaching.

Second, respondents indicated the extent of their agreement or disagreement with the following statements:

- Schools *should provide support* to teachers to encourage reflective teaching (e.g., paid release time, workshops, etc.).
- I *have received support* from my school(s) to practice reflective teaching ...

For these items, a rating of '1' indicated strong disagreement while a rating of '9' indicated strong agreement. The means and standard deviations for these ratings are given in Table 8.4.

The mean of 5.69 and standard deviation of 2.61 indicate that there was not strong agreement among the respondents as to whether employers should *require* some type of reflective teaching. However, there was strong agreement that schools should *support* teachers who undertake reflective teaching (mean = 7.88, SD = 1.68). These data suggest that teachers want the freedom to choose whether to engage in reflective teaching, but having done so, they would like to receive administrative support. When viewed in tandem with the experience ratings given in Table 8.2, these data may indicate that many language teachers engage in reflective practices without administrative support.

In terms of these respondents' experience, there was a relatively low average rating on the item that asked if they had been required by their employers to do reflective teaching (mean = 4.71, SD = 2.88). There was an even lower average rating on the item about whether the teachers had been supported by their schools in doing reflective teaching (mean = 4.27, SD = 2.85). We should note that these relatively large standard deviations (nearly three points on a nine-point scale) indicate wide variability in the ratings.

We should also acknowledge that there were some limitations with this survey, particularly with distributing it and collecting the data online. For instance, some of the answer format requirements of the program were quite rigid and as a result, some respondents got discouraged and then stopped when the program would not let them proceed. Also, because we used 'opportunistic sampling,' the respondents do not necessarily represent the full range of language teachers. Notably absent are those teaching in the primary grades, and teachers with limited formal education. In addition, in some instances the data were probably influenced by the 'digital divide' (Warschuaer, 2010). That is, teachers without readily available Internet access could not easily respond to the online questionnaire.

TABLE 8.4 Ratings regarding administrative requirements and support

Administrative category	*Mean*	*SD*
Employers should require some form of reflective teaching	5.69	2.61
Employers have required some form of reflective teaching	4.71	2.88
Schools should support reflective teaching	7.88	1.68
Schools have supported reflective teaching	4.27	2.85

Reflection: reflective teaching as an innovation

We believe these survey data suggest that reflective teaching is largely a grassroots innovation, which seems to have been influenced by dissemination through an increasing number of publications on the topic. However, there is an element of unstructured diffusion at work as well. The data suggest that many language teachers engage in reflective teaching activities without being required to do so and without much administrative support. To the extent that these respondents are representative of the wider profession, we can also say that teachers engage in a wide range of reflective procedures.

Much of the published literature about innovation in language education is about top-down programmatic or curricular developments (see, e.g., Markee, 1993) and how to get teachers engaged in the innovation process (Stoller, 2009; White, 1987). But as Stoller (2009: 75) notes, '[T]op-down innovations are rarely successful without teacher enthusiasm and endorsement. Similarly, bottom-up innovations rarely sustain themselves without the support of the administration.' White (1988: 142) echoes this point: '[E]ven bottom-up grassroots innovation will require forms of support which can only be provided by superordinate top-down parts of the system.' The data in Table 8.4 suggest that the respondents would like to get more support than they have gotten for practicing reflective teaching.

Here, however, we are concerned with what Widdowson (1993: 261) has called 'the micro-level of classroom processes' – that is, what teachers actually do. This view is echoed by Rudduck (1988: 209): '[I]ndividuals need to feel that change is not something that happens to them, and which they cannot control, like bereavement, but instead something which they are principally seeking and welcoming.' She adds that 'revisiting and reflecting on one's professional experience' (p. 210) is an important avenue to understanding change.

Our survey data indicate that many individual language teachers from around the world are utilizing (or have used) reflective teaching practices, such as those listed in Table 8.2. The appeal ratings also indicate that teachers are willing to try out reflective teaching, a finding which suggests a general openness to experimentation. As Rudduck (1988: 212) notes, 'We need to give attention to the behaviours and attitudes that individual teachers bring to the innovation context.' For this reason, we turn now to a discussion of one teacher's development as a reflective practitioner.

We have chosen at this point to complement the more abstract concepts introduced earlier in this chapter with a first-person account, which Shulman (1992) defines as a case report – that is, the case is written in the voice of the person who experienced it. It exemplifies Wallace's (1991) elements of reflective practice and highlights the dynamic influence of and interplay between each of these elements as well as related frameworks, as shown in Figure 8.1.

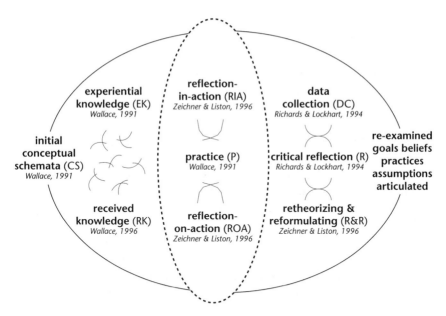

FIGURE 8.1 Development of a reflective practitioner (adapted from Wallace, 1991: 49)

In the narrative, we see that conceptual schemata (CS) are not brought clearly into juxtaposition with newly introduced concepts in the MA curriculum (received knowledge – RK) until a summer of teaching in the new context (practice – P) precipitates an internal struggle of sorts. Ingrained habits of *rapid reflection*, a form of *reflection-in-action*, generate internal conflict and a felt need for further *reflection-on-action* (RIA/ROA), and the generation of experiential knowledge (EK). The resulting cycles of more intentional practice (P), data collection (DC) and reflection (R) provide an opportunity for the teacher to examine and reconsider previously held beliefs and assumptions and to begin a longer-term process of *retheorizing and reformulating* (R&R) (Zeichner & Liston, 1996), which requires engaging with and connecting to the research and theory of the field in very personal and practical terms. (Note: abbreviations from Figure 8.1 have been inserted below to identify specific examples of these components in context.)

Case report: a reflective practitioner

I first encountered many new ideas about the nature of language, learning and teaching in 2001 when, after six years as a CELTA-trained EFL teacher in Europe, I returned to the US to begin an MA TESOL program (RK). A critical point in my studies occurred after my first two semesters, when I was hired to teach in a summer program for students from Japan (P). The curriculum focused on community-based research and involved placing the students with local community organizations. The teaching team provided linguistic and content support through courses in research methods, community language skills, and American culture. As their final project, students synthesized their findings into short PowerPoint presentations.

I had previously judged the success of my teaching by the extent to which I had successfully covered the predetermined grammatical points and lexical items contained in the course textbook, using a carefully selected sequence of textbook exercises supplemented by short 'communicative' activities (CS). Observations of my Japanese students at work convinced me that they were having a powerful educational experience, but aspects of this course conflicted with many of my prior assumptions about learning (ROA).

In order to investigate these contradictions more closely I began my reflective investigations. In the first phase, I documented the students' experiences using methods which paralleled their own: conducting background research on project-based learning, holding informal conversations with students and gathering samples of their work, making entries in my teaching journal, interviewing their faculty advisor, and surveying the students about what they had learned (DC). The realization that I eventually came to after reflecting (R) on these disparate forms of data (DC) was that in this context, more important than acquiring discrete new 'bits' of language were the ways in which they had met the challenge of using whatever language they already possessed to achieve a series of communicative goals (R&R).

When I entered graduate school, I had already spent several years working out my own practical approaches to classroom management and lesson planning (RIA). Initially my prior teaching experience (CS) seemed to enhance my ability to connect key theoretical concepts (RK) to actual classroom situations (P). However, during that summer the habits and practices that I had previously developed seemed to interfere. My teaching felt like an awkward hodgepodge of attempts to implement appealing new ideas (RK), confounded by a sudden resurgence of old instincts and approaches, once real-time decisions needed to be made in the classroom (RIA).

For my second cycle of reflective practice (ROA) I therefore decided to intervene in such a way that my prior teaching instincts would not interfere. I sought permission to observe a similar course in which I could be a participant observer, but for which I would have no explicit planning or teaching responsibilities. My goal was to become aware (EK) of new aspects of the students' use of language (RK) that I would not have been able to attend to without the measure of detachment (R) afforded by the opportunity to spend time in a colleague's classroom.

In this phase, I observed an eight-week ESL course, and collected the following types of data (DC): running field notes during class, retrospective journal entries, audio recordings of classroom interactions, an archive of assignments and students' work, and recordings of student interviews conducted during the final two days of the course. I then selected representative sections of the classroom recordings for transcription and analysis. As a result I was able to identify examples of four qualitatively different types of language use (RK). This analysis confirmed in very concrete terms (EK) my vague impression that project-based classes offer substantially different opportunities for using language (RK) than I previously would have expected (CS).

I also analyzed (ROA) the role the teachers had played in providing pedagogical scaffolding for the students on three levels (RK): in the design of the overall curriculum, through the structure of each daily lesson, and during individual interactions with students. One final, unexpected result was an increased awareness of the extent to which students' beliefs (CS) about the effectiveness of project-based curricula can have a powerful impact on their learning.

Constructs such as learner autonomy, learner training, communicative competence, alternative assessment and scaffolding (RK) are commonly encountered during MA TESOL programs, as are assignments that require candidates to record and analyze classroom discourse, conduct survey research (DC), and maintain a teaching journal (P). However, it wasn't until I had the opportunity to experience and reflect (R) on a series of very concrete situations (P) that I could begin to integrate the disparate areas of theory, research and practice in a way that resulted in true shifts in my own subsequent teaching practice (R&R).

Concluding comments

This chapter incorporates both quantitative and qualitative data from the survey, and qualitative data from the case report. The case report was written in 2003, and in the intervening years this teacher's responsibilities have shifted from working directly with language learners to training language teachers. This subsequent change in teaching responsibilities proved to be rich in opportunities to explore the dynamic interplay between practice, reflection, data collection, and the integration of received and experiential knowledge in the pursuit of further professional development. The teacher wrote:

> Based largely on my earlier experiences with data-based reflective practices, I am much less likely to assume that my own relatively superficial impressions are anything more than that – a starting point for further investigation. Likewise, I still regularly seek out opportunities to spend time in classrooms other than my own, both within and beyond our degree program. I value this rather time-intensive endeavor because by engaging in peer observations and reciprocal coaching I am not only exposed to alternative approaches, but am often forced to articulate assumptions about teaching and learning in post-secondary classrooms that I wasn't even aware I held.

The recent increase in publications on reflective teaching in language education indicates a groundswell of interest predominantly among teacher educators, to judge by the authors who have published on this topic. The data from our survey and case report also show that many language teachers engage in both individual and social types of reflective practice (Kelly, 1980) as well. As our case report illustrates, teachers engage in more private reflective formats (as in keeping teaching journals) as well as more public, collaborative reflective practices (peer observation, coaching, team teaching, etc.). In addition, the case shows how Kelly's (1980) criteria of feasibility, acceptability and relevance will likely vary not just from one individual to the next, but also for any given teacher across different teaching contexts.

We agree with Widdowson (1993: 270) that what is 'emerging in recent discussions about language teacher development is a recognition of the importance of teachers' own attitudes and opinions, and how these interact with influences from outside.' It appears that teachers who find reflective teaching to be useful will engage in some of these practices even without administrative support. As one survey respondent wrote, 'Reflective teaching has its own intrinsic rewards and that once you get started, the positive experience will generate its own momentum.'

The challenge that remains may be one largely for language program administrators. It represents a new opportunity for further innovation, namely: developing programmatically feasible forms of support for reflective practices that do not detract from a sense of personal initiative, autonomous choice, and ownership by teachers.

Key readings

To learn more about the reflective practices listed in Table 8.2, please see Bailey, Curtis and Nunan (2001).

We recommend Richards and Farrell's (2011) book entitled *Practice teaching: A reflective approach.*

References

Bailey, K. M., Curtis, A., & Nunan, D. (2001). *Pursuing professional development: The self as source.* Boston, MA: Heinle & Heinle.

Bartlett, L. (1990). Teacher development through reflective teaching. In J. C. Richards & D. Nunan (Eds.), *Second language teacher education* (pp. 202–214). New York, NY: Cambridge University Press.

Busch, M. (1993). Using Likert scales in L2 research. *TESOL Quarterly, 24*(4), 733–736.

Farrell, T. S. C. (2008). *Reflective language teaching: From research to practice.* London, England: Continuum Press.

Hatch, E., & Lazaraton, A. (1991). *The research manual: Design and statistics for applied linguistics.* New York, NY: Newbury House.

Ho, B., & Richards, J. C. (1993). Reflective thinking through teacher journal writing: Myths and realities. *Prospect, Journal of Australian TESOL, 8,* 7–24.

Johnson, K. E. (2000). Innovations in TESOL teacher education: A quiet revolution. In K. E. Johnson (Ed.), *Teacher education* (pp. 1–7). Alexandria, VA: TESOL.

Kamhi-Stein, L. D., & Galvan, J. L. (1997). EFL teacher development through critical reflection. *TESOL Journal, 7*(1), 12–18.

Kelly, P. (1980). From innovation to adaptability: The changing perspective of curriculum development. In M. Galton (Ed.), *Curriculum change* (pp. 65–80). Leicester: Leicester University Press.

Kwo, O. W. Y. (1994). Towards reflective teaching: Curriculum development and action research. In D. C. S. Li, D. Mahoney, & J. C. Richards (Eds.), *Exploring second language teacher development* (pp. 113–130). Hong Kong: City Polytechnic of Hong Kong.

Markee, N. P. P. (1993). The diffusion of innovation in language teaching. *Annual Review of Applied Linguistics, 13*, 229–243.

Murphy, J. M. (2001). Reflective teaching in ELT. In M. Celce-Murcia (Ed.), *Teaching English as a second or foreign language* (3rd edn) (pp. 499–514). Boston, MA: Heinle & Heinle.

Nicholls, A. (1983). *Managing educational innovations.* London, England: Allen and Unwin.

Pennington, M. C. (1992). Reflection on teaching and learning: A developmental focus for the second language classroom. In J. Flowerdew, M. Brock, & S. Hsia (Eds.), *Perspectives on second language teacher education* (pp. 47–65). Hong Kong: City Polytechnic of Hong Kong.

Richards, J. C., & Farrell, T. S. C. (2011). *Practice teaching: A reflective approach.* Cambridge: Cambridge University Press.

Richards, J. C., & Lockhart, C. (1994). *Reflective teaching in second language classrooms.* Cambridge: Cambridge University Press.

Rogers, E. M. (1983). *The diffusion of innovations.* London, England and New York, NY: MacMillan and Free Press.

Rudduck, J. (1988). The ownership of change as a basis for teachers' professional learning. In J. Calderhead (Ed.), *Teachers' professional learning* (pp. 205–222). London, England: The Falmer Press.

Russell, T., & Munby, H. (1991). Reframing: The role of experience in developing teachers' professional knowledge. In D. A. Schön (Ed.), *The reflective turn: Case studies in and on educational practice* (pp. 164–187). New York, NY: Teachers College Press.

Schön, D.A. (1983). *The reflective practitioner: How professionals think in action.* New York, NY: Basic Books.

Shulman, L. (1992). Toward a pedagogy of cases. In J. H. Shulman (Ed.), *Case methods in teacher education* (pp. 1–30). New York: Teachers College Columbia University.

Stoller, F. L. (2009). Innovation as the hallmark of effective leadership. In M. A. Christison & D. Murray (Eds.), *Leadership in English language education: Theoretical foundations and practical skills for changing times* (pp. 73–84). New York, NY: Routledge.

Swan, J. (1993). Metaphor in action: The observation schedule in a reflective approach to teacher education. *English Language Teaching Journal, 47*(3), 242–249.

Tremmel, R. (1993). Zen and the art of reflective practice in teacher education. *Harvard Educational Review, 63*(4), 434–458.

Wallace, M. J. (1991). *Training foreign language teachers: A reflective approach.* Cambridge: Cambridge University Press.

Wallace, M. J. (1996). Structured reflection: The role of the professional project in training ESL teachers. In D. Freeman & J. Richards (Eds.), *Teacher learning in language teaching* (pp. 281–294). New York, NY: Cambridge University Press.

Warschauer, M. (2010). Digital divide. In M. J. Bates & M. N. Maack (Eds.), *Encyclopedia of library and information sciences, Vol. 2,* 3rd Edn (pp. 1551–1556). New York: CRC Press.

White, R.V. (1987). Managing innovation. *ELT Journal, 41*(3), 211–218.
White, R.V. (1988). *The ELT curriculum: Design, innovation and management.* Oxford: Blackwell.
Widdowson, H. G. (1993). Innovation in teacher development. *Annual Review of Applied Linguistics, 13,* 260–275.
Zeichner, K. M., & Liston, D. P. (1996). *Reflective teaching: An introduction.* Mahwah, NJ: Lawrence Erlbaum.

9

TEACHER THINKING, LEARNING, AND IDENTITY IN THE PROCESS OF EDUCATIONAL CHANGE

Donald Freeman

Introduction: framing the change process in educational settings

Understanding how innovation and change happen in the contexts of classrooms, schools, and educational communities is a complex and tricky business. Designing, implementing, and evaluating changes and innovations in educational settings is complex in *what* you look at and tricky in *how* you look at it. Perspective assigns meaning, and changes in that perspective can change the meanings you 'see'.

This issue of perspective becomes critical for a number of reasons. First, what we consider as an educational change or innovation is framed by the perspective we take on it. A teacher who modifies an activity or uses some new material with one class of students is innovating in her classroom practice. Likewise, an academic department or school that reorganizes class levels or introduces interactive whiteboards is making a change. A school system that adopts a new testing program or reorganizes the timetable is innovating. And a country or region that develops a set of educational standards or redefines school-leaving requirements is making a change. In each instance, the definition of change depends on how you look at the situation and what you see in it. The teacher who is using the new activity or material in the classroom will probably see it as a change, while the principal or fellow teachers may not. Similarly, the educational authority that is promulgating them is likely to see new standards as an innovation, while some teachers in that school system may see the standards, though 'new', as simply articulating what they believe they are already doing.

There are two key points here: First, differences in perspective are not simply differences in scale. Were that the case, one might explain the teacher's change as less significant because it seems smaller scale than the school system's 'new' standards. However, the inverse can often be the case. Larger scale innovations in curriculum, pedagogy, and technology are not experienced by those at the chalkface as changes because these teachers either feel they are already doing what is called for, or they continue with familiar practices and rearticulate them in terms of the new (Cohen and Hill, 2001). Both ways of behaving are often labelled as 'teacher resistance' to reform. This is not intended as a cynical observation, but simply an affirmation that since educational practices, both immediate and large scale, are social practices, any change and innovation in them affects individual and collective sense-making (Weick 1995). Which leads to the second point: We could say that all change—like all politics—is 'local'. In this notion of 'localness', we capture the idea that what you see depends on where you sit in relation to the change or innovation, and what you're looking for in it.

The concepts that are used define the locus and the elements of the change process—*what* is changing—and the dynamics of that process—*how* it unfolds—orient both the work itself and how that work is understood. This sense-making is not a singular process since it too depends on where you sit: as a participant in the change or as an observer to it. This distinction, which is described in ethnographic research as 'emic' (or insider/participant) in contrast to 'etic' (outsider or observer) perspective-taking, acknowledges that making sense of any human activity, from a classroom lesson to district-mandated reform, is largely a function of one's perspective, which is a function of one's role or position in the activity or event.

Take an example of 'first period of the day', which, from a school administrator's point of view, let us say, runs from 7:50AM to 8:30AM. From the teacher's perspective it may be the 'most difficult period to teach' perhaps because of the size of the class, the group dynamics, or the content that is to be taught. From the students' point of view, that class may be 'difficult' because 'we're not awake, and the teacher just talks at us.' The point being that each perspective can be both emic and etic, depending on who you are and where you look. The administrator's view is not the teacher's or the students', and vice versa. Yet all three perspectives share—or are built around—some common concepts such as time of day, number and age of participants, ease (or difficulty) of the lesson, and so on. Blending these distinct viewpoints brings a fuller, more operational understanding of the phenomenon. Thus, planning, implementing, or studying the processes of change and innovation in educational settings (which I will refer to in this chapter by the shorthand 'educational change' after Fullan [2001]) involves close attention to the key concepts that drive the sense-making process. Therefore, to understand this sense-making, we have to examine the concepts on which it is built.

Three organizational concepts that frame change

Much of what has been written about educational change tends to discuss the process from a systemic point of view (e.g. Fullan, 2001; Hoban, 2002).

Such work looks at how the various components in a complex educational system—from central administration, to building and classroom levels—support or work against innovation. There are also more individually focused accounts (e.g., Evans, 1996; Cohen, 1990) that examine how change is lived by teachers or administrators. Although they differ in terms of scale, these macro and micro types of accounts share a calculus of key organizational concepts. The first has to do with the *locus* of change—how the focal area of change is defined. The second concept addresses the *process*—how change unfolds in that focal area. And the third concept defines the *unit*—what is changing or being changed within the focal area. The way in which each of these concepts is framed becomes integral to designing, implementing, and evaluating reforms or innovations in educational practices.

These three organizational concepts become the frames through which we make sense of educational change. When one of them—for the locus, process, or unit of change—shifts, so does the perspective on the reform or innovation, and therefore the sense that is made of it. In many instances, when an education change is described as 'successful' or a 'failure', the actual substance of the change is not different; what is altered is how we frame and ultimately make sense of what has happened. So, perspective matters a great deal. The following sections examine a sort of paradigm shift (after Kuhn, 1962) in how perspectives on educational change are shifting and the differences these perspectives make in our understanding.

The 'manifest' vs. the 'latent' as frames of the change process

This process of sense-making is evident when we contrast the two frames that are often used to analyze change. The first frame, which is most familiar, calls attention to elements that are 'manifest' in the process. These elements seem self-evident and therefore are sometimes called 'objective'. They can be observed, publicly documented, and measured. As 'manifest' as they are, however, they often fall short of capturing what is actually happening in the

KEY CONCEPT	The 'manifest' frame for the change process	The 'latent' frame for the change process
Locus of change	Teacher and student behaviour	Teacher and student thinking
Process of change	*Implementing* by practicing the new to master it	*Making sense* through professional learning
Unit of change	**Action and interaction**	**Professional identity**

FIGURE 9.1 Contrasting the 'manifest' and the 'latent' framing of the process of educational change

change process. The resulting analyses can interpret the innovation as 'resisted' or 'failed' because the evidence is not 'manifest'. The contrasting frame draws out the elements that are 'latent' in the change process. These are elements that we consider idiosyncratic and contextual; and because they can be ambiguous, they are often referred to as 'subjective'.

The balance of the chapter examines the contrasting definitions for each pair of concepts. The intent is twofold: First, the contrast shows what each frame reveals or obscures about educational change. Second, I will argue that the second frame is more coherent and this may better serve studying, designing, and implementing changes in educational settings.

Contrast #1: the *locus* of change—behavior *vs.* thinking

Classroom activity is arguably the most common *locus* in making educational change. Whether it involves implementing a new pedagogy or curriculum, integrating new technological resources, or adopting new standards or assessments, the locus of what needs to be changed is usually defined as what teachers and students are doing in the classroom. The basic formulation is that the 'new' activity or behavior will replace the current status-quo. Anchored in the broadest sense in a factory model of education (Lortie, 1975; Tyack and Cuban, 1995) in which pedagogical activities and classroom behaviors are generally seen as interchangeable parts (Freeman, 1999), this notion of 'newness' seems to drive this frame. The educational change introduces something that is not currently present or happening in the setting—'new' pedagogical practices, curricular materials, or technologies, which means the locus of such changes has to be accessible. Framing this locus as behavior or activity makes it publicly available for input, practice opportunities, monitoring, and external documentation and evaluation. Defining the locus in this way creates a currency for the educational change: It can be introduced, tracked, and measured as a 'new behavior'. Thus the 'new' is valued while current status-quo behavior is devalued and needs changing.

In the 1980s, alternative conceptions developed to this prevailing behavioral view of teaching (Freeman, 1996). These alternatives argued for a cognitive view in which the teacher's mental activity or thinking (Borg, 2006, 2003; Freeman, 2002) was taken into account. In a behavioral view, change could be measured by the new ways in which teachers and students worked in the classroom. That perspective obscured the fact that any public behavior or practice depends on some sort of thinking or reasoning, so changes in behavior must also entail changes in thinking. The third edition of Clark and Peterson's *Handbook on research in teaching,* published in 1986, brought this issue of student and teacher thinking to the fore. Chapters synthesizing the state of research noted that some approaches to educational reform, specifically in mathematics and science, were already focusing on student thinking as the locus of change (e.g. Romberg and Carpenter, 1986). Interestingly, the same handbook edition was the first to summarize early research on teacher thinking (Clark and Peterson, 1986), although this thinking did not become a locus of change in its own right until the 1990s (e.g. Rosenshine and Meister, 1994).

Contrast #2: the *process* of change—implementing *vs.* making sense of the new

Taking thinking as the locus of change has implications for how the *process* itself was understood. If the locus is behavior, the change process appears clearer and more tangible. This view is evident in framing the process of change as 'implementing' an educational innovation: Implementation understood as change is carrying out prescribed activities usually sequenced in a predetermined order. Implementing new curricula is a common instance of this view. Throughout the 1990s, major ELT curriculum reform projects assumed a hierarchical model of the change process in which curriculum 'specialists' determined pedagogical needs and designed new materials in response; these materials were then taught by teachers (Johnson, 1989). This view of implementation was anchored in a fidelity view of curriculum in which the goal was to accurately teach the new material as it was designed and prepared (Graves, 2008). The localness of the teaching situation—the school, classroom, students, and community—were a set of variables to be managed so that implementation was carried out 'accurately' (according to the designers' intent). Similarly, evaluation of a new curriculum in this model usually focused on the degree to which the material, as originally written, was being taught (Kennedy, 2010).

Framing the change process as implementation renders the teacher largely invisible. Localizing innovation involves thinking, both about the new and about the current status quo in new ways. This thinking must be done by the people doing the work, the teachers and students; it defies common sense to say it should be done in some centralized way on their behalf. Whether the innovation involves teaching new materials or using technology, or teaching within new standards or towards a different assessment, it is difficult to argue that the teacher is not central to successful change. In the fidelity view of change, the teacher is the implementational vehicle for new activity and behavior. Redefining the locus of change as thinking, redefines the roles of the protagonists. The change process involves making sense of the new (however it is understood); basically it is a process of professional learning.

Understanding change as a learning process allows for both intended outcomes and unintended consequences within the same frame. Smyth (1999: 67) offers a succinct definition of teacher learning as 'how teachers make sense of their world and their work of teaching.' This spare statement repositions the work involved in teaching, which is largely the focus of the fidelity view, within the teacher's wider world, or what Walberg (1976) referred to as the teacher's 'mental life.' This world is social; it involves and is co-inhabited with others. The 'mental life' of the teacher cannot be separated from the interactive and participatory settings in which it is lived. As Cohen, Raudenbush, and Ball (2003: 120) point out:

> What we casually call 'teaching' is not what teachers do, say, or think, though that is what many researchers have studied and many innovators have tried to change. Teaching is what teachers do, say, and think with learners, concerning content, in particular organizations and other environments, in time.

Thus, any process of professional learning involves both teacher and students (and/or others in the school community); it is inherently relational work (Freeman, 2002). To understand change in this frame, we have to think more broadly. The change process is not simply achieving a specifically intended outcome. It includes, or, better put, is situated within a social fabric of sense-making, which is, by definition, local. So we arrive at the point that both the locus and process of educational change are inherently local or situated.

This view of professional learning as making sense of the new within the circumstances of the local setting[1] calls into question two conventional metrics often used to evaluate the impact of educational change: scale—how widespread—and sustainability—how 'permanent'—the new practice becomes. These constructs provide the currency by which the 'success' of educational reforms is often measured in many political contexts (e.g. Rothstein, 2004). It is beyond the scope of this chapter to offer a detailed critique of scale and sustainability as constructs, except to point out that if educational change entails professional learning in the local context, then assessing its success or even impact cannot depend on rigidly standardized notions of coverage in space (i.e. scale) and stability in time (i.e. sustainability). Instead, we need a more nuanced set of constructs to better define and capture what exactly is happening in the change process as it unfolds for and through participants.

Contrast #3: the *unit* of change—action/interaction *vs.* professional identity

The French mathematician, Henri Poincare, observed that the accuracy of a particular measurement depends on the instrument used to make it—the more sensitive to differences the instrument, the more 'accurate' the measurement. Measuring an object with a ruler marked in inches gives it one length; measuring the same object with a ruler marked in eighths of an inch will give it a slightly different length. Thus, measurement depends on the instrument more than it does on the object being measured; and since the measurement itself can never be identical to the object itself, it will never be 'completely accurate.' Rather, the relationship between the object and the instrument is asymptotic, the 'accuracy' of the measurement will approach the 'length' of the object but will never actually reach or be identical to it.

Poincare's maxim applies to documenting and evaluating the change process. It is easier to talk or write about what we can see changing, the 'manifest' aspects, than what may underlie this layer of visible, tangible evidence, what is 'latent' in the process. The maxim can be extended to suggest that we tend to document the units of change that we know how to see, the phenomena we have the tools to capture, and not necessarily what there is (or may be) to document in the process. Unfortunately, the substance of an educational change often lies in these difficult-to-document elements.

This contrast in how the unit of change is defined, as manifest or as latent, echoes the issues raised by the preceding two contrasts. Given the investment of time, money, and other resources, as well as the aims for sustainability and scale, it is not surprising that the conventional view of change focuses on what participants do—their actions and interactions—as the unit. New pedagogical practices, new curricula and technologies, new standards and assessments aim at transforming teachers' and students' actions in some way. The teacher who uses new material in the lesson is acting differently; in the classrooms in which the curriculum or technologies are being implemented, students and teacher interact in new (and also familiar) ways. New standards and assessments call on teachers and students to focus their time and attention differently, which often come down to interacting differently. Because these actions and interactions are largely public, they become accessible to planning and documenting. While this focus is useful as a unit of change, as Poincare's maxim points out, it may be measuring what is manifest, and avoiding or not seeing what is latent.

The challenge is that it is people who do the acting and interacting. Part of what they do is manifested through what is visible and accessible; part is latent. When teachers and students undertake an educational change, aspects such as different ways of acting and interacting with each other, with the content being taught, and perhaps with the classroom, school, and community as a setting for learning are manifested through the process (see Cohen, Raudenbush, and Ball, 2003). In this process of acting differently, however, participants take on new roles and become different people in the context of the classroom and perhaps the school. Consider the example of a pedagogical innovation like 'cooperative learning' (Slavin, 1980), in which the teacher groups students in different ways to do different types of tasks that ask them to interact in explicitly articulated roles in their 'table groups'. These are changes in behavior that are visible and audible; they can be monitored and documented.

Latent in the situation, however, is what these changes may mean to participants. The teacher may feel that she is giving up a familiar sense of control over the classroom. Some students may welcome the greater autonomy that cooperative learning activities afford them, while others may be frustrated by the change in classroom expectations. For both, these are changes in what they do and who they are in this setting: these are changes in their classroom identities. I am using the term 'identity' here in the sense of socio-cultural participation: how people act—and are seen by others as acting—as they participate in a setting. These identities are functions of the person in the situation; they arise out of the situation and the knowledge that is inherent in it. They become evident in how the individuals act and react, as well as how others in the setting respond. James Gee (2008) outlines this notion of identity as the interplay between knowing and doing in social settings:

> Any actual domain of knowledge is first and foremost a set of activities (special ways of acting and interacting so as to produce and use knowledge) and experience (special ways of seeing, valuing, and being in the world. Physicists do physics. They talk physics. And when they are being physicists, they see and value the world in a different way than do non-physicists.

While implementing a new way of doing things such as cooperative learning may show up in teacher–student actions and interactions, underlying these visible patterns are latent changes in who does, or is expected to do, what. Initiating and sustaining these new ways of doing things requires changes in teacher–student identities in this classroom context; these changes to social identities may be subtle and evanescent, or durable and profound.

In a broader biographical sense, becoming a teacher involves forming a new professional identity. Learning this new identity happens from the start of a teacher's career as a student. It begins with socialization in school, during the 15 or more years spent as a student observing teachers and participating in their work in what Lortie called the 'apprenticeship of observation' (1975). It continues in explicit ways through preservice professional preparation as Lampert (2010: 9) describes this formation of teacher candidates who are becoming elementary mathematics teachers:

> Learning the practice of teaching ...is learning 'what teachers do' in common rather than learning what a particular teacher does by apprenticing with a more proficient individual. It is about more than acquiring skills or best practices. It involves adopting the identity of a teacher, being accepted as a teacher, and taking on the common values, language, and tools of teaching.

When innovations or changes in practice are introduced into a situation, they 'land' in the participants' on–going negotiations of identity in the school and in the classroom. At times, these changes may initiate new ways of thinking and being. At other times, they may ride on the tide of shifts that are already at play. Consider, for example, a high school teacher who, while in implementing project work, decides to give over greater autonomy and decision-making to a class of 17-year-olds. The change lands in an ongoing ebb and flow of who does what in the classroom and the school. Perhaps it rides a developmental wave of greater independence that is part of young adulthood (see, for example, Gieve and Miller, 2006). But it will be sustained to the extent that the new identities make sense. The latter might suggest why, in spite of extensive investments in technology for classroom teaching, there are few examples of sustained integration leading to improved student learning outcomes. This is not a cynical affirmation of the status quo. On the contrary, it is an affirmation of human nature: that people do what makes sense to them. This sense-making process is latent in any educational change.

Case study: putting the three frames together

The following case study, which is a classic study of how teachers take up curricular innovation, assembles these three frames in the context of a single innovation. In the early 1980s, Kelly (1980) examined the experiences of British secondary school teachers who were involved in the Nuffield science curriculum reform. The researchers were interested in the interplay between teachers' intentions in the reform curriculum and how those intentions played out in their classroom teaching. The researchers did not assume a primary locus of change, either teachers' thinking—what teachers said they would do—or their behavior—what they did in their teaching. Instead, the researchers looked at the interplay between these two loci, which produced a usefully messy and complex analysis.

At the close of the summer training on the new curriculum, 142 teacher-participants were asked about their plans for using it in their teaching in the coming school year. Kelly (1980) called this 'teachers' intentions.' They divided the responses into those who said they planned to 'adopt' the new curriculum; those who said they 'would try out parts of the new curriculum and then likely adopt it'; those who would 'try out' aspects; and those who said that they 'might try some things out.' Figure 9.2 summarizes the teachers' intentions across the bottom row.

As might be expected, about a quarter of the total falls into each of the four categories: 30 percent 'would adopt early'; 27 percent 'would try out and then adopt'; 21 percent 'would try out'; and 22 percent 'might try out.'

The researchers then returned to visit the teachers at the end of the following school year to ask what had actually happened. These responses were again divided across four possibilities, which generally reflected at what point during the year the teacher had actually taken up—or what the researchers termed, 'adopted'—the new curriculum. The researchers distinguished between those teachers who 'adopted the curriculum early' or 'late' in the school year; those who adopted it 'partially' (in essence, continued the 'trying it out' phase), and those who 'did not adopt it at all.' The column on the far right in Figure 9.2 shows those totals. Perhaps not surprisingly, the largest number of teachers—over a third (36 percent)—were in the group that had 'partially adopted' the new science curriculum.

		WHAT THEY PLANNED TO DO ──────────────────────→				When implemented
		Plan to use	Plan to try out then use	Plan to try out	May try (undecided)	TOTALS:
WHAT THEY ACTUALLY DID	Implemented **early** in the school year	5	4	12	6	27
	Implemented **later** in the school year	7	13	6	9	35
	Implemented **partly** over the school year	19	19	5	8	51
	Didn't implement	11	2	7	9	29
TOTALS: *Planned to do*		42	38	30	32	113 teachers

FIGURE 9.2 What they say and what they do: teachers' responses to curriculum innovation

Data drawn from: Kelly, P. (1980). From innovation to adaptability: The changing perspective of curriculum development. In M. Galton (Ed.), *Curriculum change*. Leicester: Leicester University Press. pp. 65–80.

This study distills a frequently heard story about the educational change process. It is a story of the normative adoption of innovation. At the start of the change process, participants' intentions to adopt the new curriculum were fairly equally distributed. A year later, a third of the total, which is the largest group, had done something with the new curriculum. Within the 'manifest frame', the story appears to be that, although more may have intended to do so, the teachers' *actions and interactions* with the new curriculum were only *implemented* in a third of the *teacher and student behaviors* a year later. This story, which is a common one in educational reform, seems to be one of resistance to change. The initial of intentions, which are distributed almost according to probability (about 25 percent in each of the four categories), only ultimately leads to a partial uptake of the innovation among about a third of the participants a year later.

Parsing these data within the 'latent' frame, however, takes us inside the change process. Following a normative distribution of initial intentions at the close of the summer training, consider the possibility that the 20 percent of participants who 'did not adopt' the new curriculum went home to find their personal or professional lives altered by things beyond their own control. Perhaps someone had been reassigned to a new grade level or school; another may have had a family change (a new baby, or a sick parent or relative). Still others may have encountered more subtle contextual factors; some may have started the new school year with a class in which they were to use the new curriculum, but found the group difficult to manage so they may have felt they could not continue with implementation. Or perhaps the teacher was assigned other classes that were new and/or demanded additional time and attention. Any of these situations, as well as others we might imagine, would demand that these participants *think differently* about their intentions as they worked to *make sense* of these unexpected conditions. These conditions, perhaps *personal,* perhaps *professional,* might well have brought about a shift in *social identity.* Consider the change when a teacher becomes a new parent with less time and energy to give to teaching. Or the change in identity for the teacher is assigned to a new class in which she needs be more disciplinarian in managing students. Such 'new' ways of behaving mean new ways of participating in the familiar social settings of the school and classroom.

The latent frame suggests that for these 29 teachers who did not 'adopt', their intentions may have shifted in the face of these new situations in which they found themselves. Another view might be that since half—15 of these 29—seemed to express some initial skepticism—they planned to 'try out' rather than 'adopt' the new curriculum—these teachers might have been voicing initial skepticism at the end of the summer about what can feel like the constant pendulum of classroom reform. They were drawing on their experiences, and the perhaps cautious view these experiences may have engendered, to *make sense* of the innovation. And there may be additional individual stories that could help us to understand the 'non adopters.'

The story behind the remaining 80 percent of teachers who did something with the new curriculum could well be equally complex, particularly if we look at the artificiality of using a school year to measure change. While the researchers did not claim that full reform in science teaching should have happened, or indeed been evident, after a school year, the linking of intention to change with what actually happened suggests that interpretation. Namely, if you say you will do something and then have not done it a year later, this marks some sort of shortcoming. But from the standpoint of the latent frame, this arbitrary use of this time period as a metric is suspect. Where is it written that innovating or changing something as complex and situated as what teachers and students do together in the classroom should happen within a school year? If we return to Poincare's maxim, the measurement may itself be the cause of the confusion. Simply put, we may yet lack metrics that are sensitive enough to *thinking, sense-making,* and the pressures on and shifts in *personal* and *professional identity* to be able to 'measure' and assess the impacts.

Closing: towards 'the creation of a new order of things'

> There is nothing more difficult to plan, more doubtful of success, nor more dangerous to manage than the creation of a new order of things.
> *Niccolo Machiavelli,* The Prince *(1513)*

To say that change is relative would misread this argument. Rather 'the creation of a new order of things', to use Machiavelli's phrase, is a complex, situated, and inherently messy business, especially in the relational work of classroom teaching and learning. Researchers, program designers, implementers, evaluators, and even funders of projects in educational change can try to clean up this messiness through the constructs they use. The notion that change is about *behavior,* that it involves classroom actors in *implementing* new or different *actions* and *interactions,* which are amenable to being observed, documented, measured, and assessed, frames innovation in terms of its 'manifest' elements. There are ways in which this frame works and can be useful. Questions about the scale and sustainability of innovation can productively focus on common elements that are manifest in the change process that can be tracked and managed.

However, if we accept the premise that the core of relational work in classrooms involves sense-making—how the protagonists themselves understand what they are doing and what they are to do—then the manifest frame leaves us short-handed. When a reform becomes messy and partial, as they did in the Kelly Nuffield Science curriculum study, we are left with explanations about how imperfectly the new material may have been transmitted and/or how resistant the teachers were to the change, or how inhospitable their schools may have been to new ways of teaching. These explanations center principally on deficits in student and teacher *behavior,* and not on the *thinking* that underlies and indeed may motivate these behaviors. Thus, it is useful to have an alternative frame that can help tease out what is latent in the situation: How are the participants making sense of the innovation? What do they think will be gained and lost in doing it? How will it alter who does what in the classroom? Who will be the 'winners' and 'losers' in the new status quo?

Change is essentially a zero-sum game, especially in classrooms and schools. The new innovation has to replace something in the status quo, whether that something is consciously held or not. But the status quo is itself dynamic. The degree to which participants recognize, and even articulate the trade-off, may suggest a path of successful change. Articulating the status quo can be challenging if only because we are all living it. Some years ago, in a workshop on classroom innovation with Brazilian secondary teachers, one participant put her finger on the dilemma when she pointed out that 'teaching always involves managing what you cannot control.'

This teacher's aphorism captures the dynamic of doing things differently in the classroom: There are aspects a teacher can 'manage' and thus choose to do differently; there are likewise aspects that the teacher 'cannot control' and thus cannot change. If we assume the line that separates the aspects of managing and controlling is bright, fixed, and given, then we work within a manifest frame in which change involves implementing new ways of doing things. But if we accept that the line that distinguishes what teachers can manage from what they believe (rightly or mistakenly) they cannot control is itself a shifting one, then we enter into a different type of change process, in which elements of thinking, sense-making, and identity that are latent in any context, must come into play.

Note

1 'Local' means closely linked to the activity and the participant. In this world of virtual interactions, it doesn't necessarily mean geographically proximate.

Key readings

Cohen, D.K. 1990. A revolution in one classroom: The case of Mrs. Oublier. *Educational Evaluation and Policy Analysis*, 12(3): 311–329. In this paper, Cohen examines the ways in which an individual teacher participates in and experiences major school reform. It is an invaluable account for those planning and/or taking part (voluntarily or not) in an educational change. An excellent companion to the Evans book just below.

Evans, R. 1996. *The human side of school change*. San Francisco: Jossey-Bass. This is a well-developed account of educational change from the point of view of a school administrator. Evans speaks to issues of teacher participation and resistance, to the role of school structures in supporting or impeding change, and to how curricular and pedagogical innovations can play out within these factors.

Hoban, G. 2002. *Teacher learning for educational change*. Buckinghamshire: Open University Press. This book brings together research on teachers' professional learning and identity development, and relates this work to the context and processes of educational reform. Hoban relates studies of larger systemic factors in reform to the individual learning of teachers.

References

Borg, S. 2003. Teacher cognition in language teaching: A review of research on what language teachers think, know, believe and do. *Language Teaching*, 36 (2): 81–109.

Borg, S. 2006. *Teacher cognition and language education*. London: Continuum.

Clark, C. and P. Peterson. 1986. Teachers' thought processes. In M. Wittrock (ed). *Handbook of research on teaching* (3rd edition). New York: Macmillan.

Cohen, D.K. 1990. A revolution in one classroom: The case of Mrs. Oublier. *Educational Evaluation and Policy Analysis*, 12(3): 311–329.

Cohen, D.K. and H. Hill. 2001. *Learning policy: When state education reform works*. New Haven: Yale University Press.

Cohen, D.K., S.W. Raudenbush, and D.L. Ball. 2003. Resources, instruction, and research. *Educational Evaluation and Policy Analysis*, 25(2): 119–142.

Evans, R. 1996. *The human side of school change*. San Francisco: Jossey-Bass.

Freeman, D. 1996. The 'unstudied problem': Research on teacher learning in language teaching. In D. Freeman and Jack C. Richards (eds). *Teacher learning in language teaching*. New York: Cambridge University Press. pp. 351–377.

Freeman, D. 1999. Changing teaching: Insights into individual development in the context of schools. In C. Ward and W. Renandya (eds). *Language teaching: New insights for the language teacher*. Singapore: SEAMEO Regional Language Centre, pp. 28–46.

Freeman, D. 2002. The hidden side of the work: Teacher knowledge and learning to teach. *Language Teaching*, 35(1): 1–14.

Fullan, M. 2001. *The new meaning of educational change*. New York: Teachers College Press.

Gee, J.P. 2008. Game-like learning: An example of situated learning and implications for opportunity to learn. In P. Moss, D. Pullin, J. Gee, E. Haertle, L. Young, (eds). *Assessment, equity, and opportunity to learn.* New York: Cambridge University Press, pp. 300–321.

Gieve. S. and I. Miller (eds). 2006. *Understanding the language classroom.* Basingstoke, Hampshire: Palgrave Macmillan.

Graves, K. 2008. The language curriculum: A social contextual perspective. *Language Teaching,* 41(2): 149–183.

Hoban, G. 2002. *Teacher learning for educational change.* Buckinghamshire: Open University Press.

Johnson, R.K. 1989. A decision-making framework for the coherent language curriculum. In R. K. Johnson (ed). *The second language curriculum.* Cambridge: Cambridge University Press, pp. 1–23.

Kelly, P. 1980. From innovation to adaptability: The changing perspective of curriculum development. In M. Galton (ed). *Curriculum change.* Leicester: Leicester University Press, pp. 65–80.

Kennedy, M. 2010. Approaches to annual performance assessment. In M. Kennedy (ed). *Teacher assessment and the quest for teacher quality.* San Francisco, CA: Jossey-Bass, pp. 225–249.

Kuhn. T. 1962. *The structure of scientific revolutions.* Chicago: University of Chicago Press.

Lampert, M. 2010. Learning teaching in, from, and for practice: What do we mean? *Journal of Teacher Education,* 20(10): 1–14.

Lortie, D. 1975. *Schoolteacher: A sociological study.* Chicago: University of Chicago Press.

Romberg, T.A. and T.P. Carpenter. 1986. Research on teaching and learning mathematics: Two disciplines of scientific inquiry. In M. Wittrock (ed). *Handbook of research on teaching* (3rd edn). New York: Macmillan.

Rosenshine, B. and C. Meister. 1994. Reciprocal teaching: A review of the research. *Review of Educational Research,* 64(4): 479–530.

Rothstein, R. 2004. *Class and schools: Using social, economic, and educational reform to close the achievement gap.* Washington, DC: Economic Policy Institute.

Slavin, R. 1980. Cooperative learning. *Review of Educational Research,* 50(2): 315–342.

Smyth, J. 1999. Researching the cultural politics of teachers' learning. In J. Loughran (ed). *Researching teaching: Methodologies and practices for understanding pedagogies.* London: Falmer Press, pp. 67–82.

Tyack, D. and L. Cuban. 1995. *Tinkering toward utopia: A century of public school reform in America.* Cambridge MA: Harvard University Press.

Walberg, H. 1976. Psychology of learning environments: Behavioral, structural, or perceptual? *Review of Research in Education,* 4(1): 142–178.

Weick, K. 1995. *Sensemaking in organizations.* Thousand Oaks, CA; Sage Publications.

SECTION 3

Innovation and change in the language curriculum

10

INNOVATION IN LANGUAGE POLICY AND PLANNING: TIES TO ENGLISH LANGUAGE EDUCATION

Joseph Lo Bianco

Preamble

This chapter introduces concepts and practices from language policy and planning, both the academic field of analysis and the practical field of action, to English teaching, and specifically to the idea of innovation and change in global English education. The first part of the discussion considers the sources of change and innovation in language education and discusses some differences between these notions. Both are considered in relation to the 'world events' which have bequeathed English its hegemonic position in contemporary global communication arrangements. The chapter next discusses language problems, a crucial construct in academic study of language policy and a crucial idea for planners, teachers, curriculum writers and teacher trainers. Language problems often appear to be straightforward when in reality what counts as a language problem is often contested. A large part of language policymaking consists of the struggle by different interests to have their interpretation of language problems prevail. The chapter then moves to discuss the role of innovation, rather than change, understood as different kinds of 'renewal' of English language education, prior to tying these various pieces together in a consideration of language planning for English language education today. Examples illustrate the points being argued, to highlight key arguments and to underscore the global scope of the enterprise of English language education.

Driving innovation and change

In recent decades, the driving forces for more and better English language education have originated in wide and deep pressures within society, economy and politics, rather than from education concerns and interests. From empire to emporium, from Britain to America, English is sometimes construed today as a post-identity language, even as a basic skill (Graddol, 2006; Cha and Ham, 2008). Educators are increasingly called upon to incorporate new notions of variety in English, highlighted by English as Lingua Franca, ELF, (Seidlhofer, 2011) which is sustained by large corpora of spoken and written text samples, supporting its claim to be a distinctive entity whose communicative and sociolinguistic presence poses unfamiliar challenges for teaching. Innovation in English language education that derives from sources close to educational endeavours, such as curriculum design, teacher preparation, textbook writing, or classroom pedagogies, are also influenced by the wider envelope of change usually labelled globalisation. However, as English traverses new terrain, from local and national to international and global, to glocal and new iterations of each (Facchinetti et al., 2010) policymaking is also challenged and specialists and non-expert policymakers are required to develop new protocols and innovative conceptual and practical tools.

Standardisation of reasoning

Most countries and major education jurisdictions are involved in language policy measures regarding English language education (Cha and Ham, 2008) and increasingly draw on more or less identical legitimations to do with national economic competitiveness and other kinds of commercial and neo-liberal concepts. In these systems of reasoning competitive ranking of universities and statistical ranking of school effectiveness (e.g., the OECD Programme for International Student Assessment, PISA, which surveys 15-year-olds in the 'principal industrialised countries' on 'knowledge and skills essential for full participation in society'), are the latest instalments in world standardisation that tend to favour English (PISA, 2011). All this trade, and talk of trade, reflects and intensifies the commodification of language and certified study (Tan and Rubdy, 2008) and poses ever sharper challenges to traditional cultural, humanistic and intellectual legitimations for language study.

The rapidly escalating worldwide demand for more and better English education (Graddol, 2006) is differentiated according to sector and purpose. In universities, the prominent link is the concentration of scientific research and publishing in English with cross-border validity of certification (Lo Bianco, 2010). These characteristics position English learning needs around academic proficiency outcomes and have led to expansion in English as language of instruction, particularly in Asia (Tollefson and Tsui, 2004).

Language policy without planning: an example from Malaysia

The increased demand for learning of and learning through English produces language policymaking, however, this increase in language planning has rarely involved the specialist input of professional language planners. This is an important point to grasp since it is a key argument of this chapter that language planning is a distinct field of academic and practical action, organised around a coherent body of concepts and procedures. Neglecting the concepts and methods of language planning relegates decision making about communication issues to government fiat, political pressure or market-based structural adjustments.

We can see precisely this dilemma in recent English education moves in Malaysia. In 2002, Prime Minister Mahathir Mohammad announced the policy of Teaching Mathematics, Technology and Science in English (PPSMI, in its Malay acronym) commencing in 2003 and disrupting the longstanding national project of replacing English with Bahasa Melayu (BM) as the primary medium of instruction.

In 1957, on the occasion of its independence from Britain the new state that would become today's Malaysia was a multiracial and multilingual compact. Current population and language data reveal a continuation of the broad ethnicity distributions with a significant consolidation in language claimants for BM (Malaysia, 2011): at independence about 54 percent identifying as 'Malay', 26 percent as Chinese, 12 percent as 'indigenous' and about 8 percent as Indian (Gill, 2007; Azirah, 2009). In the immediate aftermath of independence, English persisted as a convenient language of administration and preserved its link to domains of market prosperity and opportunity but only a small number of people, mainly in urban areas, actually spoke it. While language planning acknowledged a pragmatic pluralism the clear preference was for consolidation and assimilation to BM as the unifying and symbolic national language (Gill, 2007). From 1967 BM was adopted as the medium of instruction in all government maintained and funded schools, with partially funded Chinese and Tamil language primary schools required only to teach BM as a subject, while secondary schools would convert to exclusive use of BM as medium, with English reduced to a timetabled subject.

These arrangements were ultimately disputed by minority language interests, perceiving themselves to be disadvantaged in curriculum access, employment opportunities and social participation. From the late 1990s, concern was raised by business interests about labour market access and portability of qualifications stimulating Dr Mahathir to begin innovations in language education, expressed, in an interview quoted by Gill, as requiring a move away from 'nationalism' towards pragmatic acceptance of English's domination of science and technology fields, to ensure Malaysians were not 'working as servants to other people' (Gill, 2007: 119). The new language policy was therefore a new economic policy, often the case when language issues are recruited to serve wider socio-political and economic agendas.

From its inception PPSMI was controversial, practically as well as symbolically, provoking both embrace and rejection and conflicting claims about what the real and urgent language problems of Malaysia should be taken to be, which groups of students were in greatest need, and what the appropriate language policy for them, the nation and the economy should be (Azirah, 2009). Because PPSMI was adopted with little input from specialist language planners it lacked an informing language ecology model, i.e. a sense of what realistic communication aims against current communication realities could be, and so it accumulated an ongoing baggage of problems. In turn, poor conceptualisation aggravated the ultimately insurmountable problem of practical delivery. Despite provision of guidelines, resources and often highly innovative professional development programs, buttressed by financial incentives and rewards, the fundamental absence of an ecological communication strategy hampered implementation, and on July 8, 2009 (Chapman, 2009), PPSMI was terminated. From 2012, instruction in the nominated subjects reverted to BM.

PPSMI became a source of controversy, not only for substantive questions of defence of the national language but also because of hasty implementation; even the precise nature of its termination is unclear, it has either been abandoned, or simply modified to allow more English organised differently, according to rival perspectives of various participants (see Chapman et al., 2011). Nevertheless, protests such as those led by defenders of the national language, culminating in a large hostile public demonstration on March 7, 2009 in Kuala Lumpur, suggest that language education is difficult to quarantine from wider symbolic and practical questions of identity and opportunity. Behind the pragmatic capacity to efficiently deliver PPSMI were complicating questions of equity and opportunity, since access to English is influenced by disparities according to rural/urban, social class and ethnic/racial divides (Bernama, 2009).

The reasoning behind the initiative is evident in the selection of subjects to be taught in English. It draws on a long-standing desire in post-colonial nations of seeking to quarantine two types of curriculum orientation; a utilitarian externally oriented one, from an intrinsic internally oriented one. Separating curriculum content that is concerned with national formation and the cultivation of national citizens, on the one hand, from content presumed to be solely about instrumental links to global trade and international competitiveness (Lo Bianco et al., 2009) on the other; a distinction increasingly tenuous and difficult to draw.

One way in which this distinction is tenuous can be seen in Gill's (2004) study of higher education language policy in Malaysia. Gill isolates the question of 'bifurcation' in higher education pathways, a structural change that undermined the country's ability to complete its project of replacing English with Malay. Bifurcation refers to legislative reforms that permitted private universities to operate through the medium of English alongside public institutions operating in Malay-medium. These reforms were the catalyst for a wider dismantling of the post-independence Malay-only policies and were eventually to seep down to school level, due to the marketplace advantages of English-proficient bilinguals destabilising the position of the majority population, mostly educated mono-lingually in Malay.

This example highlights how language planning operates as a kind of ecology, since the total communication resources of a speech community are interconnected and planners cannot hope to effectively quarantine their decisions from system-wide repercussions. This complication calls into question the likely effectiveness of innovation in English education which ignores existing communicative realities. These realities refer to the existing communication abilities of a population and sociological realities of class, ethnic and regional disparities in the acquisition of English. Internal social stratifications, especially in post-colonial settings, are invariably connected with disparities in social opportunity, and so acquisition, especially of prestige forms of speech and literacy, can never be isolated to what institutions do, but must be understood as part of the hierarchy of how opportunities are distributed within societies. Prestige kinds of talk are not only fostered in education, but in the social circles and networks of communication in which speakers are immersed. If government authorities had drawn on concepts and methods devised by language planning specialists they could have grounded their new policy in analysis of the communication ecologies pertaining across the ethnic, cultural, economic and institutional domains of the society, increasing the likelihood that the eventual policy would have been both innovative and feasible.

A related situation typifies Sri Lanka (Lo Bianco, 2011) where language policy and planning in a multilingual and stratified social context provoked immense dislocation and ethnic conflict. The originating language policy, the Official Sinhala Act of 1956, despite later ameliorative measures, was a significant contributor to the deterioration of social relations between the nation's main ethnic groups. Today, at the conclusion of decades of armed conflict, the nation has embarked on exactly the same tri-lingual policy, Sinhala, English and Tamil, which was one of the policy options discarded in 1956.

A critical lesson of these examples is that innovation in language policy and planning for English language education must be sensitive to how an existing communication order aligns with social opportunity, ethnic and racial backgrounds, geography and social class. This is reinforced by ELE innovation writing. In a comprehensive survey, Waters (2009) addresses the overall scene of innovation theory, and its specific connections with the 'current state of the art of managing innovation in ELE' (p. 451).

This reveals a burgeoning literature on innovation design and management, much of it fostering improved practice and reflective implementation. However, despite wider geographic coverage, contexts, innovation types and a variety of design and management processes, work in English language education innovation appears to lack tight and evident connection to concepts and procedures within the innovation management literature, and especially to the body of experience accumulated by the 'science' of language planning.

The inheritance of history: 'world events' and English today

In much of the world, whether in post-colonial settings such as those cited above, and similar cases in Africa, as well as in settings in which English was never directly or indirectly a colonial language, such as in Eastern Europe and most of Latin America, English prevails as the naturalised choice of preferred foreign language. Often this choice for English accompanies adoption of English as language of instruction. This convergence of choices suggests that English is perceived to offer greater returns on investment than other potential language choices, and so the apparently ubiquitous presence of English is sometimes perceived as an ancient condition of global communication arrangements. However, even a cursory look at recent communication choices shows that the prevalence of English is recent and can be attributed to dominant economic, political and military conditions and world events of the past 50 years. This is a unique conjunction in history, in that recent world events and conditions: US centred military, economic and cultural sway, has not overturned the pre-existing linguistic order (British colonial spread of English), as happened throughout the world's longer-term linguistic history (Ostler, 2005), but has consolidated it.

Survey research conducted by Cha and Ham (2008) documents historic patterns of foreign language preferences. During 1875–1899 only six percent of secondary school curricula worldwide nominated English as the first foreign language, a figure which increased to 70 percent of primary and 80 percent of secondary curricula by 1990–2000. Across Asian settings, English was represented in only 33 percent of primary curricula during 1945–1969; growing to 83 percent in primary and 100 percent for secondary by 2005. However, by 2006 practically all instances in which foreign languages were employed to teach mainstream subject matter in Asian settings involved English as the First Foreign Language.

The pattern of growth in English is independent of whether countries were British colonies or under American political influence at any time in the past. Instead, it is tied to the dominant world events of the past century, World War One, World War Two, the Cold War, the Fall of the Berlin Wall, and the commencement of economic liberalisation in China from the mid to late 1980s which effectively meant the emergence of interlinked financial-services and goods markets.

This world produced in the twentieth century is also of that century. In ideologies of the right and left it is both a 'borderless world' (Ohmae, 1999) and a 'runaway world' (Giddens, 2003). In Ohmae's confident prescriptions of a future fit for commerce and untrammelled international trade, there is uncritical acceptance of universal English as facilitator and producer of this world-as-economy, above and beyond nations.

Giddens's notion, by contrast, is of how tradition is required to explain itself, to account for its claims on people, and peoples, whose nations would once have taken those traditions completely for granted, whether they were the idea of national allegiance or the uncontested place of national official languages, notions seen as indispensable to citizenship and belonging.

Language planning and policy was born into and of that same world of secure bounded nations with distinctive and official or at least dominant national languages, and mostly monolingual populations. These standard national languages and internally oriented education systems were assumed to be the sole jurisdictions of how languages were organised and transmitted, in their literate and educated forms, for citizenship, national culture and political loyalty to national states.

However, since global English is both recent and contingent, the apparently tenacious hold it has in education globally can be neither inevitable nor unalterable. All past 'empires of the word', as Ostler terms global communication regimes, have met disruption and been dismantled due to changes in the underlying economic, military, technological and intellectual order of things. In Ostler's own view (2010), a future reorganisation of communication is already gathering pace and will foster the 'return of Babel', an unprecedented world multilingualism powered by cyber-techno communication possibilities. These emergent technology-enhanced communication arrangements will render obsolete the need for a lingua franca function through the use of sophisticated multilingual technologies, instantaneous translations and speech processing.

The consequences of such speculations represent a major challenge for an invigorated and innovative language planning. Unanticipated language planning challenges arise when we do acknowledge the relative recency of the prominence and the predominance of global English.

Language problems and diverse modes of language planning

The activity of writing and implementing policies on language and education is usually seen by government agencies such as education departments as just another kind of policy making. However, making policy and undertaking planning around sensitive issues of communication and language is different in important ways from general public policy. We can see policy and planning in the context of more general issues of social change, innovation and development, including criticisms of how language planning has traditionally been enacted and understood (Lo Bianco, 2010).

A key focus of language planning historically has been the nature of language problems and how and why some communication problems come onto the agenda of public authorities, while others remain marginalised or ignored. Many societies with multilingual populations seek to regulate the role and function of languages in institutions, such as government offices, law courts and procedures, hospital and medical procedures, public administration, signage, commerce, and other fields beyond education.

Describing how different societies and diverse actors regulate the roles and status hierarchies that are established for different languages and language varieties is an increasingly important dimension of language policy research.

Teachers as language planners

The very acts of classroom management, communication and teaching are a zone of semi-autonomous language planning in the hands of teachers (Lo Bianco, 2010). In the sovereign space of the classroom, teachers enact, as do countries and education departments in their distinctive realms, language plans. These reveal their underlying view about what language problems exist and which are elevated to attention and what will be the desired and implemented solution. Interactive classroom communication is replete with choices from the available communication forms, those of the students, those authorised by school and education authorities and those favoured and known to the teacher, all exposing the often unexpressed operations of teacher language planning. We can observe this in the micro-interactions between single students and teachers in coaching and explaining or in classroom oriented communication. What teachers model in their own speech and what they favour or discourage from students, what they praise and what they discourage, what they facilitate for reading or for online and web-based authoring, are all instantiations of an underlying theory of language problems and a set of choices about language solutions.

Analysis of language planning

Alongside the growth of real-world language policy and planning, whether in institutions or in the choices and patterns of communications of individual teachers in classrooms, there has been a related expansion in academic analysis, description, teaching and theorising about the field of language policy and planning. Today, language policy and planning represents a significant part of all applied linguistics, and although the 'ideal' state is one in which specialists trained in language apply their skills and knowledge to help public authorities solve problems of language and communication in society, for the most part actual language policymaking ignores professional language planning theory.

While education is a major focus of language policy and planning activity there are many other domains of intervention to direct and shape language and communication. These include trade and commerce, social questions such as the integration of minority populations into mainstream institutions or the labour market, and diverse aspects of society and culture.

Because language is a sensitive area that connects with the identity and other symbolic resources and self-view of a community, and at the same time influences the life chances, economic and educational opportunities of individuals, language planning can be a controversial activity.

Language politics

Language planning is never conducted in a social, political or economic vacuum, instead it occurs in culturally and historically specific circumstances, in which the interests and language of dominant groups sometimes collide with the interests and languages of minority, dominated or otherwise excluded populations. A key innovation in the policy and practice of language planning in recent decades has been the emergence of awareness of how language planning has often been used by state agencies, or powerful groups, to entrench their social, economic or political domination over others. A key example is the history of language in South Africa.

Under the racist assumptions of Apartheid, which operated until 1994, language policy played a central role. On June 16, 1976, student protests broke out contesting the compulsory use of Afrikaans as a joint medium of instruction with English, for arithmetic and social studies, in public schools. The violent suppression of the protests represents the beginning of the end of the overall policy of Apartheid. The student protestors opposed the second class education they perceived in the bilingual program, describing it as 'gutter education', intended to entrench the economic inferiority of black children. As *'the immediate cause of the ... Soweto uprising'* (Juckes, 1995: 147–149) a language education policy measure provoked widespread and ultimately decisive social protest. Because large numbers of students were killed, 16 June is today commemorated as Youth Day. The post-Apartheid constitution recognises eleven official languages, including Afrikaans and English, but language policy, and bilingual education, and the roles of English and Afrikaans in the society and education system of South Africa remain controversial.

This example highlights the wide array of activities, and the deeply socially and politically situated nature, of language planning realities. Because language planning is linked to the interests of various groups in society, it is tied to politics and the play of interests and power in social groupings.

Categories of language policy and planning

In this section, three categories of language policy and planning are discussed, (see Lo Bianco, 2010).

Actions that formalise or elevate the status of language or varieties

The formal status of a language, dialect or other variety refers to the legal standing and public functions envisaged by constitutional arrangements in a particular setting. Status is typically ascribed via public texts, such as constitutional provisions, and is undertaken within the realm of exclusive state sovereignty. However, sub-national groupings, such as regions or provinces operating under autonomy statutes, can modify or elaborate or even contradict public texts and laws issued by authorities with overlapping sovereignty. Supra-national groupings, whether governmental or non-governmental, such as the European Union, the Association of Southeast Asian Nations, or the African Union, the Red Cross or the World Trade Organisation, can also attribute and formalise status to languages or they can utilise pooled sovereignty to issue language influencing decisions.

Actions that modify the corpus of a language or variety

Policy actions to impact on the status of languages are usually undertaken by politicians and policy makers working within official domains, as described above. Actions that modify the corpus of a language are more specialised, usually taken forward by professional linguists, for technical innovation, and occasionally for adoption and dissemination, in collaboration with a community of speakers. Corpus planning involves modifications to the internal meaning making resources of a language, such as writing reforms, terminology development, standardising translation, or disseminating the use and adoption of new norms.

Actions that promote the learning of languages or the acquisition of literacy

A variety of agents undertake actions to facilitate learning of additional or extended language skills or literacy, through a process involving interaction between teachers, researchers, curriculum writers, assessment agencies, credentialing authorities and learners and their families.

Innovation as renewal

Innovation is ultimately about renewal of organisations, practices or technologies. Innovation emerges from responses to internal criticism, from failure of methods or understandings to grapple with language problems, from interaction with other disciplines and openness to their ideas and operations, from new problems and possibilities in technology, economics and culture. Open innovation refers to those processes of innovation in which a field is engaged in dialogue with external actors and disciplines, while closed innovation refers to planned change that comes from internal processes, including criticism or contest. The need for greater efficiency and effectiveness can lead to innovation, because this feedback about the need to change is from commissioning agents and others with power to offer consultancies and contracts to language planning specialists.

The knowledge economy of recent decades, in which economic competitiveness is seen to reflect the degree of investment in education, has stimulated a great deal of language planning on behalf of English. This is evident from science publishing and technology innovation. If knowledge is seen as a stimulus to economic growth and expansion, then language barriers to accessing this knowledge come under pressure.

The field of language policy and planning is still developing and isn't yet sufficiently coherent and unified to allow a smooth spread of innovations. The journals that exist, especially *Current Issues in Language Planning*, *Language Policy* and *Language Problems and Language Planning*, are niche publications but the notions of language ecologies, overlapping domains of language use, the relation between learning language and its use in differentiated social domains, linked to patterns of bilingualism in society are language planning and sociolinguistic concepts that are beginning to shape innovation, education and English teaching.

Renewal of English language education to embrace the presence of English in spoken interaction as well as its presence within classrooms is underway in South Korea's ambitious creation of immersion villages and towns and in Content and Language Integrated Learning schemes in non-English speaking parts of Europe. Such initiatives seek renewal and innovation for English learning by systematically linking formal learning with informal acquisition. These sociolinguistic insights open classroom teaching to the lived presence of languages in community domains.

In many EFL settings, English use is encountered in quarantined form, since more extended presence of second languages in society can give rise to resistance and concern on behalf of the discourse range, social functions and communicative domains of national languages. This means that effective long-term renewal of English language education in EFL and even ESL settings requires comprehensive language planning involving status, corpus and acquisition actions that are multilingual, building English into strongly other-language promoting measures. This kind of wide-ranging language planning is rare, as the PPSMI example in Malaysia shows. Some public policies rhetorically affirm the value of multiple languages, but in effect privilege only dominant languages in curriculum time, teacher support and public promotion, failing to see that the ultimate success of the very policy itself is influenced by taking language planning concepts seriously.

Innovation in language planning for English

For these reasons, innovation in language policy and planning is necessarily different in kind from innovation in English language education in general. Even when language policy and planning is directed to some aspect of English language education, as it is so often today, what counts as innovative practice in language policy making, in language planning processes and content, cannot be directly compared to the object of its efforts, i.e., English language education. Instead it will need to look at the wider communicative situation of a given community. This characteristic will distinguish language planning innovation from innovation in English education in other contributions to this volume, in that it deals with a practice for decision making around and about English language education rather than aspects of English teaching, learning, assessment or curriculum per se.

First and second order change

Innovation in language education can be usefully divided into change of two broad types, or orders, according to their depth of penetration and effect. Scholars often distinguish between a more superficial order of change, *first order change*, which seeks to improve efficiency and effectiveness of what is currently done without disturbing basic organisational features. By contrast, *second order change* seeks to alter the fundamental ways in which organisations exist, including new goals, structures, and roles (Fullan, 2004). The wider or surrounding context determines whether language education policy is first order or second order change, and involves sensitivity to and awareness of the roles and value of other semiotic and linguistic systems.

For example, in settings in which there is poor or absent English language education, given that the most effective second language education outcomes require both socialisation and education, immersion and study, and new cultural knowledge, skills and habits, effective English language education requires second order change. The language policy innovation required is deeper and more extensive than traditional second language designs allow.

To succeed, innovation must not give rise to changes that counter the aims of the innovation, such as social pressures and concerns that rival or contest the aims of the innovation. Although in one respect all innovation involves change, innovation differs fundamentally from change, which can be random, undesired and undirected. By definition, innovation contains a certain element of intentionality, a willed change that is desired by those planning the future of an enterprise, a school system, a language teaching enterprise or any other project. The rise in the historic fortunes of English have come about at macro and micro levels, in first order change and second order change, through change in world events of great magnitude, for the most part, rather than innovative practice in pedagogy or in cultural esteem. However, innovations are critical to all educational process. In the review of innovations that Fullan canvases in his writings, he notes that governments can effect change in one or more of three broad modes: through the imposition of accountability measures on the various actors involved; through applying incentives (pressure or support); and through capacity development, which essentially involves 'reculturing' and assuming that internal professional motivations will contribute to effecting shared and negotiated change (Fullan, 2004).

The PPSMI example highlights the essentially ecological nature of education innovation extended even further than Fullan's categories allow, into the wider communication networks of the society, to see teachers, schooling and teaching as integrated into social and national interests. English language education innovation therefore, in many world settings, requires sensitivity to wider symbolic and practical issues bound up with communication, national identity and political and economic independence. Unlike more inert innovation and change schemes, such as the introduction of computers or web-based teaching, language planning changes are less containable in their effects and meanings and require processes of debate and research which include actors and interests well beyond those located in schools or universities.

Fullan's insights have been derived from observing failed and successful innovations within education systems, and include a commitment to seeing education as part of wider cultural systems. However, languages are more than normally present within wider ecological systems, they are often symbols of those very systems, including nations and national identities, and so languages are comparable to Fullan's ideas about overlapping and mutually constituting systems, but even more deeply so. Top-down language planning, as discussed above in relation to PPSMI, is an unproductive first order change, ultimately made vulnerable by its failure to engage with deep social questions of the wider communicative culture and the professionalism of teachers and other educators.

University instruction and language planning

A critical domain for long-term English language education planning is its role in university instruction. Here, too, context and ecology are critical notions for deliberate language planning innovation.

It is evident that there are significant advantages for English-language based authors and institutions compared to those operating in other languages (database costs, products and resources, closer experience in editing and housing journals and procedural advantages in peer review and academic writing), advantages not exclusive to American or British settings, but also shared by academics in English medium institutions in settings such as Hong Kong and Singapore. Acquiring competitive status can involve prohibitive cost barriers for developing country institutions, compounded by pervasive, subtle operations of linguistic advantage in preferred rhetorical style, argument modes and diverse academic disciplinary traditions. Language planning innovation is required to dislodge unfair advantages and pluralise modes of expression that retain rigour of scholarship without entrenching inherited advantages accruing to certain transactional styles, expressive modes or rhetorical power. In Altbach's (1998) analysis, China and India represent 'gigantic peripheries' to American and other English-centred academic globalisation. In both settings English has a long and differentiated history of presence, rejection, and embrace but in the past decade there has been immense investment in public education in and through English in each of these giant systems.

Especially marked is China, where in 2001 the Ministry of Education required 5–10 percent of undergraduate instruction in foreign languages (MinEd, 2001), stimulating great expansion in university level English-Chinese instruction. A proliferation of course types and language teaching combinations has emerged raising dilemmas about the role, purpose and consequences of mass and required English (Lo Bianco et al., 2009).

Deliberation and language planning

The most critical language policy and planning innovation in contexts such as these is process based deliberation. Language problems which public authorities 'resolve' through top-down rules, laws, regulations and accountability, fail the test of innovation if they provoke reaction and rejection by professionals responsible for their implementation or students and the wider community affected by their adoption. PPSMI in the Malaysian case strongly suggests this weakness in innovation design.

Deliberative, professionally informed language planning innovations can secure more multilingually sensitive English language education innovation that can be supportive of pluralistic language futures as well as providing opportunity and portable valid qualifications for students.

Future development in English language education innovation management and research should also pay attention to the wider communicative context within which English language education occurs and, in dialogue with language planning literature, evolve new models of innovation that incorporate insights on language and communication ecologies from language planning and policy studies.

Key readings

Lo Bianco, J. (2010), Language Policy and Planning, in Nancy H. Hornberger and Sandra Lee McKay (eds.), *Sociolinguistics and Language Education*, Bristol, UK: Multilingual Matters, pp. 143–176. This article traces the origins and development of the field of language policy and planning. It addresses the kinds of language planning that exist at a national level with celebrated case studies discussed. However, the key emphasis of the article is to widen the classical definition of what counts as language policy and planning to include the specific role of teachers and teaching, arguing that language modelling in classroom, and teachers' language behaviour within multilingual and multicultural contexts, are micro but critical kinds of language planning.

Lo Bianco, J. (2004), Language Planning as Applied Linguistics, in A. Davies and C. Elder (eds.), *Handbook of Applied Linguistics*, Blackwell: London, pp 738–763. This article discusses the difference between applied linguistics and linguistics applied, tracing the disciplinary history of language planning as an emblematic kind of applied language studies. The latter is distinguished from 'linguistics applied' since the focus is 'real world problems' featuring communication problems rather than the application of an academic discipline. The article traces the intense criticisms of language planning of the 1990s and early 2000s, and shows how its reinvigorated contemporary life can be traced to the population mobility and denser interconnectedness produced by globalisation.

References

Altbach, P. (1998), Gigantic Peripheries: India and China in the World Knowledge System, in P. Altbach (ed)., *Comparative Higher Education*. Greenwich, CT: Ablex, pp. 133–146.

Azirah, H. (2009), Not plain sailing: Malaysia's language choice in policy and education. *AILA Review, 22:* 36–51.

Bernama, (2009), *Teaching of Science and Mathematics back to Bahasa Melayu*, July 8. Retrieved November 2, 2011 from http://www.bernama.com/bernama/v5/ newsgeneral.php?id=423799.

Cha, Y-K. and Ham, S-H. (2008), The Impact of English on the School Curriculum, in B. Spolsky and F. M. Hult, *Handbook of Educational Linguistics*. Malden, MA: Blackwell, pp. 313–327.

Chapman, K. (2009), *It is Bahasa again but more emphasis will be placed on learning English*. July 9. *The Star Online*. Retrieved November 10, 2011 from http:// thestar.com.my/news/story.asp?file=/2009/7/9/nation/4286168&sec=nation

Chapman, K. et al., (2011), *PPSMI policy should be carried on for many generations* Sunday November 6. *The Star Online*. Retrieved November 10, 2011 from http:// thestar.com.my/metro/story.asp?sec=nation&file=/2011/11/6/nation/985056.

Facchinetti, R., Crystal, D., and Seidlhofer, B. (eds.), (2010), *From International to Local English – And Back Again*. Frankfurt am Main: Peter Lang.

Fullan, M. (2004), *Leading the Way from Whole School Reform to Whole System Reform*. Jolimont, Vic.: IARTV.

Giddens, A. (2003), *Runaway World: How Globalization is Reshaping our Lives*. London: Routledge.

Gill, S. K., (2004), Medium of Instruction Policy in Higher Education in Malaysia, in J. Tollefson, and A. B. M. Tsui (eds.), *Medium of Instruction Policies*. Mahwah, N.J.: Erlbaum Publishers, pp. 135–152.

Gill, S. K. (2007), Shift in language in policy in Malaysia. *AILA Review, 20:* 106–122.

Graddol, D. (2006), *English Next*. London: The British Council.

Juckes, T. J. (1995), *Opposition in South Africa*. Praeger, Westport, CT.

Lo Bianco, J. (2004), Language Planning as Applied Linguistics, in A. Davies and C. Elder (eds.), *Handbook of Applied Linguistics*. Blackwell: London, pp. 738–763.

Lo Bianco, J. (2010), Language Policy and Planning, in Nancy H. Hornberger and Sandra Lee McKay (eds.), *Sociolinguistics and Language Education*. Bristol, UK: Multilingual Matters, pp. 143–176.

Lo Bianco, J. (2011), A Friendly Knife? English in the Context of Sri Lankan Language Politics, in L. Farrell, U. N. Singh and R. A Giri (eds.), *English Language Education in South Asia: From Policy to Pedagogy*. Cambridge University Press India, pp. 36–60.

Lo Bianco, J., Orton, J. and Yihong, G. (eds.), (2009) *China and English: Globalisation and Dilemmas of Identity*. Clevedon, UK: Multilingual Matters.

Malaysia (2011), *Department of Statistics, Population and Housing, 2010*. Retrieved November 10, 2011 from http://www.statistics.gov.my.

MinEd, (2001), *Standard of English Courses for 9-Year Compulsory Education and General Senior High Schools*. Retrieved November 2, 2011 from http://www.tefl-china.net/2003/ca13821.htm.

Ohmae, K. (1999), *The Borderless World: Power and Strategy in the Interlinked Economy*. Harper Collins: New York.

Ostler, N. (2005), *Empires of the Word: A Language History of the World*. London: Harper Collins.

Ostler, N. (2010), *The Last Lingua Franca: English Until the Return of Babel.* Allen Lane/Penguin: London.

PISA (2011), *OECD Programme for International Student Assessment.* Accessed November 2, 2011 from http://www.pisa.oecd.org/pages/0,2987,en_32252351_32235731_1_1_1_1_1,00.html.

Seidlhofer, B., (2011), *Understanding English as a Lingua Franca.* Oxford: Oxford University Press.

Tan, P.K. W. and Rubdy, R. (eds.), (2008), *Language as Commodity.* London and New York: Continuum.

Tollefson, J and Tsui, A. (eds.), (2004), *Medium of Instruction Policies.* Mahwah, N.J.: Erlbaum.

Waters, A. (2009), Managing innovation in English language education. *Language Teaching, 42*, 4: 421–458.

11

CHANGE AND INNOVATION IN PRIMARY EDUCATION

Beverly Derewianka

Introduction

A key motivator of educational change is the curriculum mandated by the state. Internationally, curriculum reform is a major ongoing project as nations endeavour to improve student learning outcomes in a globally competitive environment. In the UK, for example, the National Curriculum is being significantly revised in order to identify the essential knowledge that students need to acquire and to provide greater autonomy to teachers and schools. In the USA, Common Core State Standards are being adopted by the majority of states in an effort to provide a consistent, clear understanding of what students are expected to learn in order to succeed in further education and careers and to compete in the global economy. In Australia, a national curriculum is in the process of implementation, following several attempts in the past. This chapter will focus on the Australian experience, as it throws up several issues confronting other countries as they grapple with curriculum reform and innovation. In particular, it will consider issues involved in the development of the English curriculum – and more specifically, the area of 'knowledge about language' (KAL) at the primary level.

In order to provide guidance for the writing team, Professor Peter Freebody was commissioned to produce a Framing Paper, outlining the theoretical framework for a robust and future-oriented English curriculum. Rather than simply replicate the generally accepted view of subject English – typically organised around the 'modes' of speaking, listening, reading/ viewing and writing – Freebody determined to ask the fundamental question of what constitutes English as a body of disciplinary knowledge. He proposed that the curriculum should give equal weight to an informed appreciation of literature, an expanding repertoire of literacy practices, and an explicit knowledge about how language works. The proposal was controversial in that it required secondary English teachers to take on the responsibility of teaching literacy – an area often assumed to be the province of primary schooling. It also meant that primary teachers would need not only to foster an enjoyment of literature, but to cultivate a critical awareness of literary qualities. But perhaps most contentious of all was the recommendation that knowledge about the English language be given comparable prominence – indeed, that it should be the backbone informing the other two strands.

The media, politicians, employers and the general public applauded the decision to place language at the centre, interpreting it as a return to a mythical golden age where a knowledge of spelling, punctuation and grammar would 'fix' all the problems of education. The Framing Paper (2008: 9), however, conceived of a knowledge about language as a much more comprehensive and rigorous enterprise:

> All students need to develop their understandings of how language functions to achieve a range of purposes that are critical to success in school. This includes reading, understanding, and writing texts that describe, narrate, analyse, explain, recount, argue, review, and so on.
>
> Students need to grow in their knowledge of how language enables people to interact effectively, to build and maintain their relationships, and to express and exchange their knowledge, skills, attitudes, feelings, and opinions. It can enable students to reflect consciously and with precision on their own speaking and writing, its efficacy, fluency and creativity, and to discuss these matters productively with others.

The aims of a 'knowledge about how language works' were envisaged as:

- extending students' language resources in ways that support increasingly complex learning throughout the school years;
- helping students deal with the language demands of the various curriculum areas;
- supporting students in moving from the interactive spontaneity of oral language towards the denser, more crafted language of the written mode;
- raising students' awareness of interpersonal issues such as how to take and support a stand in an argument, how to express considered opinions, how to strengthen or soften statements and how to interact with a variety of audiences;
- enabling students to engage with, analyse, and construct a wide range of texts, and negotiate evaluations of the social and aesthetic value of texts; and
- expanding students' understanding of how language builds knowledge and beliefs about the world. (pp. 9–10)

An appropriate model of language

Such a vision would require a powerful model of language, well beyond the scope of traditional school grammars, with their emphasis on labeling the 'parts of speech' and conforming to often arbitrary rules. In Australia, a more contemporary alternative based on Halliday's Systemic Functional Linguistics has a history of being employed fruitfully in school contexts. The initial and ongoing motivation was one of social justice – making the linguistic demands of schooling explicit so that learners – particularly those from ESL (EAL/D) and disadvantaged backgrounds – might be better supported in meeting these demands.

Halliday (1986) sees language as a resource, a meaning-making system. It is through language that we interactively shape and interpret our world and ourselves. According to Halliday, the language system can be seen as a complex network of choices. These choices have evolved to serve our needs, clustering into three major functions:

- representing our experience of the world (the experiential function);
- enabling interaction (the interpersonal function); and
- shaping texts (the textual function).

In a functional model, there is an intimate and systematic relationship between certain factors in the context and the choices made from the language system:

- the *field* (what is the subject matter being developed? e.g. everyday, personal, literary, technical, abstract, specific, generalized);
- the *tenor* (what are the social relations between the interactants? e.g. differences in terms of status, power, expertise, age, gender, familiarity);
- the *mode* (what mode and medium are being used? e.g. written, spoken, face-to-face, distanced, visual, electronic).

Given a particular field, certain choices are likely to be made from the experiential system. If, for example, the field being developed is an explanation of how an ecosystem works, we might expect language choices involving relations of causality, technical lexis, nominalisation, adverbials of manner, and action verbs in the 'timeless' present tense.

Given a particular tenor, certain choices are likely to be made from the interpersonal system. In the case of a student writing a book review for the school newsletter, for example, we might anticipate the use of persuasive language choices to align the reader, including some expression of emotion regarding the writer's feelings about the story or characters, evaluative language appraising the qualities of the text, an element of judgement of the characters' behaviour in developing the moral theme of the story, and some use of modality.

And given a particular mode or medium, certain choices are likely to be made from the textual system. A written historical recount, for example, will display a more prominent degree of 'crafting', greater lexical density, more considered sequencing in time, and a higher level of internal cohesion than a spontaneous, oral recount of personal experience.

Beyond the context of the specific situation, a functional model also locates language choices within the broader cultural context. In particular, following the work of Martin (Martin & Rose, 2008), it describes the various purposes for which language is used in a particular culture or sub-culture, allowing us to identify the genres that have arisen in that culture to achieve these purposes. In the context of schooling in a democratic culture, for example, students are expected to be able to debate the merits of a particular position employing one of the 'arguing' genres. A great deal of research has been undertaken in Australia into the ways in which the various school genres unfold in stages and their characteristic language features, forming the basis of many syllabus documents, the writing criteria for the national literacy assessment tests, and English textbooks.

In summary, a functional model:

- sees language as a system of choices that have evolved to serve different functions;
- seeks to describe authentic language in use;
- views language development as the ongoing expansion of learners' resources for making meaning;
- provides students with tools to investigate and critique how language is involved in the construction of meaning;
- takes into account the relationship between texts and their contexts of use, enabling teachers to identify the language demands typically made in each context and teach to them explicitly;
- operates at the level of the text but also explains how the text embodies language choices at the level of the clause through to the word.

In responding to the challenge of the Framing Paper, it was decided to draw on a functional model of language to inform the knowledge about language strand of the curriculum. The sub-strand dealing with experiential meanings was labelled 'Expressing and developing ideas', the sub-strand dealing with interpersonal meanings was labelled 'Language for interaction', and the sub-strand dealing with textual meanings was labelled 'Text structure and organization'. While these sub-headings are not entirely satisfactory, they sufficiently captured the intent for a lay audience.

Classroom implementation

As part of a small-scale project to observe how classroom teachers might interpret and apply the curriculum, the author worked with teachers from the local school, recording the teachers' first encounters with the document and how they drew on its contents to design and implement learning activities.

The teachers were initially nervous about the perceived complexity of the curriculum, but could see its potential and were keen to see how it might work in practice. Two upper primary teachers worked together to develop a series of lessons around the theme of 'community', including notions of relationships, belonging and identity. In the preamble to the English curriculum, they noted that there were three designated priority areas, one of which was Indigenous and Torres Strait Islander histories and cultures:

> The Aboriginal and Torres Strait Islander priority involves students actively engaging with the world's oldest continuous living cultures and the principles and virtues that are deeply embedded within these communities.

They determined that this would become a focus: investigating traditional and contemporary indigenous cultures and communities.

The first challenge was to consider how they might integrate the three strands: Literature, Language and Literacy. They decided that the Literature strand would provide a context for exploring the theme of community, and also for work on the students' knowledge about language and their literacy development. They noticed in the Literature strand a recommendation that:

> Students should experience a range of literatures from different cultures including the inscriptional and oral narrative traditions of Aboriginal people and Torres Strait Islander people, as well as the contemporary literature of these two cultural groups.

With that in mind, they introduced the students to the significance in indigenous communities of storytelling as a way of passing on cultural values and beliefs. They learned from members of the local indigenous community that the storyteller custodian's role was that of cultural educator, passing on the accumulated knowledge, spirituality, and wisdom, from when time began. The students watched videos of traditional Aboriginal communities sitting round the campfire following their evening meal and listening to the storyteller recount the stories from the Dreamtime:

> The bilby is digging for grubs that live in the roots of the witchetty bush. The bilby was digging and sniffing around for witchetty grubs. He dug, he pulled them out and ate them. He dug for more until he became very tired. If the roots were tough, the bilby would start singing, infesting the grubs with maggots to rot them and then he would just leave it and walk away ...

In addition to learning about storytelling in traditional rural communities, the students investigated how these stories were being made more widely available using contemporary technologies. In particular, they explored a website called Dust Echoes, a collection of twelve beautifully animated

Aboriginal dreaming stories collected from the Wugularr Community in Arnhem Land in the Northern Territory, Australia. The philosophy informing the development of the website was to create a broader community who could come to know and appreciate Aboriginal lore and heritage.

The teachers chose one of the animated stories to focus on more closely. The story of The Mimis (see Table 11.1) was one that dealt with the search by a young boy for his identity within the community. They began by looking at the overall structuring of the text into stages and phases, as indicated in the curriculum:

> Understand that different types of texts have identifiable text structures and language features that help the text serve its purpose.

The students compared the structure of this modern version of the story with the way in which the traditional campfire story of the bilby had unfolded.

When it came to looking in greater detail at the language features of the story, the teachers felt somewhat less confident as functional grammar was new to them. Following a couple of meetings with the researchers, they decided to try working on the experiential function of language – in this case, how the grammar is used to represent 'what's going on' in the story.

The original text had been modified to remove any complex grammatical structures that could cause a distraction and to make the story sound more 'oral'. The students began by learning how the clause helps to construct the story world. As the students watched the animated version, the teachers stopped the video at relevant points and asked the students to create clauses describing the visual image, responding to the questions suggested in the curriculum:

> What's happening here?
> Who or what is participating in the activity?
> What are the circumstances surrounding the action?

Gradually they were introduced to the terms Process, Participant and Circumstance as the beginnings of a shared metalanguage. They read through their clauses, asking each other the questions above and colouring the Processes in green, the Participants in red, and the Circumstances in blue, visually revealing the simple patterns in the clauses.

The teachers then guided them to identify the Processes representing various kinds of 'doings and happenings' in the story. They first looked for the physical activities that the participants were engaging in, such as when the mimis tended the land:

> In the evening, the mimis **come up** from the underworld
> and they **prepare** the land for the next day.
> They **groom** the bushes,
> they **feed** the fish
> and they **fix** broken branches.

TABLE 11.1 Structure of the story of the Mimis

	The Mimis (modified version)
Orientation *Introduction of character*	The boy is sitting at the camp while the rest of the tribe are hunting. He wants to hunt, but he can't throw a spear and he can't track an animal.
Event *Reaction* *Response* *Event* *Setting in place and time*	In the late afternoon, everyone returns with heaps of fish and kangaroo, and the boy feels ashamed and embarrassed. So he gets up and leaves the camp. He takes a sharpened stick because he wants to catch an echidna. He walks all the way up to the hills, but he can't find a single echidna! But as the sun sets, a magical thing happens. The hills begin to move and they change shape. All around him the hills begin to part as the shadows stretch into the dusk.
Event *Introduction of characters*	In the evening, the mimis come up from the underworld and they prepare the land for the next day. They groom the bushes, they feed the fish and they fix broken branches.
Description of characters	The mimis are very tall and thin. They are human-like stick people. The mimis are spirit creatures, who leave no tracks! They are also fun, playful, and magical. They are good spirits, happy spirits!
Event **Complication**	The boy looks on in amazement as the small group of mimis tidy the land. The mimis enchant him with their magic and they carry him into their home in the hill. The mimis take the boy into their underworld and they dance all night long. The boy forgets about his world.
Response *Introduction of character* *Reflection* *Response*	In the meantime, his father is waiting all night. He worries about his son. So the boy's father walks out of the camp at the crack of dawn. He follows his son's footsteps into the distance. But suddenly the tracks finish. So he sits on the ground, and he begins to chant, and eventually he goes into a trance. With his magic he can hear the dancing and singing of the mimis. He wants to reach this underworld. The old man's hair grows and grows. It seeps into the ground and creeps deep into the earth in search of his son. His chanting follows his hair and the son begins to hear the chanting of his father as his hair grows closer and closer!
Resolution *Reflection* *Evaluation*	The old man's hair grows until it coils itself right around the boy, and the father pulls up his son out of the earth. The boy snaps back into reality, and his father takes him back to the camp. The boy then realizes that the camp needs all kinds of people with all kinds of skill and he is no longer envious of his fellow hunters.

Then they noted those Processes that represented what the Participants were thinking:

> The boy **forgets** about his world.
> The father **worries** about his son.
> The boy **realizes** the camp needs all kinds of people.

... and feeling:

> He **wants** to hunt.
> He **wants** to catch an echidna.
> He **wants** to reach the underworld.

They discussed what these Processes contributed to the story in terms of providing an insight into the inner thoughts and feelings of the participants. They identified those points in the story where they, as readers, would have liked to know what the characters were thinking or feeling. In a 'freeze frame' activity, they dramatised the story and froze the action at those points so that the class members could ask the character such questions. When the boy was sitting alone in the camp while the others were out hunting, he was asked to reveal what he was thinking and feeling:

> I **am feeling** as if I don't belong.
> I **want** to be part of the group.
> I **hope** I can show my father that I **know** how to hunt.

The students then incorporated these sentences into the story, creating the kinds of 'spaces for reflection' that characterise much good literature.

When they came to the description of the mimis, they discussed the function of 'are', with one student volunteering that it was a 'joining Process':

> The mimis **are** very tall and thin.
> They **are** human-like stick people.
> The mimis **are** spirit creatures who leave no tracks!
> They **are** also fun, playful, and magical.
> They **are** good spirits, happy spirits!

They observed the pattern of these clauses, with the Process forming a relationship between the thing being described and its description, as in Table 11.2.

The teachers decided to set them a task finding out more information about the mimis from the Internet. Following the pattern above, they came up with clauses such as those shown in Table 11.3, which were then incorporated into the story.

TABLE 11.2 Pattern of 'describing' clause

The mimis	*are*	*tall and thin.*
'thing being described'	'relating Process'	'description'

TABLE 11.3 Relating Processes linking 'the thing being described' to its description

'thing being described'	*'relating Process'*	*'description'*
Mimis	**are**	dreaming spirits of Arnhem Land.
They	**are**	extremely long with thin stretchy bodies that move with the wind.
They	**have**	elongated fingers that move in and out of the trees as they fix the broken branches, feed the fish and groom the bushes.
They	**are**	trickster spirits that are playful and joyful.
They	**are**	like humans but they live in a different dimension.
They	**are**	shadow spirits that dance around the shrubs in the wind.

As can be seen from the clauses in Table 11.4, the teachers had also done some work on the 'description' part of the clause, focusing in particular on rich noun groups with vivid pre- and post-modifiers.

Together, the teachers and the students were developing an understanding of the grammar of the text. The teachers had been able to find their way around the curriculum and draw on the three strands – language, literature and literacy – to design a successful sequence of lessons.

The teachers' reflections reveal an overall satisfaction with what they and the students were able to achieve, despite their initial trepidation:

> One of the things I became more aware of was all the different types of processes!! It was great to understand how to explicitly present these to the students in context. I was amazed at how they understood and were able to use the new terminology so readily – even the slower ones could do this. The class was very motivated to participate in all the activities which was quite intriguing as we have some reluctant writers. We were very excited about the standard of their work. I noticed that their enthusiasm and ability to describe things showed a marked improvement.

TABLE 11.4 Noun groups describing the Mimis

pre-modifiers	head noun	post-modifiers
dreaming	spirits	of Arnhem Land
thin stretchy	bodies	that move with the wind
trickster	spirits	that are playful and joyful
elongated	fingers	that move in and out of the trees
shadow	spirits	that dance around the shrubs in the wind

We both feel we have so much more to digest – we're still on the learning curve. So far we have only touched the tip of the iceberg but I'm certainly glad that we have done that much. Personally, I gained a lot from this experience. Firstly, a greater understanding of the new curriculum and how it can be used to enrich the students' writing. I also learnt that by using scaffolding, students who are low achievers are able to achieve and feel good about their work. Functional grammar has a purpose when it is taught and used in the way it is intended.

This is obviously only an anecdotal account of a very small-scale initiative, but it highlights a number of issues surrounding curriculum innovation, and in this instance, the introduction of a functional approach to language.

Reflections: issues and discussion

As with any major curriculum innovation, mandating an explicit knowledge about language throws up a number of issues. Here we will consider three key factors that mitigate against the success of this initiative: feasibility, degree of innovation and innovation fidelity.

Feasibility

The term 'feasibility' is being used here in a broad sense to capture a number of widely acknowledged factors that can potentially impact upon the viability of an initiative. Towndrow et al. (2010: 246), in discussing 'the problematic enactment of educational innovations', point to *scale* as a key factor in determining what might be reasonable expectations for a specific innovation. In contrast to the example above of a single attempt at classroom application, the scale of national curriculum adoption and implementation is considerable, involving tens of thousands of schools, teachers and students. A functional approach has been successfully implemented at the level of the individual class, school and even system. In Queensland, for example, the government school system recently provided a five-day professional development program in a functional approach to language and literacy for all 25,000 primary teachers. Resources (both human and material) to replicate this at the national level, however, would be stretched very thin.

Compounding the difficulty is the unrealistic *timeframe*, with a lead-up of only a couple of years, during which the various states need to interpret the curriculum to suit their own contexts, trial the content and validate the achievement standards. Key personnel responsible for the implementation need to be trained, textbooks and other resource materials need to be produced, and systems and infrastructure need to be put in place. Even if this proved manageable, would it result in *uptake* by classroom teachers? The mandatory nature of the curriculum, backed by state and commonwealth governments, implies a level of compliance, particularly when the curriculum is linked to the national testing system and the results of the tests are linked to teacher accountability. But this can result in false buy-in unless the teachers are convinced that the innovation will 'solve problems that educators see as urgent, are relatively usable, and require only modest professional learning' (Cohen and Ball, 2007: 32). Student knowledge about language might not be regarded as a high priority and might receive only superficial attention if it is perceived as yet another intrusion imposed on an already crowded curriculum, with little obvious and immediate pay-off in terms of learning outcomes.

Despite such apprehension, however, the response of teachers who have attended inservice programs on an introduction to functional grammar has been generally very positive. Teachers who have participated in full-day workshops presented by the author, for example, have provided feedback such as the following:

- Meaning-based grammar makes sense.
- Useful for working with young children (especially those who may have language delays/difficulties).
- I am very excited about having an understanding of a functional grammar and the language and terminology of this, to use at school with students who have little or no understanding of grammar. This is just what I needed.
- Really like the focus on meaning and form. The terminology participant, process, circumstance makes so much sense and is a logical way into the structure of language for both reading and writing.
- I love grammar and, compared to many, have good grammatical knowledge. I found invaluable the distinction between function and form – and how one needs to deal with both – and why. This will make my grammar teaching more relevant, useful.

Degree of innovation

Cohen and Ball (2007: 19) define innovation as a 'departure from current practice—deliberate or not, originating in or outside of practice, which is novel' and caution that innovations involving substantial change from current instructional practices are less likely to be adopted broadly. The teaching of an explicit knowledge about language across all years of schooling in all states represents a high level of innovation in the Australian context and is thus susceptible to a low level of adoption. It is not only a matter of a massive renovation of teachers' professional knowledge-base with regard to knowledge about language, but also the challenge of implementing contemporary pedagogic practices which involve the explicit teaching of grammar in the context of authentic use in the various curriculum areas. As recommended by the Framing Paper:

> The goal of teaching grammar and textual patterns should go beyond students' labelling of various grammatical categories; it should centre on goals such as clearer expression of thought, more convincing argumentation, more careful logic in reasoning, more coherence, precision, and imagination in speaking and writing, and knowing how to choose words and grammatical and textual structures that are more appropriate to the audience or readership. (p. 6)

The deliberate extravagance of the functional model also works against its uptake. Hallidayan theory is multi-layered and multi-dimensional in its efforts to capture the richness and complexity of authentic language in use. An understanding of a functional approach requires a very different way of conceiving of language and grammar. Although it has been widely drawn on over a period of three decades, it is by no means fully institutionalised throughout the school system.

Even if the knowledge about language strand was based on a traditional model of grammar, the innovation level would be very high for most teachers. A small-scale survey by the author confirmed previous findings (e.g. Andrews, 2007) about teachers' knowledge of grammar. With regard to the sentence *I might go to the beach tomorrow*, all managed to identify and label the noun and verb, but only 50 percent were able to identify the definite article, the other respondents labeling it as a *pronoun, noun, joining word,* or *preposition.* Only 30 percent were able to identify the modal auxiliary 'might', the others referring to it as an *adverb, adjective, quantifier, qualifier, conditional tense, thinking verb,* or *preposition.* And only 12 percent were able to recognize 'tomorrow' as an adverb/adverbial, the rest labeling it as, for example, a *proper noun, abstract noun,* or *adjective.* In response to an item on the difference between compound and complex sentences, fewer than ten percent were able to give anything close to a coherent definition, the others providing attempts such as:

Compound sentence
- 'Joins two pieces of information together'
- 'Joins two phrases'
- 'One has a comma or a number of commas'
- 'Separated by a conjunction – has one clause'
- 'I think – contains a dependent clause'
- 'Contains simple clauses'
- 'Something to do with the subject, where it is in the sentence + how much other information is included (maybe) + the verb is important too!!!'

Complex sentence
- 'Cannot be separated independently'
- 'You can turn it around'
- 'A complex > phrased'
- 'May or may not have conjunction but contains adjective'
- 'Many parts'
- 'Includes consequences for a particular condition'

Given the high degree of innovation, critical to teacher uptake is the provision of substantial in-service opportunities, as recognized by the teachers' feedback from the above survey:

- I feel that I need quite a deal more professional learning in this area in order to improve. I feel inspired to begin working on these areas with my class.
- I pity those who have no background at all for their base and I also fear for those who have no professional learning at all in this area.
- There's a saying about a little bit of knowledge being dangerous and I fear that so many of us, with our little bit of knowledge, will be dangerous.

Among many others, Carless (1997: 352) recommends that 'in-service training is an essential preparation for a new curriculum. Teachers need to be retrained with new skills and knowledge, particularly when the required methodology is highly different from the existing one'.

Innovation fidelity

Towndrow et al. (2010) discuss the degree to which implementation retains fidelity to the intent of the innovation. It is generally recognized that with any curriculum innovation there is a process of recontextualisation, where the theoretical knowledge developed in academic contexts is appropriated by policy developers, providers of professional development, and producers of materials and made accessible to the end users (Bernstein, 1990; Chen and Derewianka, 2009). Priestley (2011: 2), for example, notes that 'policies mutate as they migrate from setting to setting' mediated by professionals with different values, interests and levels of expertise. In the present case, systemic functional theory has been interpreted in Australia with a relatively high degree of fidelity to the intent of the original theory, primarily due to close collaboration over a number of years between researchers, theory developers, teacher educators and classroom practitioners.

With the advent of large-scale implementation, however, there is considerable risk that the integrity of the theory is compromised by the 'Chinese whispers' mode of professional learning, whereby the content of the national curriculum is open to interpretation at state level by curriculum developers with only a passing familiarity with systemic functional theory. This interpretation is then taken up by a variety of providers of professional development and commercial publishers, with increasing simplification of content and accommodation towards the status quo. Teachers attending workshops are then charged with the responsibility of returning to their schools and sharing their understandings with colleagues. By this stage there is the potential for the original intent to become so distorted as to be almost unrecognizable.

In the case of the knowledge about language strand, fidelity is further eroded by the lack of clarity regarding the intent on the part of the developers of the national curriculum. Because the politicians and media commentators were expecting a return to traditional grammar, it was considered prudent to heighten the visibility of familiar terminology such as 'nouns' and 'verbs'. Systemic functional linguistics, in fact, operates both at the level of function (e.g. Process) and form (e.g. verb) – and the relationship between the two. So, terminology referring to grammatical class (e.g. pronoun, conjunction, preposition) is encompassed by the theory. In the content descriptions, this was dealt with by first mentioning the form and then introducing its function, e.g.:

- understand that verbs represent various processes (doing, thinking, saying, and relating);
- understand how adverbials work in different ways to provide circumstantial details about an activity.

This was done with a view to reassuring the politicians that familiar terminology would be evident in the curriculum – and also keeping in mind previous failed attempts to introduce a functional approach into curricula (e.g. the LiNC project in the UK) due to bureaucratic apprehension. But, with the foregrounding of 'traditional' terminology, it would be very easy for someone unfamiliar with functional grammar to assume that what was intended was indeed a return to traditional grammar.

Conclusion

So what might constitute 'success' in this instance of curriculum innovation? If we were to base such a judgement on the ideals of the Framing Paper, it might be that teachers and students were developing an explicit, evolving knowledge about how language works – not only out of intrinsic interest, but in order to explore and evaluate the texts of others and to achieve greater clarity, interest and precision in their own texts. This would be accompanied by the development of a shared metalanguage that focused initially on meaning and function, but which then, when appropriate, would consider how these meanings are realized by various grammatical forms. Such an objective would best be attained through a functional approach to language, which enables us to observe how language is used to represent what is going on in the world, how language is used interpersonally to interact and appraise, and how language is used to shape cohesive and coherent texts.

Given the constraints canvassed above, it is highly unlikely that, certainly in the short term, the majority of teachers will be implementing such a curriculum with high fidelity – or at all. But perhaps such high compliance is not a reasonable (or even desirable) goal. Fullan and Miles (1992) note that change is not simply compliance, but involves new learning – coming to grips with new personal meaning. They see curriculum change as a recursive process – a guided journey loaded with uncertainty, where the most significant outcomes occur at the local level.

Similarly, Hargreaves and Shirley (2009: 94) suggest that there is a 'Fourth Way', superseding previous top-down, bureaucratic, accountability-driven curriculum change:

> In the Fourth Way, professional learning communities develop curriculum and don't just deliver it. They set ambitious targets together rather than running a furious and frantic race to meet the targets imposed by others.

The Fourth Way advocates a democratic process which supports and trusts teachers' professionalism as they work collaboratively with colleagues, drawing on relevant research, to explore the challenges of their practice. From such a perspective, highly trained teachers apply their expertise to find out 'what works' for their students in their context.

The fact that a functional approach to language has endured and grown in Australia over a period of several decades – despite ill-informed political opposition – is due to the professionalism of educators who have worked collegially to develop practice grounded in sound, relevant theory because they observe that it makes a difference to student learning outcomes. A reasonable expectation might therefore be that committed teachers, energized by the possibilities of the new curriculum and supported by high quality, intensive and sustained professional learning, will continue to work closely with colleagues in cycles of learning, practice, reflection and improvement, documenting and disseminating their observations through professional association journals and newsletters and at meetings and conferences. Such bottom-up, incremental change is, in the long run, more likely to result in real change than accepting low-fidelity, superficial, mandated compliance by the masses as an indication of 'success'.

Key readings

Christie, F. (2005). *Language Education in the Primary Years.* Sydney: UNSW Press. Following a discussion of various approaches to language and literacy, Christie outlines how a functional approach can contribute to students' academic achievement in the primary years and beyond. A practical and comprehensive guide for teachers based on contemporary, relevant language education theory.

Hargreaves, A., & Shirley, D. (2009). *The Fourth Way: The Inspiring Future for Educational Change.* Thousand Oaks, CA: Corwin Press. The authors provide a framework for educational change that calls for deep and demanding learning supported by a high level of professionalism. The approach includes developing a common, inspiring vision pursued by collaborative learning communities involving teachers, students, parents, and education systems.

Wilson, A. (1999). *Language Knowledge for Primary Teachers.* London: David Fulton Publishers. In the context of changing curriculum expectations, Wilson tackles the issue of teachers' and students' explicit knowledge about language. Drawing on both functional and traditional approaches, she emphasizes the need to teach about language through rich activities using authentic texts.

References

Andrews, S. (2007). *Teacher Language Awareness.* Cambridge: Cambridge University Press.

Bernstein, B. (1990). *The Structuring of Pedagogic Discourse.* London: Routledge.

Carless, D. (1997). Managing systemic curriculum change: A critical analysis of Hong Kong's Target-Oriented Curriculum initiative, *International Review of Education – Internationale Zeitschrift für Erziehungswissenschaft – Revue Internationale de l'Education, 43,* 4: 349–366.

Chen, H. & Derewianka, B. (2009). Binaries and beyond: A Bernsteinian perspective on change in literacy education, *Research Papers in Education,* Special Issue on Shaping futures: Literacy policy in the twenty-first century, *24,* 2: 225–257.

Cohen, D. K. & Ball, D. L. (2007). Educational innovation and the problem of scale. In B. L. Schneider & S. K. McDonald (Eds.), *Scale-up in Education: Ideas in Principle* (Vol. 1, pp. 19–36). Plymouth: Rowman & Littlefield.

Fullan, M. & Miles, M. (1992). Getting reform right: What works and what doesn't. *Phi Delta Kappan, 73,* 10: 744–752.

Halliday, M. A. K. (1986). *Language in school.* Lecture 4 in a series of lectures at the University of Singapore, University of Singapore Press.

Hargreaves, A. & Shirley, D. (2009). *The Fourth Way: The Inspiring Future for Educational Change.* Thousand Oaks, CA: Corwin Press.

Martin, J. R. & Rose, D. (2008). *Genre Relations: Mapping Culture.* London: Equinox.

National English Curriculum: Framing Paper (2008). Australian Curriculum, Assessment and Reporting Authority.

Priestley, M. (2011). Schools, teachers and curriculum change: A balancing act? *Journal of Educational Change, 12*: 1–23.

Towndrow, P., Silver, R., & Albright, J. (2010). Setting expectations for educational innovations, *Journal of Educational Change, 11*: 425–455.

12

INNOVATION IN SECONDARY EDUCATION: A CASE OF CURRICULUM REFORM IN HONG KONG

David Carless and Gary Harfitt

Introduction

The New Senior Secondary Curriculum (NSS) stands as a key element of Hong Kong's post-colonial education reforms. Its genesis lies in proposals to revamp the educational system launched at the turn of the millennium (Education Commission, 2000) and related curriculum reform initiatives (CDC, 2001; CDC & HKEAA, 2007). The NSS component has been implemented across Hong Kong secondary schools since September 2009.

The NSS includes changes to the structure and content of the senior secondary curriculum (i.e. years 10–12). The structural element is a move from a four-year to a three-year program with students entering university one year earlier than previously. An adjunct to this is that instead of undergoing high-stakes examinations at years 11 and 13, as per the previous British-influenced system, students are involved in only one public examination in year 12 via the new Hong Kong Diploma of Secondary Education (HKDSE). This includes school-based assessment (SBA), where grades awarded by their own teachers for work in schools count towards the high-stakes examination results.

The content aspects of the NSS aspire to provide: a more flexible, diversified curriculum to cater better for learners' varied interests, needs and capabilities; a broad-based curriculum replacing one that required specialization in either science or humanities; stronger synergies between schooling and future career or higher education options; and greater emphasis on preparation for lifelong learning through nine generic skills, including collaboration, communication and creativity.

This chapter aims to provide a critical analysis of the English Language components of this NSS curriculum. The chapter is organized as follows. First, we outline a framework which guides our analysis of reform in secondary education in Hong Kong. We then describe the English language components of the NSS and outline its implications for teaching, learning and assessment. We use recently collected data to illustrate teacher and student views of the early implementation of the NSS. We draw out wider implications for educational reform, focusing particularly on potentials and challenges in using assessment as a lever for pedagogic change.

Conceptual framework: technological, political and cultural perspectives on reform

We frame our analysis through the lens of an influential framework developed by House (House, 1979, 1981; House & McQuillan, 2005). This framework argues that an adequate understanding of school reform requires three perspectives: technological, political and cultural. The technological perspective assumes a rational-linear model of educational change and sees reform as mainly a process of research, development and diffusion. This rationalized model is often favored by government planners who are attracted by the hierarchical control it appears to bring. The political perspective views innovation as a process of conflicts, negotiation and compromise between groups and factions. Central to such an orientation are issues such as power and legitimacy. The cultural perspective relates to meanings and community values, and reflects an ecological perspective. It examines innovation within the specific culture and sub-cultures of the educational setting in which reform is being implemented. We use this tri-partite framework to analyze below selected pre-existing features of school curriculum reform in Hong Kong. At the end of the chapter, we relate it to our discussion of the NSS initiative.

Technological

A technological perspective on school reform in Hong Kong is represented by the way in which reforms have typically been developed. Within this perspective, we address two elements: first, centralized and bureaucratic processes; and second, policy borrowing or policy transfer.

Curriculum development in Hong Kong has long been characterized as centralized and bureaucratic (Morris, 1995; Morris & Adamson, 2010), with teachers having little input to or influence on curriculum reform proposals. Well-presented visions, guidelines and syllabi are compiled, but there is relatively modest detail or attention to classroom implementation. A repercussion is that there is frequently a mismatch between curriculum *intentions*, what the syllabus suggests should take place in the classroom and curriculum *realities*, what actually occurs in the classroom (Morris & Scott, 2003). The lack of teacher ownership and participation in reform in Hong Kong has meant that innovative curricula have usually only been adopted superficially. This is a recurring theme in the wider literature as teachers often rely excessively on superficial similarities between their current practice and reform ideas, and may lose important aspects of a reform in the desire to assimilate it into existing knowledge structures (Spillane et al., 2002). Furthermore, teachers in Hong Kong are faced with their own priorities, such as guiding students through competitive examinations which affect university entrance. If pedagogic reform is not aligned with congruent assessment change, it is unlikely to be taken seriously by teachers (Carless, 2013).

A second strand within a technological perspective is that of policy borrowing. This typically involves the transfer of policies, whereby one country seeks to ameliorate its educational problems by adopting a policy or practice deemed successful in another country (Phillips, 2006). Hong Kong has traditionally looked to major Anglophone countries for ideas about curriculum reform and many borrowed innovations have failed to embed themselves successfully as they contained elements which were not congruent with local norms and values. This has been particularly the case when inquiry-oriented or student-centred approaches have met resistance from Hong Kong teachers or students, more accustomed to conventional practices.

Political

A key political dimension to educational reform in Hong Kong involved the retrocession to mainland China in 1997. The incoming post-colonial government sought to establish its legitimacy by launching curriculum reforms which were, or appeared to be, different from the previous government (Morris, 2002). The NSS is one of the major initiatives of the post-colonial government, and notably the structural reform brings the school system in line with the Chinese system of six years of secondary school and a four year Bachelor degree.

A weakness of the Hong Kong political system is that there is only a limited form of democracy, so governments tend to lack legitimacy in the eyes of various sectors of the population. This sometimes results in protracted negotiations between factions, inevitable compromises and reversal or amendment to policies deemed unpopular. Within education, influential forces include representatives of elite schools, well-connected business leaders, teachers' unions and parents. A repercussion is that there has been a tendency for reforms to be viewed as a tacit compact between government and schools in which reforms are mainly symbolically promoted and symbolically implemented (Morris & Scott, 2003). In such cases, the visions of reform are often only partially implemented.

Cultural

Hong Kong is a setting influenced by Confucian cultural values, although Confucianism itself has a contested and evolving identity (Wong & Wong,

2002), and Chinese beliefs span a huge spectrum of differing and contradictory ideas (Ryan & Louie, 2007). Wider societal orientations are also enacted through existing and changing sub-cultures at professional, school or individual levels (Morris & Lo, 2000). Following from these points, discussion of culture is fraught with risks of stereotyping and over-simplification, but despite this danger we do wish to attempt an outline of some conventional culturally based teaching, learning and assessment practices which impact on the prospects of pedagogic reform.

The traditional authoritative teacher role in Confucian-heritage cultures (CHCs) as source of knowledge and wisdom is often supplemented by close personal relationships between teachers and students. Teaching often contains elements which are both 'teacher-centered' and 'student-centered' (Biggs & Watkins, 2001) in that the teacher orchestrates, but a concern for students' and their needs is at the forefront. The role of teacher as orchestrator of classroom activities is exemplified by interactive whole-class teaching being much more common than independent student work, individually, in pairs or in groups.

There is also a strong cultural element to assessment practices in CHCs. Assessment in the form of competitive examinations is deeply rooted in the Chinese tradition and can be traced back over 2,000 years to the Han dynasty. This historical and culturally based orientation sees major purposes of assessment as providing through examinations a level playing-field and a means for social mobility. Whilst these aims are laudable, their practice in Hong Kong has often led to emphasis on reliability at the expense of validity, and limited modes of assessment. An unintended adjunct has been that the de facto goal of education is to pass examinations.

Summary in relation to the three perspectives

To sum up, we note a number of features which have characterized attempts at reform in Hong Kong. Reform ideas are usually sound and draw on good practice internationally and regionally in line with global trends. They are expressed within a number of documents that outline the goals of reforms and contain curriculum guidelines. Teachers rarely have strong objections to the substance of the reforms, although they often perceive that they are not directly integrated with the priorities of schools and teachers. Schools and teachers are generally left to adopt, adapt or downplay reform initiatives in that there is limited support for change or pressure to do more than pay lip-service to reform rhetoric. This suits the needs of both parties, because government does not have the confidence or will-power to pursue energetically the implementation of potentially challenging or unpopular reforms, whilst schools are often too busy with their own priorities and agendas to have time to engage with multiple innovations. Cultural aspects are particularly relevant in relation to reform of English language teaching because Chinese ways of learning the mother tongue through, for example, painstaking practice of the written form of Chinese characters are very different to more communicative orientations to learning English as a second or foreign language.

The English language curriculum in the NSS

English is one of four core subjects in the NSS, the others being Chinese, Mathematics and a new subject, Liberal Studies – worthy of brief comment because it exemplifies some of the broad-based aspects of the reform. Liberal Studies contains elements of science, humanities and liberal arts with the aim of broadening students' knowledge base and enhancing their social awareness through the study of a wide range of issues.

The English language component of the NSS is framed around three interconnected strands. These comprise English for interpersonal communication, for developing and applying knowledge, and for responding and giving expression to real and imaginative experience (CDC & HKEAA, 2007). The third strand represents an extension of previous curricula, in terms of strengthening the provision of language arts. This is incorporated within an elective section of the NSS (25 percent of curriculum time) consisting of eight modules categorized into four language arts subjects (learning English through poems and songs, short stories, drama and popular culture) and four other electives (learning English through workplace communication, debating, social issues and sports communication). Through these eight electives, students are presented with opportunities to apply subject knowledge and other generic skills including communication, critical thinking, creativity and collaboration. These electives represent the major innovative thrust to the NSS English curriculum.

The elective modules have a number of commonalities: they are mostly aimed at encouraging students to engage with authentic materials highlighting the use of English language in context; they are all designed to be exploited through a series of task-based activities; and they seek to promote student productive skills, orally and in writing. Materials for the NSS often include texts with different styles, registers and genres with varying levels of difficulty. The aspiration as stated in the NSS documents and suggested schemes of work, is that teachers will exploit the use of imaginative texts because they are by nature open to multiple interpretations and so can facilitate genuine interaction among learners. Emphasis is placed on arousing students' emotional experiences and their responses to the text instead of a sole focus on its mechanical aspects. The curriculum makes frequent references to the importance of students' sharing experiences, their personal involvement in texts, and the development of their attitudes and values. The curriculum documentation also invites schools to develop their own assessment methods for these electives, and proposes innovative methods, such as multimedia presentations, portfolios, projects and creative tasks.

Schools are expected to select two to three electives from both the language arts and other electives that best suit the interests and abilities of their students. The choice of elective modules then aspires to promote greater creativity in English lessons so, for example, students who embark on the poems and songs elective are encouraged to engage in tasks that lead to them rewriting song lyrics and producing their own poems. The short stories elective invites students to write and present (or perform) their own story. At the same time, the electives emphasize the practical nature of English outside the classroom such as in the context of the workplace or a debate, and in the discussion of social issues and current affairs around them.

The implementation of the three-year senior secondary academic structure in Hong Kong also aims at developing a stronger alignment between curriculum, pedagogy and assessment. We address the relationship between these core components next.

Teaching, learning and assessment in the NSS

The NSS invites English teachers to move their practice further towards notions of teacher as a facilitator who supports the development of independent student learning capabilities. In a specific section of the curriculum document (CDC & HKEAA, 2007: 68), teachers are given guidance on how to make this shift possible, including negotiating learning goals and content with learners, adapting teaching to student responses and enhancing the quality of interaction in the classroom. The same document also calls for teachers to adopt a flexible approach to the organization of their classrooms so that pair work and group work become more frequently used tools for promoting peer collaboration during lessons. Teachers are also encouraged to develop higher-order thinking skills in their students through the use of more open-ended questions.

These suggestions about fostering more open, probing questions in class, resemble the type of dialogic classroom talk that has been discussed by international authorities, such as Robin Alexander (e.g. Alexander, 2008) and Neil Mercer (e.g. Mercer & Littleton, 2007). The implementation of this kind of interactive English language classroom in Hong Kong carries, however, a number of challenges. The conventional view of a teacher in CHCs is to see their main role as imparting knowledge to students, who accordingly may be placed in a mainly receptive role. Attempts to introduce a more communicative orientation to language teaching in Hong Kong over the last twenty years or so have had only limited success (e.g. Carless, 2004).

A further barrier to interactive pedagogy is student reticence and anxiety about active participation in English lessons (e.g. Tsui, 1996). These issues are exacerbated by issues of Chinese identity and resistance to English as a foreign language of colonial ancestry (e.g. Lin, 1999). Under these influences, local students may be reluctant to pose questions or negotiate with their teacher, thereby hindering the NNS curriculum planners' aim of promoting learner enquiry in English language classrooms. This is illustrative of a number of tensions facing ELT in Hong Kong. English is simultaneously an important language for study, wider communicative purposes and a subject that most students in the lower half of the achievement scale find difficult or even unpleasant. In the secondary school arena, English becomes a subject for examination purposes more than a means of communication. Accordingly, we turn next to this critical issue of assessment.

The assessment and examination system is a key factor impacting on pedagogy and curriculum reform. This is the case in most contexts, but particularly so in CHCs where examinations take on an almost religious fervour (Kennedy et al., 2008). Previous ELT reforms in Hong Kong have often foundered on the rocks of an examination system which during the 1980s and 1990s moved at a slower pace than curriculum innovation proposals. An important initiative in regard to the NSS is SBA (Davison, this volume). SBA is intended to promote a positive washback on language pedagogy by encouraging student oral work and engaging students with extensive reading of texts and viewing of non-print material, such as movies. SBA involves teachers in the high-stakes grading of their students, and also encourages all stakeholders to engage with the published assessment criteria.

From a technological perspective, SBA has many positives. It went through a detailed research, development and diffusion process. It has a number of technical attributes: it permits a wider range of assessments than traditional pen-and-paper tests; it acts as a tool to encourage extensive reading; and it can activate student involvement in assessment. Through the latter, students become more aware of standards and criteria; and their classroom role as participants in peer- and self-assessment is strengthened.

Political perspectives on reform are also highly relevant to the SBA initiative, particularly in view of the highly politicized nature of assessment reform (Pizorn & Nagy, 2009). SBA has experienced some criticism from teachers and teachers' unions in view of the considerable additional workload for teachers in terms of preparation and implementation of SBA tasks; training sessions for SBA; marking, moderation, retention and storage of samples. Whilst some of these challenges relate to perceptions and school decision-making that does not necessarily match with the views of the SBA developers, this does not detract from the reality that SBA does increase the workload of the already heavily burdened English teachers in Hong Kong. These concerns about SBA led to some dilution of the proposals in that the results of two tasks are submitted for grades instead of the original plan of four. This pragmatic and politically driven compromise reduced teachers' burden, but it also decreased the diversity and richness of assessed tasks.

Also significant in relation to assessment are cultural elements which are still being played out. The extent to which SBA can operate fruitfully on a large scale in a CHC setting remains unclear. A number of socio-cultural barriers to its successful implementation arise: a preoccupation with reliability and fairness at the expense of validity (Pong & Chow, 2002); a lack of trust in the ability of teachers to grade their own students fairly, although the HKEAA evidence (e.g. Lee, 2008) indicates that they are able to do so; and the challenges of using assessment formatively in an examination-oriented setting (Carless, 2011).

The implementation of elective modules

We now use semi-structured interview data from an ongoing case study of an 'average' school in the New Territories of Hong Kong to illustrate teacher and student views of the early implementation of the NSS. Some salient issues emerged in relation to the elective modules; as indicated earlier, this is one of the key innovative elements of the NSS. We provide some teacher comments on some of their perceptions of school selection of electives:

> We chose short stories because we have always been teaching reading and in the popular culture elective there is a section on newspapers which is familiar to all of our students.
>
> We didn't ask our students what they wanted to study in the electives. It's easier to teach certain electives based on our experience and knowledge.
>
> Our teachers are not literature experts so we stayed away from things like drama and poems.

From these comments, and others omitted due to lack of space, we infer that the selection of electives is based more on what teachers are comfortable with, and what has gone on before, than on the needs and interests of students as suggested in the government documents. Although the English curriculum is accompanied by detailed 'Suggested Schemes of Work' which outline examples of task-based lessons, specify target knowledge skills, provide helpful resources and suggest time allocation for each elective module, schools and teachers are concerned about teaching unfamiliar subject matter, such as drama and poems. Our interaction with teachers also reveals that while teachers appreciate using creative texts, many feel that they lack confidence in using language arts materials in their own classrooms.

Teachers also commented on teaching, learning and assessment in the elective modules, for example, as follows:

> We don't ask the students to produce any substantial learning tasks for their electives. We just give them more input because it is easier that way. If we have to spend time marking portfolios and projects we would lose time for the core course.
>
> The electives are courses for students to see language in different settings. But the HKDSE does not have a paper on the electives. The exams are mainly the same as the old ones, so we prefer to teach students

the skills for that. The students like language arts but they want exam practice more. Teachers and students are under pressure to get good grades in HKDSE.

The first quote indicates tensions, such as time and workload, and teachers preferring tried and tested methods of providing input rather than more complex learning outcomes and assessments envisaged in the curriculum documents. The second quote reinforces some of the tensions of examination-oriented education in relation to the elective modules.

A further theme in our data related to professional development and support. Some examples of teacher comments are as follows:

The teachers in this school are not confident about those new types of subjects and I don't think the training from the government will help very much.

Language arts is new and colleagues worry that they are not teaching it the right way, they are not trained for language arts

The Education Bureau gives out lots of ideas, handbooks and PowerPoint presentation after PowerPoint presentation but they don't help much. We are not told or shown how to use the ideas. We need trainers who know the real life of the classroom.

We infer from these quotes that there is professional development available, but that it does not appear to be meeting the needs of the teachers. A potentially positive initiative, however, is the use of financially generous English Enhancement Grants to buy in school-based professional development tailored to the needs of schools. An advantage is the flexibility this entails, but a drawback reported by teachers is that it involves them in carrying out new administrative responsibilities in relation to liaising with providers, drafting tenders and compiling reports on how funding has been utilized.

In sum, the small-scale evidence we have compiled indicates that the reforms have generally been welcomed. Our data has reinforced, however, a view that in developing school curricula, a gap tends to arise between the goals of the planned curriculum and what is actually achieved at the school level. Policies like appreciation of literary texts, poems and song lyrics may well show the Government's desire to promote change but when teachers have minimal support for implementation, they are uncertain how to proceed. This reinforces the point made by Morris and Scott (2003) that reform in Hong Kong has often been symbolic rather than real.

Student voices

Linked to the challenge of how to implement the new curriculum is the issue of how students respond to it. Students are an important voice in educational reform and it is valuable to gauge how students are reacting to the NSS. Based on focus group interviews carried out with year 11 students in our case study school, the following extracts provide perceptions of how students are responding to the electives:

> We looked at different social issues like assisted suicide, unemployment, the popularity of reality TV shows and urban development in Hong Kong. These are interesting topics for teenagers like us because they are new. We need to know what is happening around us.
>
> I liked poems last year. I used to be afraid of poems because they have difficult language but my teachers introduced us to some humorous poems. I wrote a free verse poem. It gives me confidence.
>
> I liked short stories most of all. Reading different types of stories improves my vocabulary and I prefer the style of a short story. The twists at the end of the stories are memorable.

The general picture that emerged was that students perceived English under the NSS as being more enjoyable and permitted them a more active role in engaging with stimulating English material.

We also collected a number of comments which cast light on students' perceptions of the kind of learning that was ensuing:

> In the junior form we looked at advertisements ... print and non-print and we had to design our own advertising slogan and poster for a product we designed. The adverts in the class were very creative. I can't imagine how creative they could be.
>
> We can work together in class to talk about the stories. I like talking to my classmates and sharing ideas. We can be more creative that way.
>
> Our teacher tells us that there is no fixed answer when we are giving opinions on a story so we try to think of more ideas. It is fun to hear other points of view.

A common theme running through these comments is that of creativity, one of the generic skills which the reforms are designed to develop. A stated goal of the NSS is to allow for the personal involvement of students through the use of creative texts and the positive student comments point to the elective element of the NSS being seen by students as motivating and rewarding. Importantly, these students' responses seem to present a counter-point to the previously mentioned concern of barriers to these types of open-ended dialogue communication. The students seem to appreciate and value creativity, which indicates a different image to stereotypical views of a CHC learner as relying excessively on memorization and rote-learning.

More complex was the relationship between the electives and student perceptions of their priorities. Two student comments illustrate this aspect:

> I like the electives because they are a break from the normal curriculum.
> They are fun and we can try new things.
>   The electives are not part of the final exam in school so we don't
> study seriously for them.

The first comment, which implies that the electives are a welcome break from the regular curriculum, indicates a lack of understanding that the electives form part of that same curriculum. Our further discussions with students revealed tensions in relation to dichotomies between enjoyable learning and examination-oriented education. Whilst the electives were viewed positively, they were taken less seriously because they did not count as part of the HKDSE. The intention in the syllabus was that the electives are important means of developing student competence in English language (which by implication should help them in all forms of study, including examinations). The narrower interpretation of students and teachers was that if there is no formal assessment of the elective, it does not demand a significant amount of study time. In these students' eyes, if there is no direct assessment of knowledge gained from the elective modules then there is no need to study seriously for them. This kind of interpretation undoubtedly weakens one of the aims of the NSS which was to reduce students' examination pressure through the implementation of a broad-based, process-oriented approach that placed emphasis on aesthetics as well as academic knowledge.

Overall, the tentative evidence from our small-scale data collection appears to suggest that students are responding positively to the NSS in terms of enjoyment. This is a positive verdict because a lack of motivation to engage with English has been a challenge for ELT in Hong Kong for several decades. The issue of assessment represents various tensions and we return to this important aspect of reform in the conclusion.

Conclusion

In this chapter, we have explored the NSS in Hong Kong through the lens of a tri-partite framework on educational reform. From a technological perspective, the reforms are plausible at rhetorical levels and draw on themes which could be seen as international good practice (e.g. promotion of authentic materials, task-based language teaching, and a focus on needs and interests of students). We have also suggested that whilst some aspects of the NSS, such as use of language arts to promote active and enjoyable learning, have been taken up, there has been some evidence of surface implementation rather than the more extended reforms envisaged in the documentation.

Drawing on political dimensions, we have reinforced previous work suggesting that the weak political legitimacy of the Hong Kong government leads to compromises in educational reform, and a surface approach to policy implementation. Striving too hard to implement policy may lead to unwanted conflicts with schools, so is best avoided (Morris & Scott, 2003).

From a cultural perspective, we have been mindful of the dangers of oversimplified or culturally deterministic statements. These caveats, notwithstanding, we have reviewed some of the tensions between well-established teaching practices in CHCs, and those which are more in tune with the international trends referred to above. Cultural issues are also at play with regard to how classrooms might be organized, and how assessment should be conducted. A notable finding which reinforces the complexity of discussions of culture relates to students' positive comments about their appreciation of creativity as an aspect of the NSS. A stereotypical viewpoint of the CHC learner would not necessarily bring creativity to the forefront.

A key implication for the management of change arising from this chapter relates to the role of assessment in promoting change in schools. Whereas exhortations to modify pedagogy or the curriculum can be downplayed or ignored, changes to assessment are invariably heeded by teachers and students because of their high-stakes impact. So whilst our data show that the NSS electives were viewed positively by teachers and students, they were not seen as a major part of the curriculum because there was no high-stakes assessment explicitly attached to them. Conversely, SBA profoundly affects the behaviors and responses of students and teachers because it is a core element of the HKDSE examination grade. Like most innovations, SBA is reinterpreted in line with teachers' own personal assumptions and experiences. In assessment reform, teachers' reinterpretations often lead to partial and incomplete implementation of the ideas of test developers. Following from this, teacher beliefs mediated through societal values are probably even more significant in affecting what goes in classrooms than the washback of high-stakes examinations (Deng & Carless, 2010).

Key readings

Kennedy, K. J., & Lee, J. C. K. (2008). *The Changing Role of Schools in Asian Societies – Schools for the Knowledge Society*. London and New York: Routledge. This work focuses on the nature of modern schooling in Asia and argues for a fundamental restructuring of schools whilst maintaining long-held cultural values.

Morris, P., & Adamson, B. (2010). *Curriculum, Schooling and Society in Hong Kong*. Hong Kong: Hong Kong University Press. This introduction to the Hong Kong school curriculum discusses various socio-cultural factors affecting the implementation of innovations.

Waters, A. (2009). Managing innovation in English language education. *Language Teaching*, 42(4): 421–458. This authoritative and accessible overview suggests that innovation in English language education needs to be better informed by concepts from the management of change.

References

Alexander, R. (2008). *Towards Dialogic Teaching: Rethinking Classroom Talk* (4th edn). Cambridge: Dialogos.

Biggs, J. & Watkins, D. (2001). Insights into teaching the Chinese learner. In D. Watkins & J. Biggs (Eds.), *Teaching the Chinese Learner: Psychological and Pedagogical Perspectives.* Hong Kong: Comparative Education Research Centre and Australian Council for Educational Research (pp. 277–300).

Carless, D. (2004). Issues in teachers' re-interpretation of a task-based innovation in primary schools. *TESOL Quarterly,* 38(4): 639–662.

Carless, D. (2011). *From Testing to Productive Student Learning: Implementing Formative Assessment in Confucian-heritage Settings.* New York: Routledge.

Carless, D. (2013). Innovation in language teaching and learning. In C. A. Chapelle (Ed.), *The Encyclopedia of Applied Linguistics.* Oxford: Wiley-Blackwell.

Curriculum Development Council (2001). *Learning to Learn: The Way Forward in Curriculum Development: Consultation Document Summary.* Hong Kong: Government Printer.

Curriculum Development Council & Hong Kong Examinations and Assessment Authority (2007). *Senior Secondary Curriculum Guide. The Future is Now: From Vision to Realisation (Secondary 4–6).* Hong Kong: Government Printer.

Deng, C. R. & Carless, D. (2010). Examination preparation or effective teaching: Conflicting priorities in the implementation of a pedagogic innovation. *Language Assessment Quarterly,* 7(4): 285–302.

Education Commission (2000). *Learning for Life, Learning through Life: Reform Proposals for the Education System in Hong Kong (September 2000).* Hong Kong: Government Printer.

House, E. (1979). Technology versus craft: A ten year perspective on innovation. *Journal of Curriculum Studies,* 11(1): 1–15.

House, E. (1981). Three perspectives on innovation: Technological, political, and cultural. In R. Lehming & M. Kane (Eds.), *Improving Schools: Using What We Know.* Beverly Hills, CA: Sage Publications (pp.17–41).

House, E. & McQuillan, P. J. (2005). Three perspectives on school reform. In A. Lieberman (Ed.), *The Roots of Educational Change.* Netherlands: Springer (pp.186–201).

Kennedy, K., Chan, J. K. S., Fok, P. K. & Yu, W. M. (2008). Forms of assessment and their potential for enhancing learning: Conceptual and cultural issues. *Educational Research for Policy and Practice,* 7(3): 197–207.

Lee, C. (2008). The beneficial washback of the introduction of a school-based assessment component on the speaking performance of students. Paper presented at the conference of the International Association for Educational Assessment, Cambridge, 11 September, 2008.

Lin, A. M. Y. (1999). Doing-English-Lessons in the reproduction or transformation of social worlds? *TESOL Quarterly,* 33(3): 393–412.

Mercer, N. & Littleton, A. (2007). *Dialogue and the Development of Children's Thinking: A Sociocultural Approach.* New York: Routledge.

Morris, P. (1995). *The Hong Kong School Curriculum: Development, Issues and Policies.* Hong Kong: Hong Kong University Press.

Morris, P. (2002). Promoting curriculum reforms in the context of political transition: An analysis of Hong Kong's experience. *Journal of Education Policy,* 17(1): 13–28.

Morris, P. & Adamson, B. (2010). *Curriculum, Schooling and Society in Hong Kong.* Hong Kong: Hong Kong University Press.

Morris, P. & Lo, M. L. (2000). Shaping the curriculum: Contexts and cultures. *School Leadership and Management,* 20(2): 175–188.

Morris, P. & Scott, I. (2003). Education reform and policy implementation in Hong Kong. *Journal of Education Policy,* 18(1): 71–84.

Phillips, D. (2006). Investigating policy attraction in education. *Oxford Review of Education*, 32(5): 551–559.

Pizorn, K. & Nagy, E. (2009). The politics of examination reform in Central Europe. In C. Alderson (Ed), *The Politics of Language Education: Individuals and Institutions*. Bristol: Multilingual Matters (pp.185–202).

Pong, W. Y. & Chow, J. C. S. (2002). On the pedagogy of examinations in Hong Kong. *Teaching and Teacher Education*, 18(2): 139–149.

Ryan, J. & Louie, K. (2007). False dichotomy? 'Western' and 'Confucian' concepts of scholarship and learning. *Educational Philosophy and Theory*, 39(4): 404–417.

Spillane, J., Reiser, B. & Reimer, T. (2002). Policy implementation and cognition: Reframing and refocusing policy implementation research. *Review of Educational Research*, 72(3): 387–431.

Tsui, A. B. M. (1996). Reticence and anxiety in second language learning. In K. Bailey & D. Nunan (Eds.), *Voices from the Language Classroom: Qualitative Research in Second Language Education*. Cambridge: Cambridge University Press.

Wong, N. Y. & Wong, W. Y. (2002). The 'Confucian heritage culture' learner's phenomenon. *Asian Psychologist*, 3(1): 78–82.

13

HIGHER EDUCATION CONSTRAINTS ON INNOVATION

Denise E. Murray

Introduction

Higher education encompasses a complex array of educational delivery. However, it is a term used variously by different people in different contexts such as differences in use between the U.S. and the U.K. Some use it as a synonym for college; others use it to include both university/college education and vocational education; others use it only for programs that lead to a degree, diploma, or certificate of some sort. The only consistent elements that identify a context as higher education are that it is post-secondary education.

For the purposes of this chapter, I will use it in its narrowest sense, that is, college/university. In other words, I will differentiate it from post-compulsory education that is training for specific vocations (often called vocational education or career technical education) or adult education (sometimes called further education) that is for post-compulsory education at pre-degree level. Likewise, in English language teaching (ELT), a variety of different programs are offered in higher education. One categorization depends on whether it occurs in an Inner, Outer, or Expanding Circle (Kachru, 1986). Although Kachru's model is contested (see, for example Crystal, 1997; Modiano, 2003; Seidlhofer, Breitender, & Pitzl, 2004), especially because of the current blurring across the boundaries, it serves a useful purpose in highlighting the differences in context between learners of English in the three circles.

Thus, any discussion of innovation and change in higher education must, by necessity, focus on only one circle. In this chapter, I will focus on innovations in two Inner Circle countries—the United States and Australia. Even within each circle, a variety of different programs are offered, with their own particular curricula and socio-political imperatives. In Inner Circle countries, programs may include adjunct courses, pre-admission courses (often called intensive English programs, IEP), and stand-alone language courses for already admitted students. Furthermore, they may be for international students or for immigrants/refugees. In this chapter, I will discuss a stand-alone program for already matriculated students, and an adjunct program for international students.

Situating the programs in the world of ELT

Stand-alone programs for already admitted students are more common in the U.S. than in other Inner Circle countries. This is because the U.S. has a long tradition of the teaching of composition to freshmen. Until the 1870s, U.S. colleges taught mostly the classics, mathematics, and morals (religion) and students came from a small segment of the population (Brereton, 1995). Any English or rhetoric was taught, not as courses, but as instruction when students needed it to fulfill assignments. After 1870, came changes in the basic notion of the U.S. college, based on a German model, in response to advances in science and technology, and with a view to having English gain the same status as the classics and mathematics. Harvard was the first college to institutionalize courses in composition.

After 1885, a composition course (called English A) was moved to the freshman year and was required of all students, with additional courses in further years for students who needed it. This requirement spread across the country, although the actual models differed. As the student body was drawn from a much larger cross-section of the population, colleges felt students were not prepared for the academic writing they would need to be successful in college and so additional pre-English A courses were developed, called 'basic writing,' 'developmental writing,' or 'remedial writing.' Both types of classes traditionally have been taught in English departments and usually include students writing a number of themes during the course, in response to a reading or short prompt. Instruction includes models of types of compositions such as compare and contrast, argument, exposition, as well as in grammar. Readings are usually drawn from a handbook, a collection of different readings.

Adjunct courses are usually considered a form of content-based instruction (CBI), which is an approach to curriculum design used in a variety of settings and uses a variety of different delivery mechanisms (Brinton & Master, 1997; Brinton et al., 1989; Chamot, 1995; Crandall, 1995; Kasper, 1999; Mohan, 1986; Mohan et al., 2001; Snow & Brinton, 1997; Williams, 2004). Some adjunct courses may fall more readily under the rubric of English for Academic Purposes (EAP) because they focus only on the grammar and discourse types of the academy (see, for example, Benesch, 2001 for a critique of EAP). However, most adjunct courses involve

the integration of content learning with language teaching aims. More specifically, it refers to the concurrent study of language and subject matters, with the form and sequence of language presentation dictated by content (Brinton et al., 1989: vii).

A CBI curriculum is designed around specific content, and syntax, functions, and vocabulary result from that content. English for specific purposes (ESP), a form of CBI, tends to be used more in EFL settings (Master, 1997) and its research is grounded in linguistic analysis, discourse studies, pragmatics, and discourse communities (Johns, 1992). Adjunct courses in the Inner Circle refer to a model that requires collaboration between a content teacher/professor and an English language instructor. The content teacher is responsible for the content, while the English instructor provides classes that support that content by teaching the language syntax, functions, and vocabulary specific to the content. In some adjunct programs, the language instructor attends the content lectures and builds the language instruction around these lectures; in some programs, the two instructors plan the lessons/lectures together; in some, course assignments are graded by both instructors, while in others, each aspect of the course receives a grade.

The effect of context on innovation and change

This chapter takes the position that innovation is dependent on characteristics of the local context. While many writers use 'innovation' and 'change' synonymously, Stoller (1997: 34) distinguishes between them: 'change is predictable and inevitable, always resulting in an alteration in the status quo but not necessarily in improvements'. Change can, however, lead to innovative responses. Scholars who recognize the complexity and conflicting beliefs and attitudes towards change accept that innovations inevitably are adapted and revised because of local contexts (Carless, 1999; Rogers, 2003). Three local contexts contribute to the introduction and diffusion of innovation—the structure of the organization, its leadership, and people's perceptions of innovation.

Organizational structure and innovation

In her landmark book *The Change Masters*, Kanter (1983) examines innovation and change in corporate America, researching companies where innovation is suffocated and those where innovation flowers. Kanter characterizes two types of organizations: integrative and segmental. The integrative approach, one which fosters innovation, demonstrates

> the willingness to move beyond received wisdom, to combine ideas from unconnected sources, to embrace change as an opportunity to test limits. To see problems integratively is to see them as wholes, related to larger wholes, and thus challenging established practices—rather than

walling off a piece of experience and preventing it from being touched or affected by any new experiences. (p. 27)

The approach to organizational structure that suffocates change she calls 'segmentalism':

> because it is concerned with compartmentalizing actions, events, and problems and keeping each piece isolated from the others. Segmentalist approaches see problems as narrowly as possible, independently of their context, independently of their connections to any other problems. Companies with segmentalist cultures are likely to have segmented structures: a large number of compartments walled off from one another —department from department, level above from level below, field office from headquarters, labor from management, or men from women. (p. 28)

For innovation to take place, organizations need a number of characteristics, ones present in integrative organizations and absent in segmentalized ones. First, employees must be able to identify problems as unique and view their solution as new challenges. Integrative organizations foster this process by 'making the familiar strange' and promoting unrestricted communication among people likely to be able to contribute to the problem solution. Employees feel they belong to a family, one in which respect is mutual and ties and relationships criss-cross the organization. Segmentalized organizations, on the other hand, discourage people from seeing problems – or, if they are seen, it is only from a small, departmental view. Employees are discouraged from seeing other manifestations of the problem and, even more importantly, employees' jobs are strictly defined so that they do not think beyond their immediate tasks. Secondly, innovation requires people to look to the future, not the past. In segmentalized organizations, employees are rewarded *after* they have achieved. In integrative organizations, rewards are future-oriented, they occur at the time a project is approved, not after. Third, innovation occurs if employees are all looking forward towards the same goal. Integrative organizations have long-range plans and create a sense of community, with all the respect for individuals that implies; in segmentalized organizations the system is trusted more than the individuals, and individuals are defined by their category, not by their ability to contribute.

Leadership for innovation

Kanter notes that for innovation to blossom, organizations and innovations must be managed effectively:

> First are 'power skills'—skills in persuading others to invest information, support, and resources in new initiatives driven by an 'entrepreneur.'

Second is the ability to manage the problems associated with the greater use of team and employee participation. And third is an understanding of how change is designed and constructed in an organization—how the microchanges introduced by individual innovators relate to macrochanges or strategic reorientations. (pp. 35–6)

People's perceptions of innovation

For innovations to spread and continue is dependent not only on the organizational structure and its leadership, but also on people's perceptions (Markee, 1993; Rogers, 2003; Stoller, 1997; White, 1993), as opposed to the reality of the innovation. Stoller (2009) identified what she calls a 'zone of innovation,' that is, a range of characteristics perceived to be sufficiently present. When an innovation falls within this zone, adoption is more likely. She identifies the following parameters of this zone:

- compatibility, which refers to the innovation being sufficiently compatible with current practice
- complexity, which refers to the innovation being not completely simple, nor being too complex
- explicitness, which refers to how clear adopters are on exactly what the innovation involves
- flexibility, which refers to the innovation being sufficiently flexible for some variation in implementation to be possible
- originality, which refers to the innovation not being so novel that adopters don't understand it
- visibility, which refers to the extent to which the innovation will increase the visibility of the organization (positively).

The two cases that are described below, demonstrate the importance of organizational structure, leadership, and people's perceptions in the development and adoption of curricula innovation in these two contexts.

The U.S. case: a stand-alone freshman academic English program

Background and context

San José State University (SJSU) is a large, public university situated in Silicon Valley, California. The state and city are magnets for large immigrant populations. The innovation discussed here was in response to meeting the needs of a diverse immigrant/refugee population, first identified in a 1987 study of the language backgrounds and use of SJSU students (Murray et al., 1992). This study found that one-third of the student population was born in a non-English speaking country, with almost half (46.4 percent) having at least one parent born in a non-English speaking country. The majority of these immigrants/refugees (73.6 percent) had lived in the U.S. for more than five years and had received their high school education in the U.S. while 30 percent had received their entire education in the U.S.

As mentioned above, all entering freshmen were required to take freshman composition and those who did not pass the English placement examination were required to take one or two basic writing courses. These were all offered in the English department, which offered a few sections in ESL for students who self-identified as ESL. Other students in the basic writing courses were native English speakers of standard American English, as well as dialect speakers. Our survey research was sponsored by the Associate Vice President for Academic Affairs, who had a keen interest in serving these students. He was supported in this by the Vice President for Academic Affairs, who herself was a professor of English with an equally keen interest in social justice.

In 1990, when a new Dean of the College, with some exposure to ESL learners, arrived, he was surprised at the lack of focus on ESL, given the large number of second language speakers on campus. In addition, upper level administrators had read the research report and were keen to help this large population of students. To address their need, after broad consultation across different stakeholders, the Dean, with upper level support and encouragement, decided to start a new department that would be responsible for all basic writers, whether second language speakers, native speakers, or dialect speakers. In addition, it would house the Masters and Bachelor degrees in linguistics, which had been a sub-program in the English department. In addition, a new Masters degree in TESOL was established as a stand-alone degree, whereas formerly it had been a strand in the linguistics Masters.

The innovation

While the department of Linguistics and Language Development (LLD) itself was an innovation, the innovation of particular interest here is the basic writing courses. It was decided to teach all students who failed the English placement test in the same classes (approximately 50 percent of entering freshmen). The LLD faculty decided to call these courses Academic English, in order to focus on both reading and writing, since students had reading difficulties that impeded the development of their writing. Further, we took the position that what all these students needed to be successful in college was academic English—they all had varying proficiencies in oral language, but limited skills in academic language, a distinction Cummins (first formulated in 1979) has made in his description of BICS (basic interpersonal skills) and CALP (cognitive academic language proficiency). We were the only university in the 23-university state system that chose this path. Others had separate departments for ESL students or they were taught in separate classes. Our contention was, however, that identifying students as ESL was impossible.

At SJSU, ESL students had self-identified, but, in our research, we found that many students did not consider themselves to be ESL, even though they exhibited ESL characteristics. Others had been in ESL classes in high school and did not want to be identified as being 'different' from other students. Further, we were very conscious of the large number of students who had received their entire education in the U.S. or had been born in the U.S., but had received no formal instruction in English and who are therefore often called 'ear' learners (to distinguish them from 'eye' learners who have studied English). These students have since been identified 'as 'Generation 1.5,' in acknowledgement that these students have language backgrounds and educational needs somewhere between those of recently arrived *first generation* immigrants and U.S.-born *second generation* immigrants' (Goen et al., 2002). The term 'Generation 1.5' was first used by Rumbaut and Ima (1988) in their study of Southeast Asian youth in the U.S., and was then used in the TESOL literature. Therefore, we chose to teach all these students together, but ensured that teaching staff were well qualified in understanding language, language varieties, and second language teaching strategies for both reading and writing.

Classes were supported by a Language Development Center, where students had one-on-one tutoring on their writing, small-group tutoring in reading, as well as practice on language skills via the computer. Many of these tutors were graduate students in the MA degrees, many of whom later became instructors in the Academic English program. Those who did not have experience teaching reading and writing to ESL students were required to take a course in tutoring academic English. Academic English has been a very large program, with, for example, 67 sections of 20 students each in fall semester.

The curriculum consisted of extensive and intensive reading, explicit instruction in writing and English syntax, and writing to a variety of prompts, both timed and non-timed, usually around eight per 15-week semester. Students produced many drafts of these assignments, receiving feedback from their peers, teacher, and tutors. Students also kept journals and took a common timed-essay final examination, which required students to respond to a prompt based on a short reading. Following the tradition of freshman composition, which these students would take on successful completion of academic English, the common final was blind-graded on a six-point scale by two faculty and the final score was the sum of the two scores.

While universities traditionally are segmentalist in structure and SJSU is organized along parallel college lines, one of the factors that helped the birthing of the innovation was the administration's bringing together faculty from across the university to participate in its design—from education, English and communication studies. Traditional barriers were broken down in these cross-discipline conversations, leading to the birthing of an innovative department, with innovative approaches to 'remedial' English. Further, leaders came together to support the new venture with a common goal of helping these disadvantaged students. I would contend that the innovation fell within Stoller's zone of innovation on all criteria. Therefore, initially, all three contributors to innovation development and diffusion were present.

Challenges

The department and the Academic English program were started in 1991 and over the 20-year period of their implementation, there have been significant challenges. The most difficult have been increasing budget cuts to the California State University system by state government. This has led to increasing class sizes. Initially, we considered 16 to be an ideal number so students would have many opportunities for writing and feedback on their writing. Over time, largely because of budget cuts, this has gradually increased to 20. Along with these budget cuts has come a changing position at the Chancellor's level, a belief that the state university system should not be providing basic writing. While many at that level and among the general public have labeled these young people as remedial, LLD faculty (and other TESOL professionals) have shown that 'remedial' refers to having to relearn something one has already been taught. But, for these students, academic English (CALP) is a new language. However, over time, because of budget cuts, the Chancellor's level has hardened its position.

Many different proposals have been announced and some implemented. One program has had university faculty work with high school English teachers in an effort to help them understand what students need in the way of academic writing at the college level. Another has been testing students in their sophomore year so that they can be given help in their junior and senior years and so place directly into freshman composition. Another has been summer programs prior to the start of their freshman year. Another has been a move to have all basic writing taken at the community college. These programs have had limited success for a number of reasons, almost all of which have been thwarted by budget cuts across educational sectors in California: the class size in high school, lack of funding to provide the additional help needed, budget cuts to community colleges. The other reasons are to do with the characteristics of these students, who are mostly the first in their family to go to college and who come from families with few financial resources: the level of unpreparedness as high school students which needs addressing at elementary school, their need to work to help support their families, and the cost of summer school courses.

A further challenge has been changes in leadership in the deanship and levels above, people who had no background in language, in disadvantaged students, or interest in them. These changes resulted in pressures to consolidate the department with another one, such as foreign languages, and have the English department responsible once again for 'basic writing.' The department has constantly fought this proposition because it neither saves money, nor provides improved instruction for these at-risk students. The quality of instruction in LLD has always been high and the synergy provided by combining graduate degrees in language with classes in academic English has proven to be an excellent model.

Reflection

Why, then, has the Academic English program come under threat, especially over the past decade? Clearly, from the discussion above, while leadership at SJSU was supportive initially, this was substantively reduced with new leadership and budget cutting taking precedence over quality of instruction for this group of students, especially with leadership with no history of the needs of language minority students.

One of the abiding legacies of this innovation, however, is the importance of faculty teaching and leading in language programs is a) their understanding of the nature of language(s) and language development, b) their ability to be able to convey that understanding to non-specialists, especially management, and c) the importance of hard data from research to support instructional needs.

The Australian case: a content-based adjunct program for international students

Background and context

The innovative program to be discussed here is a content-based adjunct program for international students in accounting and finance at Macquarie University, Australia. In Australia in the 1980s and 1990s, the Federal Government cut operating grants to universities and imposed larger tuition fees for students, with international students having to pay full fees. As a result, Australian universities began to vigorously recruit international students to help meet their shortfalls. By 2003–2004, Australian universities had attracted one in ten of the world's international students, bringing in revenue of Au$5.6 billion, making this the ninth largest export industry in Australia (Jopson & Burke, 2005). In 2010, it brought in Au$18 billion (Harrison, 2011). Initially, focus was on increasing market share and recruitment, with little attention being paid to the educational experiences of these students.

With one in five students being international, many faculty were perplexed about how to adjust to students for whom English was not their primary language. Many positioned international students as deficient in learning styles, as well as English. At the same time, many international students considered they were not receiving value for money in their Australian degree (Jopson & Burke, 2005), especially those who were failing courses, often multiple times.

At Macquarie University, two of the degree programs that attracted large numbers of international students were the postgraduate diploma in accounting and the Master in accounting (PGDA/MAcc). This was largely because many students assumed accounting did not need much English and because the Federal Government had made an immigration policy that granted additional points towards immigration eligibility to students graduating from Australian universities in fields that were in great demand in Australia, and accounting was one of those fields. Traditionally, accounting, like other professional fields, had focused primarily on the acquisition of technical competencies. However, as the field of accounting changed, the focus shifted to the competencies needed for a successful professional career. Consequently, the Accreditation Guidelines for Universities was published by the two Australian professional accounting bodies, CPA Australia and the Institute of Chartered Accountants. They noted that graduates needed competencies in skills such as logical thinking, critical analysis, oral and written communication skills, and interpersonal skills, often referred to as soft skills or generic skills (CPA Australia & Institute of Chartered Accountants in Australia, 2005).

As a result of these requirements, Australian universities undertook a number of generic skills projects, making generic skills explicit to students and even mapping them across program curricula (for example, de la Harpe et al., 2000). However, such efforts do not necessarily lead to student learning outcomes; further, discipline faculty often report not knowing how to teach some of these soft skills. Consequently, Macquarie University chose a different path, rooted in the research literature that contends that development of such generic skills is most effective when it is integrated into program content, and in CBI.

The innovation

In 2002, the Director of the PGDA/MAcc approached the Head of the English Language Program Unit of the National Centre for English Language Teaching and Research (NCELTR) because NCELTR was already preparing many international students for these degree programs in the intensive English pre-entry program for accounting students. Several meetings followed between PGDA/MAcc faculty and NCELTR staff. These meetings were both informational and relational, fostering trust between the two groups that would allow for future collaboration. As these meetings developed, NCELTR appointed a coordinator to develop what was to become the Language for Professional Communication in Accounting project (LPCA). This collaboration required the language specialists to become members of the accounting community of practice. By the end of 2005, the program had grown, largely by word of mouth among accounting faculty, until 23 English language teachers and 36 accounting faculty were involved, teaching 1164 students across 16 different accounting courses.

The program included NCELTR teachers teaching alongside accounting faculty, assisting accounting faculty in re-designing assessment tasks, jointly assessing assignments, with the language specialists grading for language and the discipline faculty for content. The program began with a language audit of students at the beginning of each trimester, as a basis for intervention. Although NCELTR staff are primarily ELT specialists, the LPCA program was for all accounting students in the collaboration because all needed to acquire the soft skills and the discourse of the accounting profession (Evans et al., 2009).

The program was awarded two successive curriculum research and development grants by the university to evaluate the program and make necessary changes based on the evaluation. In addition to the strengths of the research proposals, the program itself had a high profile among administrators who were grappling with the influx of international students and seeking a solution that would enhance both the experience and success of international students. The research used a collaborative action research model. The research involved interviews with those teaching on the program, focus groups with students, a survey of recent graduates, interviews with employers, interviews with representatives of the two accounting professional bodies, analysis of students' work, observation of LPCA workshops, and review of LPCA materials. Students and teaching faculty were all positive about the program, but did offer suggestions for improvement. Through this collaborative action research, various changes were tried in the program, such as new approaches to assessing the portfolio in one course, new approaches to addressing plagiarism, a new compulsory referencing skills workshop, support for students in establishing study groups, and additional voluntary workshops such as presentation skills. Other findings led to a new focus for ongoing staff professional development for accounting faculty, revisions to orientation processes for new students, including involvement of continuing students and intercultural orientation sessions.

The research documentation of the project (Evans et al., 2009) showed that its success was due to the integrated approach to delivering both academic content and professional communication skills and the close interdisciplinary collaboration between NCELTR staff and accounting faculty. Further, the approach to change was critical, being one of 'bottom up,' not 'top down' as well as being an incremental approach. All participants volunteered to do so.

In 2007, a new Vice Chancellor (President) was appointed to Macquarie University. His goal was to increase research output and increase Macquarie's standing in the rankings of research universities. To that end, the colleges were reorganized, new deans appointed, and new research centers established. The college in which accounting resides had a new dean in 2008, with new priorities. Consequently, the LPCA program was discontinued. Key staff from NCELTR and the Director of the PGDA/MAcc moved to other colleges.

Like the situation at SJSU, Macquarie University also has a typical segmental structure. However, because NCELTR had taken it upon itself to work with faculty in discipline areas to develop pre-entry programs, horizontal structures were already in place for the collaboration between accounting and

NCELTR staff. As already indicated, the original innovation, starting with only a couple of collaborations, developed exponentially by word of mouth and the improvement in students' soft skills. Also, like SJSU, there was strong leadership by higher level administrators as well as locally. Further, all of Stoller's characteristics of the zone of innovation were initially present. Although the local contexts were very different, the innovations were successful and diffused because the contexts had the three features essential to innovation—breaking down of vertical silos, the zone of innovation, and leadership. However, despite the similarities of the challenges of changes in leadership common to both, those at Macquarie finally led to the discontinuation of the program. In both cases, the need continued to exist, but at Macquarie, under the new Vice Chancellor, the focus was on research more than on teaching, and the imperative to increase international student enrolment was diminished. These changes in priorities resulted in lack of support for collaborative, softs skills teaching.

Reflection

Although the program was discontinued, the model of innovation used by NCELTR and Accounting showed how a bottom-up, incremental approach can lead to very quick uptake by other colleagues. Further, it demonstrated the value of collaborative action research as a tool for curriculum improvement.

Conclusion

Public institutions of higher education in Inner Circle countries are buffeted by changes in government policy, both ideological and fiscal. Over the past decade, these changes have included immigration, international student visas, reduced public funding, and competition from for-profit higher education colleges. Although the case studies above are from very different institutions, they demonstrate that English language education in public higher education can respond innovatively and creatively to such external pressures. However, for their innovations to be fully implemented and sustained over time requires characteristics beyond the immediate English language faculty. It requires breaking down the organizational and cultural structural barriers endemic to higher education. It requires sustained leadership from higher level administrators.

Key readings

Christison, M. A. & Murray, D. E. (Eds.). (2009). *Leadership in English language education: Theoretical foundations and practical skills for changing times.* New York: Routledge. This edited volume provides a basic understanding of the role of leadership in ELT. It includes chapters that discuss innovation, organizational structure, and the role of emotional intelligence.

Kanter, R. M. (1983). *The change masters: Innovation and entrepreneurship in the American corporation.* New York: Simon and Schuster, Inc. Although over two decades old, this is a seminal book on the role of organizational structure in impeding or facilitating innovation.

References

Benesch, S. (Ed.) (2001). *Critical English for academic purposes.* Mahwah, N.J.: Lawrence Erlbaum Associates.

Brereton, J. C. (Ed.) (1995). *The origins of composition studies in the American college, 1875–1925.* Pittsburg, PA: University of Pittsburg Press.

Brinton, D. M. & Master, P. (Eds.). (1997). *New ways in content-based instruction.* Alexandria, VA: Teachers of English to Speakers of Other Languages.

Brinton, D. M., Snow, M. A. & Wesche, M. B. (1989). *Content-based second language instruction.* New York: Newbury House.

Carless, D. R. (1999). Large-scale curriculum change in Hong Kong. In C. Kennedy, P. Doyle & C. Goh (Eds.), *Exploring change in English language teaching* (pp. 19–28). Oxford: Macmillan Heinemann.

Chamot, A. (1995). Implementing the Cognitive Academic Language Learning Approach: CALLA in Arlington, Virginia. *Bilingual Research Journal, 19*(2): 221–247.

CPA Australia, & Institute of Chartered Accountants in Australia. (2005). *Accreditation guidelines for universities.* Melbourne & Sydney: CPA Australia & ICAA.

Crandall, J. (1995). *ESL through content-area instruction.* McHenry, IL: Delta Systems.

Crystal, D. (1997). *English as a global language.* Cambridge: Cambridge University Press.

Cummins, J. (1979). Linguistic interdependence and the educational development of bilingual children. *Review of Educational Research, 49*(2): 222–251.

de la Harpe, B., Radloff, A. & Wyber, J. (2000). Quality and generic (professional) skills. *Quality in Higher Education, 6*(3): 231–243.

Evans, E., Tindale, J., Cable, D. & Mead, S. (2009). Collaborative teaching in a linguistically and culturally diverse higher education setting: A case study of a postgraduate accounting program. *Higher Education Research & Development Journal, 28*(6): 597–614.

Goen, S., Porter, P., Swanson, D. & Vandommelen, D. (2002). Generation 1.5. *The CATESOL Journal, 14*(1): 103–105.

Harrison, J. (2011, June 6). Report warns of fall in overseas students. *Sydney Morning Herald,* from http://www.smh.com.au/national/education/report-warns-of-fall-in-overseas-students-20110705-1h0t1.html.

Johns, A. (1992). What is the relationship between content-based instruction and English for specific purposes? *The CATESOL Journal, 5*(1): 71–75.

Jopson, D. & Burke, K. (2005, May 7). Campus critical: The privatisation of learning has come at a huge cost. *Sydney Morning Herald,* from http://www.smh.com.au/news/National/Campus-critical/2005/05/06/1115092690378.html.

Kachru, B. B. (1986). *The alchemy of English: The spread, functions and models of non-native Englishes.* Oxford: Pergamon Press.

Kanter, R. M. (1983). *The change masters: Innovation and entrepreneurship in the American corporation.* New York: Simon and Schuster, Inc.

Kasper, L. F. (1999). *Content-based college ESL instruction: An overview.* Mahwah, NJ: Lawrence Erlbaum Associates, Inc.

Markee, N. (1993). The diffusion of innovaiton in language teaching. In W. Grabe (Ed.), *Annual review of applied linguistics 13: Issues in second language teaching and learning* (pp. 229–243). New York: Cambridge University Press.

Master, P. (1997). ESP teacher education in the USA. In R. Howard & G. Brown (Eds.), *Teacher education for LSP* (pp. 22–40). Clevedon, UK: Multilingual Matters.

Modiano, M. (2003). Euro-English: A Swedish perspective. *English Today, 19*(2): 35–41.

Mohan, B. A. (1986). *Language and content.* Reading, Mass: Addison-Wesley Publishing Company.

Mohan, B. A., Leung, C. & Davison, C. (Eds.) (2001). *English as a second language in the mainstream.* Harlow: Longman.

Murray, D. E., Nichols, P. C. & Heisch, A. (1992). Identifying the languages and cultures of our students. In D. E. Murray (Ed.), *Diversity as resource: Redefining cultural literacy* (pp. 63–83). Alexandria, VA: TESOL.

Rogers, E. M. (2003). *Diffusion of innovations* (5th edn). New York: The Free Press.

Rumbaut, R. G. & Ima, K. (1988). *The adaptation of Southeast Asian refugee youth: A comparative study* (Final Report to the U.S. Department of Health and Human Services, Office of Refugee Resettlement, Washington, D.C.: U.S. Department of Health and Human Services). San Diego: San Diego State University. Document Number)

Seidlhofer, B., Breitender, A. & Pitzl, M.-L. (2004). English as a lingua franca in Europe. *Annual Review of Applied Linguistics, 26*: 1–34.

Snow, M. A. & Brinton, D. M. (1997). *The content-based classroom.* White Plains, NY: Longman.

Stoller, F. L. (1997). The catalyst for change and innovation. In M. A. Christison & F. Stoller (Eds.), *A handbook for language program administration* (pp. 33–48). Burlingame, CA: Alta Book Center Publishers.

Stoller, F. L. (2009). Innovation and effective leadership. In M. A. Christison & D. E. Murray (Eds.), *Leadership in English language education: Theoretical foundations and practical skills for changing times* (pp. 73–84). New York: Routledge.

White, R. (1993). Innovation in curriculum planning and program development. In W. Grabe (Ed.), *Annual review of applied linguistics 13: Issues in second language teaching and learning* (pp. 244–259). New York: Cambridge University Press.

Williams, A. (2004). *Fact sheet – Enhancing language teaching with content.* Sydney: AMEP Research Centre.

SECTION 4

Innovation and change in teaching practice

14

INNOVATION IN MATERIALS DEVELOPMENT

Brian Tomlinson

Introduction

What is an innovation?

An innovation is something new which aims to be an improvement on what already exists. It also aims to be efficient, effective, popular and enduring. It is difficult to innovate successfully in materials development because innovations threaten the powerful status quo, they are not properly understood, they seem too demanding or they are not effectively promoted. Many teachers resist materials that do not have the face validity afforded by resemblance to the norm. This is what happened to an innovative coursebook in Japan, which looked like a 'manga' comic book, and to an innovative non-linear coursebook in the UK, which did not use the conventional Presentation, Practice, Production (PPP) approach and which looked very different from other coursebooks (Shepherd et al. 1992).

Innovators need to be prepared for resistance, to persevere and to develop strategies for turning initial failure into enduring success. I remember when leading the Permantapan Kerja Guru (PKG) English Programme in Indonesia (Tomlinson 1990), that our exclusive use of Total Physical Response (TPR) Plus materials (Tomlinson 1994a) with twelve-year-old beginners in experimental classes in Indonesian secondary schools was very popular with the teachers and students but unpopular with Heads of Department, whose credibility and authority were threatened. Eventually, though, their opposition was overcome when the teachers of the experimental classes asked their Heads of Department to observe them and to give them advice. The Heads were flattered by this ploy and impressed by how enthusiastic the students were and how much they could understand after such a short time. Soon, some of them were making use of the approach themselves.

What is the current situation in materials development?

Despite recent developments in second language acquisition research and the many changes in L2 pedagogic theory in the last thirty years, coursebooks for teaching English as an L2 have remained little changed. They have more or less stuck with a commercially successful script of PPP activities focusing on discrete teaching points (Tomlinson et al. 2001; Masuhara et al. 2008). They have also retained a focus on forms and still use such theoretically unsupported practice exercises as dialogue recitation, listening and repeating, filling in the blanks, matching, sentence transformation, true/false and multiple choice.

Tomlinson (1999) analysed ten lower level coursebooks and found that such exercise types were dominant in all but one of the books and that these nine books were forms-focused. I have just analysed Unit 1 of *Global Pre-Intermediate* (Clandfield 2010) and Unit 6 of *Just Right Intermediate* (Harmer 2012). I found that the units are forms-focused and that the exercise types above are made use of in these units (though I must say in more creative ways than was typical of coursebooks thirty years ago). This focus on forms and the predominance of stereotypical practice exercises is also true of currently used coursebooks at higher levels (e.g. Redston & Cunningham 2007; Puchta et al. 2008). To be fair to commercial publishers, it needs to be said that you cannot expect them to risk innovations that threaten the face validity of their global coursebooks and put million-pound investments at risk. It has been inevitable, therefore, that most of the major innovations in materials have been pioneered in institutional and Ministry materials development projects around the world (although it should be said that each of the coursebooks referred to above does contain some small innovations, such as short sections on 'Language in chunks' in *Just Right Intermediate* (Harmer 2012)).

What does this chapter focus on?

The sections below focus on specific aspects of language learning materials and each one describes the norm and reports recent innovations. These sections focus on topic content, teaching/learning points, pedagogical approaches, design procedures and medium of delivery. They are followed by two case studies of innovations and by a conclusion in which I present my views on the current situation and my hopes for the future.

Topic content

The norm

Over the years, the typical topic content of ELT materials has moved from topics from literature in the grammar translation approach (e.g. friendship), to topics from the immediate environment of the learners in audio-visual and direct method approaches (e.g. the classroom), to topics relating to contexts in which the learners might need to use the language in situational approaches (e.g. the post office), to ways of doing things in functional approaches (e.g. ordering a meal), to macro-concepts in notional approaches (e.g. time) and to topics related to the learners' lives in the weak communicative approaches followed by most current coursebooks (e.g. hobbies). Typical topics in current coursebooks include: eating and drinking, health and fitness, work and leisure, hopes and fears, and science and technology in *Global Pre-Intermediate* (Clandfield 2010); interests, going shopping, eating, houses and travel in *Intermediate Outcomes* (Dellar & Walkley 2010); and crime, nature, the internet, male and female, and making a living in *face2face Upper Intermediate* (Redston & Cunningham 2007).

What all the commercially published materials in the last forty years have had in common has been an avoidance of any topics such as religion, politics, drugs, sex and alcohol that might cause offence to individuals or societies. This avoidance of the controversial has been criticised for resulting in a safe, bland neutrality which not only fails to achieve the affective engagement required for deep processing and acquisition but which also propagates an EFL world which is happy, healthy, harmonious and affluent. Tomlinson (2001: 68), for example, criticises the lack of preparation for using English in the real world and says that 'it is arguable that provocative texts which stimulate an affective response are more likely to facilitate learning than neutral texts which do not.' This is still my position and I have run many courses recently which have helped materials developers to make use of provocative topics which would be acceptable in their cultures and would have the potential for stimulating affective engagement (e.g. the relationship between mothers and teenage sons in Iran). A different critical position is taken by Gray (2010), who is critical of global coursebooks as commodities selling an image of the world as Western, consumerist, materialistic and aspirational.

Innovations

There are some topic innovations in current commercially published coursebooks. In addition to the fairly mundane (and sometimes trivial) topics of the eighties and nineties, you can now find more 'intelligent' topics such as art and music and individual and society in *Global Pre-Intermediate*, body talk and the blogosphere in *Just Right Intermediate* and breaking codes and cultural differences in *face2face Upper Intermediate*. This is especially true of advanced level coursebooks. *English in Mind Advanced* (Puchta et al. 2008) for example, includes such topics as logic and intuition, fiction and reality and youth and old age. Many coursebooks (e.g. *Global Pre-Intermediate* and *face2face Upper Intermediate*) also include texts about English as a global language and about such other global issues as the social effects of modern technology and ecological footprints. And, remarkably, *English Unlimited*

(Rea & Clementson 2011) deals with such 'risky' topics as dispute resolution, dealing with conflict, problems in the home, complaints, truth and lies and talking about mistakes, and includes photos of people looking angry, sad, frightened and disturbed in addition to the usual smiling faces.

A major innovation in project materials has been the use in content and language integrated language (CLIL) materials of topic content from other subjects on the curriculum (e.g. physics, biology, history) or from areas of learner interest such as fashion, film or football. The British Council Premier Skills web materials are an example of CLIL materials in that their topic content is related to football clubs in the English Premier League (http://premierskills.britishcouncil.org/).The theory informing CLIL is that whilst focussing on affectively and cognitively engaging content the learners acquire language and language skills either from recycled exposure to language in use in the strong approach, or from paying attention to form in the weak version. See Snow (2005) for reports on innovative experiments and projects using CLIL materials and Coyle et al. (2010) for information and advice on developing CLIL materials.

There have been some successful attempts to base materials on controversial topics. For example, the Namibian secondary school coursebook *On Target* (1995) was written as a text-driven coursebook by thirty teachers during a six-day workshop in Windhoek (Tomlinson 1995). The texts were chosen to coincide with some of the provocative topics which featured on a nationwide survey of student preferences and permission was then sought from a senior representative of the Ministry of Education to include them in the coursebook. Consequently, texts and tasks were used which related to commercial exploitation, alcoholism, drugs, corporal punishment, unemployment and violence (all topics considered taboo by commercial publishers of coursebooks in the UK and USA). A similar innovation in topic content is reported by Banegas (2011: 80), who describes a two-part syllabus in use at a secondary school in Argentina:

> Syllabus 1 follows a mainstream coursebook while Syllabus 2 is a negotiated syllabus driven by such teacher suggested topics as gay marriage and child abuse and such student suggested topics as divorce and single parenting. To resource this deliberately provocative syllabus the teachers have produced a sourcebook of authentic reading and listening texts to develop activities from.

Teaching/learning points

The norm

The norm for the past forty years in both commercial and institutional materials has been to focus on teaching discrete features of the language or of its use. A teaching point is selected from a predetermined syllabus and then focused on. This teaching point could be a grammar point (e.g. the present perfect), a function (e.g. offering an invitation), a pronunciation point (e.g. the vowel sound in 'cat'), a receptive skill (e.g. skimming a reading text) or a productive skill (e.g. using direct speech). It could also be a semantic family of related lexical items (e.g. popular foods) or a set of lexical chunks (e.g. to make somebody angry/happy/sad). Whatever the selected feature is, it is typically taught to the learners intensively in one unit and then maybe never taught to them again. Mukundan (2010) analysed coursebooks in use in Malaysian schools and demonstrated how dominant the teaching of discrete points is and how rarely these points are recycled.

I have just analysed three current coursebooks and I found, for example, that:

- In *Global Pre-Intermediate* (Clandfield 2010) Unit 4 'will/won't' and 'will/won't be able to' are introduced and practised with the functions of prediction and future ability/possibility. However there is no exposure to, practice in or use of these structures anywhere else in the book.
- In *face2face Upper Intermediate* (Redston & Cunningham 2007) comparatives are presented and practised in Unit 5 but are not encountered, practised or used by the learners anywhere else in the book.
- In *English in Mind Student's Book 5* (Puchta et al. 2008) modal passives are presented and practised in Unit 7 but do not feature anywhere else in the book.

Innovations

Very few published ELT materials are not driven by predetermined teaching points. Exceptions include language through literature materials, text-driven materials, content-based materials and task-based materials. *Openings* (Tomlinson 1994b) is an 'activities book' which presents the learners in Part 1 with extracts from modern literature and presents the teacher in Part 2 with creative activities to select from when using the texts in the classroom. *On Target* (1995), Search 8 (Fenner & Nordal Pedersen 1997) and *English for Life* (Tomlinson et al. 2000) make use of potentially engaging texts to drive follow-up activities, which include making discoveries about language features made use of in the texts. None of the above textbooks follows the typical procedure of being driven by predetermined discrete teaching points. Instead, they are driven by reading and listening texts selected for their potential to engage the learners. This is also the guiding principle of content-based materials (Coyle et al. 2010) and of materials designed to help learners to develop intercultural competence (Troncoso 2010).

A similar experiential approach is followed by task-based materials, which get learners to perform communication tasks with specified non-linguistic outcomes rather than to learn discrete language or skills points. In the weak form of the approach, though, the teacher might have a language learning objective that is different from the learners' task completion target. For example, groups of learners might be competing to be the first group to replicate a drawing from instructions from the only member of the group with access to the original. Their target is to replicate the drawing before any other group does but the teacher's target might be to help the learners to develop their ability to ask clarification questions. For information about task-based materials, see Ellis (2011); for examples of innovative task-based materials in action, see Van den Branden (2006).

For other recent examples of materials designed to give learners an experience of language in use rather than to teach them discrete language points or skills, see Byram & Masuhara (2013) on materials for developing intercultural competence, Fenton-Smith (2010) on materials offering creative follow-up activities on an extensive reading course, Hewings (2010) on materials for improving essay writing skills, McCullagh (2010) on experiential materials for medical practitioners, Mishan (2010) for problem solving materials and Park (2010) on materials for process drama approaches.

Pedagogical approaches

The norm

As indicated above, the pedagogic norm has been and still is Presentation, Practice, Production (PPP). This is an approach that is very convenient for administrators and teachers because it enables a discrete teaching point to be taught, to be practised and to be produced within one unit. It is focused and systematic and provides and facilitates short-term learning. Unfortunately, it is unprincipled in that it does not meet any of the pre-requisites for long-term language acquisition (Tomlinson 2010, 2011, 2013b). It does not provide the learner with sufficient exposure to the language feature in use, it does not create a psychological need for acquisition, it does not take into account the delayed effect of instruction, it does not provide the learner with the frequent and varied encounters over time required for acquisition, and it does not provide the learner with sufficient opportunities to use the feature for communication.

Innovations

In institutions around the world, there is a growing discontent with PPP-based global coursebooks and there have been many recent attempts to supplement or replace them. For example, in the University of Hue, Vietnam, in Kanda University, Japan, in Leeds Metropolitan University and in the University of Leuven, Belgium, there are teachers who begin every lesson with a performance of a potentially engaging poem, story, anecdote, dramatic scene, song or item from the news (Tomlinson 2003a). The students are not questioned on the text but take a copy of the text at the end of the lesson if they are interested in it. They keep a file of those texts that have engaged them. They frequently revisit the texts and sometimes ask their teacher questions about them. This massively increases the students' exposure to the language in meaningful use and has proved very popular with students.

Kanda University, Japan, are supplementing their global coursebooks with text-driven institutional materials (see, for example, Fenton-Smith 2010). Sultan Qaboos University, Oman, have replaced coursebooks on their academic writing courses with institutional materials which follow a text-driven approach (Tomlinson 2003b). The University of Hue are replacing their global coursebooks with institutional materials which follow a localised and personalised text-driven approach. The University of Limerick is developing problem solving task-based materials (Mishan 2010). The International Islamic University of Malaysia is replacing coursebooks with task-based institutional materials. And many institutions at primary, secondary and tertiary level in Belgium have been inspired by research at the University of Leuven (Van den Branden 2007) to base their courses on in-house materials following a task-based approach.

Design procedures

The norm

The norm used to be that teachers developed materials for their classes, found they were popular and then submitted them to a publisher with a view to publication. That was certainly how I wrote my first published coursebook (Ellis & Tomlinson 1973). Most coursebooks and institutional materials nowadays, though, are commissioned by publishers who have already decided what they want. They are written by individuals or by a small team of two or three writers. These writers are recruited because they are considered to be 'expert' professional materials developers, they follow a predetermined curriculum and they write the materials progressively from Unit 1 onwards. This process has been recorded by Hidalgo et al. (1995), who asked a number of writers in South-East Asia to write chapters on how they go about the process of materials writing and by Prowse (2011), who asked a number of well-known textbook writers in 1994 and in 2009 how they go about writing their textbooks. None of the writers in Prowse (2011) mention following a principled framework (though a few of the writers in Hidalgo et al. do) and most of them reinforce the findings of Johnson (2003) that expert writers tend to write from repertoire (i.e. make use of what seems to have 'worked' for them before).

Innovations

One innovation being pursued by a number of institutions and countries developing their own materials has been the use of large teams of teachers.

For example, in Namibia, thirty teachers from all over the country came together in Windhoek to write the secondary school coursebook *On Target* in six days (Tomlinson 1995). In Romania (Popovici & Bolitho 2003) and in Russia (Bolitho 2008), large teams of teachers wrote series of coursebooks over a number of years. This is an approach currently being followed by the University of Hue, where a large group of teachers is writing materials to replace 'irrelevant' global coursebooks on their pre-sessional English courses. The advantages of materials development by large teams of local teachers are considerable. Such teams are able to localise the materials, to pool resources, to stimulate each other, to deliver materials quickly and to sustain the creative energy needed to develop engaging materials.

Another recent innovation has been the establishment of principled criteria prior to the commencement of the writing process for use both as criteria for the development of the materials and criteria for the on-going and post-use evaluation of the materials (Tomlinson 2003a). Such criteria were developed for the materials produced by Leeds Metropolitan University and The College of St Mark and St John for the Ethiopian Teacher Language Improvement Project (a blended learning project aiming to help primary and secondary teachers to improve their English) and are being developed by the University of Hue Project mentioned above. A further recent innovation has been the development of principled frameworks to drive the development of materials (Tomlinson 2003b). Some such frameworks are reported in Hidalgo et al. (1995), the Namibian textbook *On Target* used a text-driven framework so as to engage sixteen-year-old students and the International Islamic University of Malaysia is using a task-driven framework to develop materials for undergraduate pre-sessional students in both English and Arabic.

Medium of delivery

The norm

Until recently, the norm for most courses was that they were delivered through a level specific coursebook which included everything the learners needed in one book. There was usually a teacher's book to advise the teachers on how to best make use of the coursebook and sometimes there was a student workbook to provide additional practice for the learners. In addition, supplementary materials were available in the form of specific or integrated skills books and level specific graded readers were available for students to read in their own time.

Innovations

In the last twenty years, commercial courses have expanded into multi-component courses. For example, the *Global Pre-Intermediate* course (Clandfield

2010) includes a coursebook, an e-workbook, audio VCDs, a teacher's book and teacher's resource CD and a website. It is also available in 'a fully interactive digital version with embedded multimedia assets'. All the extras are potentially very useful as they can enrich the learning experience but they are not always popular with teachers as they can add considerably to the cost and the complexity of a course. In addition to such blended learning materials, many materials are now being delivered exclusively on the web, through mobile phones and through interactive white boards. For example, English 360 is a web-based teacher community which allows teachers to draw on a range of Cambridge University Press materials in order to create their own resources (http://www.english360.com/) and Speechinaction publish innovative online pronunciation courses (http://www.speechinaction.com/). Learners are also being encouraged to interact through the use, for example, of Facebook, blogs, twitter and Skype.

For details of innovative electronic delivery of materials, see Kervin & Derewianka (2011) and Motteram (2011).

Case studies of innovations

Action research projects

There have been numerous action research projects in recent years investigating the effects of innovation in materials development. For example, in 2010, Brian Tomlinson and Hitomi Masuhara conducted vocabulary learning experiments for the English Profile project (englishprofile.org) at the Universiti Putra Malaysia (UMP), at ELS Language School, Kualu Lumpur, at the University of Portsmouth and at IES Hermanos Machado (an upper secondary school in Seville). They selected fifteen lexical items from the English Profile B1 Wordlist and then they devised a two-task test to assess the students' knowledge of the fifteen items both before and after treatment.

They then devised two different treatments to help students to learn the fifteen items. One treatment featured the extensive reading of three stories and the other featured text-based vocabulary teaching for three lessons. The stories were innovative in that they were written primarily to engage the students but each topic was selected because it lent itself to authentic use of some of the selected items, whose learning was facilitated by the meaningful and varied recycling advocated by, for example, Nation (2005). The stories were first written 'naturally' but were then revised in order to look for opportunities to insert more of the selected items without disturbing the 'authenticity' of the stories (with each item being used at least six times over the three stories). The stories were written so as to stimulate affective and cognitive engagement (Tomlinson 2003c) and mental pre- and post-reading activities were added to encourage the use of visual imaging and inner speech (Tomlinson and Avila 2007). The materials were designed to lead the students to a holistic, extensive experience of stories rather than to a discrete, intensive reading of texts.

The extensive reading treatment group increased their scores considerably in all four institutions and much more than the no-treatment control groups. At three of the institutions, the text-based teaching group increased their scores most, but at UMP, the extensive reading group improved their scores much more than the text-based teaching group, even though the latter had received ninety minutes of treatment as opposed to the forty five minutes of the extensive reading group. As a result, Tomlinson and Masuhara recommended an innovative series of vocabulary textbooks which would make use of both types of treatment. For details of the research outlined above, see Tomlinson & Masuhara (2011).

Other innovative research projects have already been mentioned above and details of some of them and other innovative materials development research projects can be found in Tomlinson and Masuhara (2010).

Innovative materials development projects

There are numerous innovative materials development projects in action around the world designed to improve the materials available to learners. These projects are innovative in that the materials are being developed locally by practising teachers and lecturers and they are using pedagogic approaches that are new to the teachers and students in the participating institutions. Unfortunately, not all of these projects are being written up and not all are being evaluated for their effectiveness.

One project which is still ongoing and is being written up and evaluated is the Explore Writing project at Sultan Qaboos University in Oman. In 2007, the Language Centre of Sultan Qaboos University decided that their coursebook-based academic writing course on their Intensive English Language Programme was not helping their pre-sessional students to communicate in writing to the standard that would be required once they began to study their academic specialisations in English. They therefore decided to replace the existing materials with in-house materials. They brought in Brian Tomlinson and Hitomi Masuhara to train a team of six writer/teachers and to orientate the senior administrators who became responsible for editing the coursebooks. It was decided to focus on the lowest level students and to develop writing and language use textbooks for levels 2, 3 and 4 of the six level academic writing course. It was also decided to make use of authentic texts in order to engage the learners in the topic they are going to write about, to stimulate the writing tasks and to serve as models for the students to make discoveries from about genre conventions, discourse features and language use (Tomlinson 2003b). Once the team started to write they developed a flexible framework which progressed as follows:

i) A readiness activity to activate the students' minds in relation to the topic of the unit
ii) A meaning-focused reading activity

iii) A personal response activity
iv) A writing task responding to the text
v) A discovery activity focusing on a salient feature of the reading text (Tomlinson 2007)
vi) Student revision of the writing task taking advantage of the discoveries made
vii) Peer editing of the students' texts
viii) Teacher feedback on students' texts
ix) Final revision of student texts
x) Completion of a student reflective 'log'.

Each unit of the book was drafted by members of the writing team and then feedback was provided by the other members of the team, by the external advisors and by the editorial committee. It was then revised, trialled and revised again. The finalised materials were then published in book form for the three levels and used for up to two semesters before being evaluated. The criteria for evaluation had been developed by the writers, advisors and editors before the writing began (Tomlinson 2003a) and they were used for the development, the feedback, the trialling and the final evaluation of the materials. The criteria were principled in relation to the team's shared beliefs about language acquisition and development (Tomlinson 2003a) and to the objectives of the courses, which had been articulated after a needs analysis had been conducted. The criteria were constantly revised to ensure that they were valid and reliable and their use in the evaluation of the published materials revealed, for example, that:

- the teachers and the students considered the materials to be engaging
- the teachers and the students considered the process approach to writing instruction to be effective
- the teachers considered the discovery approach to be very effective
- the students were not sure about the value of the discovery approach.

Comparison of the average and high level students' writing before and after treatment revealed considerable improvement in the students' ability to communicate clearly, coherently and effectively in a variety of genres, as well as a considerable increase in language awareness. However, the performance of the low level learners did not improve very much and the team are considering giving extra support and possibly a different treatment to this minority group of students.

This materials development project is innovative in that:

- it is needs driven
- it has been developed by a large local team
- it makes use of text-based, task-based and discovery approaches new to the region

- it has been developed in order to satisfy predetermined, principled and rigorous criteria
- it has been evaluated whilst being developed, after being trialled and after being used
- it is now being revised yet again in order to maximise its value to the students.

For details of the Explore Writing project, see Al-Busaidi & Tindle (2010).

Conclusion

In summary, commercially published coursebooks seem to continue to be conventionally similar in that they use a PPP approach to teach pre-determined language and skills points. They are innovative, though, in their use of blended deliveries which combine paper-based components with electronic components and which offer rich opportunities for independent follow-up to the work done with a teacher in the classroom (Tomlinson & Whittaker 2013). In contrast, institutional and Ministry of Education projects are often conventional in that they rely on paper-based delivery but tend to be innovative in that they reject PPP pedagogy in favour of more principled text-driven, task-based or process-based approaches. My hope is that in the near future commercial publishers will be able to move towards more theoretically principled approaches and that institutions and Ministries of Education will be able to make use of those electronic devices which can cheaply and reliably facilitate increased exposure, engagement, noticing and use. Both developments could be informed by the chapters in Tomlinson (2013a), a book exploring the potential for positive interaction between applied linguistics and materials development.

Key readings

Harwood, N. (ed.). (2010). *Materials in ELT: theory and practice*. Cambridge: Cambridge University Press. A book which contains a number of chapters reporting the results of innovative materials development projects in EAP.

Tomlinson, B. (ed.). (2011). *Materials development in language teaching*. Cambridge: Cambridge University Press. A book of chapters proposing and reporting innovations in materials development.

Tomlinson, B. & Masuhara, H. (eds.). (2010). *Research for Materials Development in Language Learning*. London: Continuum. A book of reports of recent research projects which have trialled innovative materials.

References

Al-Busaidi, S. & Tindle, K. (2010). Evaluating the effect of in-house materials on language learning. In B. Tomlinson & H. Masuhara (eds.) *Research for materials development in language learning: evidence for best practice*. London: Continuum, pp. 137–149.

Banegas, D. L. (2011). Teaching more than English in secondary education. *ELT Journal* (65/1): 80–82.

Bolitho, R. (2008). Materials used in Central and Eastern Europe and the former Soviet Union. In B. Tomlinson & H. Masuhara (eds.) *Research for materials development in language learning: evidence for best practice*. London: Continuum, pp. 213–222.

Byram, M. & Masuhara, H. (2013). Intercultural competence. In B. Tomlinson & H. Masuhara (eds.) *Applied linguistics and materials development*. London: Continuum.

Clandfield, L. (2010). *Global pre-intermediate*. Oxford: Macmillan.

Coyle, D., Hood, P. & Marsh, D. (2010). *CLIL: content and language integrated learning*. Cambridge: Cambridge University Press.

Dellar, H. & Walkley, A. (2010). *Intermediate outcomes*. Andover: Heinle.

Ellis, R. (2011). Macro- and micro-evaluations of task-based teaching. In B. Tomlinson (ed.) *Materials development in language teaching*. 2nd edition. Cambridge: Cambridge University Press, pp. 221–235.

Ellis, R. & Tomlinson, B. (1973). *English through situations*. Lusaka: Longman Zambia.

Fenner, A. N. & Nordal-Pedersen, G. (1997). *Search 8*. Oslo: Gyldendal.

Fenton-Smith, B. (2010). A debate on the desired effects of output activities for extensive reading. In B. Tomlinson & H. Masuhara (eds.) *Research for materials development in language learning: evidence for best practice*. London: Continuum, pp. 50–61.

Gray, J. (2010). *The construction of English: culture, consumerism and promotion in the ELT global coursebook*. Basingstoke: Palgrave Macmillan.

Harmer, J. (2012). *Just right intermediate*. 2nd edn. Andover: Heinle.

Hewings, M. (2010). Materials for university essay writing. In N. Harwood (ed.) *English language teaching materials: theory and practice*. Cambridge: Cambridge University Press, pp. 251–278.

Hidalgo, A. H., Hall, D. & Jacobs G. M. (eds.) (1995). *Getting started: materials writers on materials writing*. Singapore: RELC.

Johnson, K. (2003). *Designing language teaching tasks*. Basingstoke: Palgrave Macmillan.

Kervin, L. & Derewianka, B. (2011). New technologies to support language learning. In B. Tomlinson (ed.) *Materials development in language teaching*. 2nd edition. Cambridge: Cambridge University Press, pp. 328–351.

Masuhara, H., Haan, M., Yi, Y. & Tomlinson, B. (2008). Adult EFL courses. *ELT Journal* (62/3): 294–312.

McCullagh, M. (2010). An initial evaluation of the effectiveness of a set of published materials for medical English. In B. Tomlinson & H. Masuhara (eds.) *Research for materials development in language learning: evidence for best practice*. London: Continuum, pp. 381–393.

Mishan, F. (2010). Withstanding washback: thinking outside the box in materials development. In B. Tomlinson & H. Masuhara (eds.) *Research for materials development in language learning: evidence for best practice*. London: Continuum, pp. 353–368.

Motteram, G. (2011). Developing language learning materials with technology. In B. Tomlinson (ed.) *Materials development in language teaching*. 2nd edition. Cambridge: Cambridge University Press, pp. 303–327.

Mukundan, J. (2010). Words as they appear in Malaysian secondary school English language textbooks: some implications for pedagogy. In B. Tomlinson & H. Masuhara (eds.) *Research for materials development in language learning: evidence for best practice*. London: Continuum, pp. 291–304.

Nation, P. (2005). Teaching and learning vocabulary. In E. Hinkel (ed.) *Handbook of research in second language teaching and learning*. Mahwah, NJ: Erlbaum, pp. 581–96.

On Target (1995). Windhoek: Gamsberg Macmillan.

Park, H. (2010). Process drama in the Korean EFL secondary classroom: a case study of Korean middle school classrooms. In B. Tomlinson & Masuhara, H. (eds.) *Research for materials development in language learning: evidence for best practice.* London: Continuum, pp. 155–171.

Popovici, R. & Bolitho, R. (2003). Personal and professional development through writing: the Romanian Textbook Project. In B. Tomlinson (ed.) *Developing materials for language teaching.* London: Continuum, pp. 505–517.

Puchta, H., Stranks, J. & Lewis-Jones, P. (2008). *English in mind 5.* Cambridge: Cambridge University Press.

Prowse, P. (2011). How writers write: testimony from authors. In B. Tomlinson (ed.) *Materials development in language teaching.* 2nd edition. Cambridge: Cambridge University Press, pp.151–173.

Rea, D. & Clementson, C. (2011). *English unlimited intermediate.* Cambridge: Cambridge University Press.

Redston, C. & Cunningham, G. (2007). *face2face upper intermediate.* Cambridge: Cambridge University Press.

Shepherd, J., Hopkins, A & Potter, J. (1992). *Sourcebook intermediate: an alternative English course.* Harlow: Longman.

Snow, M. A. (2005). A model of academic literacy for integrated language and content instruction. In E. Hinkel (ed.) *Handbook of research in second language teaching and learning.* Mahwah, New Jersey: Erlbaum, pp. 693–712.

Tomlinson, B. (1990). Managing change in Indonesian high schools. *ELT Journal* (44/1): 25–37.

Tomlinson, B. (1994a). Materials for TPR. *Folio* (1/2): 8–10.

Tomlinson, B. (1994b). *Openings: language through literature.* London: Penguin.

Tomlinson, B. (1995). Work in progress: textbook projects. *Folio* 2 (2): 26–31.

Tomlinson, B. (1999). Developing criteria for materials evaluation. *IATEFL Issues* (147): 10–13.

Tomlinson, B. (2001). Materials development. In R. Carter and D. Nunan (eds.) *The Cambridge guide to TESOL.* Cambridge: Cambridge University Press, pp. 66–71.

Tomlinson, B. (2003a). Materials evaluation. In B. Tomlinson (ed.) *Developing materials for language teaching.* London: Continuum, pp. 15–36.

Tomlinson, B. (2003b). Developing principled frameworks for materials development. In B. Tomlinson (ed.) *Developing materials for language teaching.* London: Continuum, pp. 107–129.

Tomlinson, B. (2003c). Humanizing the coursebook. In B. Tomlinson (ed.) *Developing materials for language teaching.* London: Continuum, pp. 162–173.

Tomlinson, B. (2007). Teachers' responses to form-focused discovery approaches. In S. Fotos & H. Nassaji (eds.) *Form focused instruction and teacher education: studies in honour of Rod Ellis.* Oxford: Oxford University Press, pp.179–194.

Tomlinson, B. (2010). Principles and procedures of materials development. In N. Harwood (ed.) *Materials in ELT: theory and practice.* Cambridge: Cambridge University Press, pp. 81–108.

Tomlinson, B. (2011). Principled procedures in materials development. In B. Tomlinson (ed.). *Materials development in language teaching.* 2nd edition. Cambridge: Cambridge University Press, pp. 1–31.

Tomlinson, B. (ed.) (2013a). *Applied linguistics and materials development.* London: Continuum.

Tomlinson, B. (2013b) Second language acquisition. In B. Tomlinson & H. Masuhara (eds.) *Applied linguistics and materials development.* London: Continuum.

Tomlinson, B. & Avila, J. (2007). Seeing and saying for yourself: the roles of audio-visual mental aids in language learning and use. In B. Tomlinson (ed.) *Language acquisition and development: studies of learners of first and other languages.* London: Continuum, pp. 61–81.

Tomlinson, B. & Masuhara, H. (eds.) (2010). *Research for materials development in language learning: evidence for best practice*. London: Continuum.

Tomlinson, B. & Masuhara, H. (2011). *The English profile vocabulary project*. Unpublished report for Cambridge University Press.

Tomlinson, B. & Whittaker, C (eds.) (2013). *Blended learning in ELT: course design and implementation*. London: British Council.

Tomlinson, B., Hill, D. A. & Masuhara, H. (2000). *English for life 1*. Singapore: Marshall Cavendish.

Tomlinson, B., Dat, B., Masuhara, H. & Rubdy, R. (2001). ELT courses for adults. *ELT Journal* (55/1): 80–101.

Troncoso, C. R. (2010). The effects of language materials on the development of intercultural competence. In B. Tomlinson & Masuhara, H. (eds.) *Research for materials development in language learning: evidence for best practice*. London: Continuum, pp. 83–102.

Van den Branden, K. (2006). *Task-based language education: from theory to practice*. Cambridge: Cambridge University Press.

15

CORPORA, INNOVATION AND ENGLISH LANGUAGE EDUCATION

Ken Hyland

Corpora have been at the forefront of two of the most significant changes in language education in recent years. On one hand, they have provided teachers and materials designers with more robust descriptions of how language is patterned and used, revealing the pervasive occurrence of phrasal units as the basis of idiomatic language use. On the other hand, they have facilitated new teaching methodologies, contributing to a wider shift from teaching as imparting knowledge to teaching as mediating learning. Here, corpora provide a means for students to take a more active and reflective part in their learning by exploring authentic examples of language. In the last decade, then, we have seen corpora exploited in areas as diverse as syllabus design (Walsh, 2010), classroom methodologies (Chambers, 2010), student grammars (Conrad & Biber, 2009) and assessment (Barker, 2010) in what has been something of a revolution in attitudes to language teaching. In this chapter, I survey the key changes that corpora have brought to language education, concluding with an example of an online concordancer for students. First, however, I offer a basic primer on what corpora are and how they are used.

Some key ideas and concepts

Essentially, a corpus is a collection of naturally occurring, computer-readable texts, often comprising many millions of words, which is considered more or less representative of a particular domain of language use. While it does not contain any new theories about language, it can offer fresh insights on familiar, but perhaps unnoticed, features of language use, replacing intuition with evidence. Or rather, in Partington's words (1996: 1) 'it represents a resource to both test intuitions and a motor which can help generate them'. Using text retrieval and concordancing software, analysts (or students) can isolate, count and see patterns in lexical and grammatical features from large numbers of texts to better understand the ways language is used in a particular genre, register or community.

Corpora vary in size depending on the feature the analyst is interested in, with lower frequency items requiring larger corpora to provide sufficient examples. Multi-million word corpora, such as the 400 million word *Bank of English* corpus, have been used to compile learner aids such as general purpose dictionaries, grammars and course books and this necessitates retrieving thousands of examples to get a complete picture of language use. At the other end of the scale, there are numerous DIY corpora around the world, some consisting of just a few thousand words, collected for such purposes as identifying student learning needs (e.g. Nation, 2001) or teaching particular genres. Other corpora have been assembled to assist second language learning by discovering variations in how particular institutional and social factors impact on language use such as the role of discipline (e.g. Hyland, 2004) or first language (e.g. Hinkel, 2002).

By themselves, corpora tell us very little, but the analyst is able to gain new perspectives on the familiar by basing interpretations on the patterns revealed using text analysis software to display frequency, phraseology and collocation. Frequency lists are useful for identifying commonly occurring words and phrases in target texts for teaching purposes. Thus, it is not only possible to discover the most common content words in a particular domain, such as a first year undergraduate textbook, but also to see routinely occurring word sequences in particular registers, like '*a result of the*' and '*this suggest that*' in academic writing (Hyland, 2008). Lists of frequently occurring words such as the *Academic Word List* (Coxhead, 2000) have also informed specialised learning materials (Schmitt & Schmitt, 2005). Frequency lists can also assist teachers by showing the tendency of certain verbs to occur in the passive or in negative forms, or by revealing commonly occurring grammar words, such as the fact that nearly all future time reference in English conversation is marked by *will* or other modals while the present progressive, the staple of many beginner classes, occurs in less than five percent of cases (Mindt, 2000).

Beyond frequency, concordance programmes bring together many instances of a search word in its local co-text, allowing the user to see regularities that often remain hidden in everyday use. Typing in a search word or phrase produces unconnected lines summoned from all the texts in a selected corpus with the search item at the centre of the screen. Patterns become visible by the vertical display of text, giving instances of *use* when read horizontally and evidence of *system* when read vertically. Corpus examples can therefore often provide teachers and learners with more information about the use of a word than dictionaries by supplying numerous examples of its use in varied contexts. It is possible, for example, to see the pragmatic versatility of the epistemic modifier *quite*, how it boosts or amplifies the meaning of non-gradable and 'extreme' words (*right, agree, amazing, fantastic,* etc.) and modifies terms with a gradable quality (*interesting, nice, large*) by indicating a point on a scale defined by the modified word (Hyland, 1996). Similarly, teachers can turn to a corpus to help students decode frequently confused adjectives such as *interested* and *interesting,* with the former overwhelmingly preceding *in* (especially *someone is interested in something*) and the latter almost always used before a noun (*an interesting thing*) (Hunston, 2002: 10).

A further capability offered by corpus software is collocation: the statistical probability of words to co-occur. Sinclair (2004: 19) observes that the choice of one word conditions the choice of the next, and the next after that, so that collocation is a way of understanding meanings through associations between words that are not readily available to introspection. Thus, it may be useful for learners to know that *utterly* occurs before *different* but not before *similar,* or that the immediate left collocates of *of* in academic writing are mainly nouns and comprise a narrow range of terms (*form of, terms of, case of, effect of,* etc.) (Scott & Tribble, 2006: 100). Habitual collocation, moreover, produces the phenomenon of 'semantic prosody' (Louw, 1993) where a word carries an additional, evaluative, meaning due to its frequent associations. Thus, words like *cause* and *commit* are almost always associated with negative events (*cause accidents, problems; commit suicide, crimes*) while *provide* has a favourable prosody (*provide care, shelter*). Again, this may have value for learners by assisting them to construct idiomatic text (*the rot set in*) or to fashion ironic or creative uses through collocational clashes (*happiness set in*).

In the next section, I look more explicitly at some of the educational changes brought about by corpora and then discuss an online concordance tool for students as an illustrative case study.

Corpora and innovation: two influences on teaching

Corpora have brought significant changes to language teaching and learning for a number of reasons, but not least by providing students with naturally occurring, authentic data instead of invented examples, by revealing the phraseological basis of language use which has contributed to curricula developments and teaching materials, and by encouraging a more autonomous, inductive approach to language learning. Römer (2010) distinguishes between indirect applications, where research findings feed into syllabuses, references works and teaching materials, and direct applications, which refer to more hands-on involvement by teachers and learners working with corpora in classrooms.

Indirect innovations: corpora in syllabus and materials design

Corpora have led to new descriptions of language which have fed into the design of syllabuses and materials, ensuring that teaching is based on frequency of occurrence and typical collocational patterns. Most importantly, perhaps, is the revolution they have brought about in lexicography and the production of dictionaries for students such as the *Collins COBUILD Advanced Learner's English Dictionary* (2003) and the *Oxford Dictionary of English* (2010). These resources are based on very large and diverse corpora which include a range of registers and frequently different varieties of English to capture recurrent language events. These resources not only provide greater access to context and more (and more authentic) examples, but also give greater prominence to what is typical rather than what is merely interesting to the compilers (Atkins & Rundall, 2008). They also give greater attention to syntagmatic patterning of language which not only notes the part of speech of the word but also the typical constraints on how an individual item behaves. In addition, corpus-based dictionaries are beginning to provide learners with other kinds of information not usually found in dictionaries, such as typical errors taken from learner corpora to raise awareness of common difficulties and misuses.

In addition to providing the theoretical and phraseological bases for dictionaries, corpora have brought innovations to grammars used by both teachers and learners. Reference grammars for learners of English emerged from the COBUILD project, but perhaps the most renowned grammar is the 1200 page *Longman Grammar of Spoken and Written English* (Biber et al., 1999). This gives comparative frequency information for forms in four different registers, including conversation and academic writing, and provides users with lexis-dependent patterns as well as common syntactic structures. However, when compared to later 'third generation' corpus grammars, such as the *Cambridge Grammar of English* (Carter & McCarthy, 2006) which draws on 700 million words, the 40 million words which form the basis of the earlier grammar now seems rather small and its size may constrain the accuracy and coverage of items (Tucker, 2001). Critics have also argued that despite the impressive data sources of these texts, we should not equate frequency with pedagogic relevance nor forget the fact that teachers and learners may have more traditional attitudes to grammar (Cook, 1998).

Corpora have been relatively slow to inform ELT materials, despite studies showing that textbooks rarely reflect how language is actually used in real life (e.g. Yoo, 2009). The impressive 4-level *Touchstone* series (McCarthy et al., 2006), based on the massive CANCODE corpus, however, is a notable exception. McCarthy and McCarten (2012) describe the decision-making involved in selecting conversational materials from this corpus, taking into account factors such as native-user dominance and the extent to which conversation draws heavily on participants' shared understandings of the context. Despite these caveats, however, the authors relied on the statistical output of the corpus to provide guidance on 'not so much what the speakers *say* in the corpus as what they *do* to create and sustain successful spoken interactions' (ibid: 231). The activities, therefore, draw on the corpus to help learners understand general principles for organizing talk through discourse markers (*well, so, I mean*), for taking account of other speakers through face and engagement markers (*you see, you know*), and for managing the conversation using signals for opening and closing talk, interrupting and shifting topics (*anyway, OK then, going back to what you were saying*) (McCarthy & McCarten, 2012).

More generally, corpora have informed teaching by revealing the tendency of words to occur, not randomly or only in conformity with grammatical rules, but in preferred sequences. This is Sinclair's 'idiom principle' (Sinclair, 1991) which is that every word is used in a common phraseology. He argues that corpus evidence shows that meanings (and often constraints on sequence) are attached to whole phrases and the hearer hears it in this way, rather than as a unit with lexical fillers completing available grammatical slots. When text cannot be interpreted in this way, users must use the 'open choice principle' which is much less predictable. This view informs the lexical syllabus (Willis, 1990) which organizes learning according to lexical patterns rather than grammatical forms or pragmatic functions. Frequency underlies the lexical syllabus, so that level 1 contains the 700 words that make up about 70 percent of all English text, covering their most typical uses which are rarely mentioned in beginners' courses. Perhaps the greatest use of corpora in materials design has been in English for Academic Purposes courses, where corpora have informed materials in engineering (Mudraya, 2006), the social sciences (Jones & Schmitt, 2010), and doctoral studies (Lee & Swales, 2006).

Despite these efforts to base syllabuses and materials on new descriptions of language and authentic examples, some authors argue that invented examples may actually be more effective in promoting noticing of salient items (e.g. Cook, 1998) and that pedagogic relevance as perceived by teachers and learners should not be ignored in favour of frequency (Widdowson, 2003).

Direct innovations: using corpora in classrooms

In addition to the role of corpora in assisting materials and syllabus designers, they have also found a role in classrooms themselves through Data Driven Learning (DDL) approaches. DDL owes much to the pioneering work of Tim Johns (Johns, 1991) who saw the computer as a resource to be tapped by the learner, so that corpora can replace instruction with discovery and move the study of language away from correctness to typicality.

The essence of DDL is the inductive acquisition of language regularities on the part of the learner: he or she becomes a 'detective' to discover facts about language use through the process of analysing authentic corpus examples. DDL is essentially a consciousness-raising methodology as it presents learners with evidence of language use and asks them to draw conclusions. However, while DDL typically involves teachers setting up activities which encourage students to notice salient features through the recurrent phrases they find in the data, they are often guided in this process through more constructivist and *deductive* learning activities. In fact, direct learner access to corpora spread along a deductive-inductive cline (Flowerdew, 2012).

The teacher's first decision when constructing corpus activities is whether to ask students to engage with raw corpus data or to mediate the experience by prior selection (and possibly editing) of concordance lines to highlight target features. Direct access to corpora requires and can stimulate enquiry, promote independent learning and reveal unfamiliar or typical uses to students through completing research tasks. For some students, this is undoubtedly a productive teaching method, and teachers have extended this to encourage students to build and analyse their own corpora (Lee & Swales, 2006). However, DDL requires learners to interpret patterns in large numbers of concordance lines and this is an analytical process involving considerable skill. On their own, students are not always sure what they should look for nor are they always sufficiently interested in language to conduct research on it.

Such explorations of corpora, or Discovery Learning as it is sometimes called, has therefore been slow to influence teaching methodology in ELT. Its unpredictability not only presents challenges to teachers, who may be threatened by the unplanned questions such open-ended research throws up, but the expertise required to search, sort and decipher concordances also places heavy demands on all but the most motivated students. In fact, as Hunston (2002: 171) suggests, it may only be suitable for more advanced learners who are 'filling in gaps in their knowledge rather than laying down the foundations'. For this reason, teachers who are enthusiastic about the approach have recommended strategy-training to familiarise students with corpus interrogation techniques (e.g. Lee and Swales, 2006). Alternatively, others have attempted to filter the results and predigest them for learners. Teachers often create structured, companion exercises that require students to make specific searches of the corpus. One example is the academic writing materials designed by Thurston and Candlin (1998). Here, specific lexical realisations are related to particular rhetorical functions, such as hedging or reporting a literature as students are asked to search a corpus for key terms and see meanings and patterns in the surrounding text before using the items in their own writing.

Where teachers or materials writers reduce and filter outputs, however, students are denied a more learner-centred use of corpora which allows them to browse the corpus and search to find answers to their own questions. As a result, more flexible tools have been developed which facilitate this kind of independence. Krishnamurthy and Kosem (2007) have criticized the complexity of corpus query tools and simpler interfaces have now emerged for classroom use. Three of the best known are the *Compleat Lexical Tutor* (www.lextutor. ca), the *Virtual Language Centre* (http://vlc.polyu.edu.hk/) and the *Academic Word List* site (www.nottingham.ac.uk/~alzsh3/acvocab/). These typically include concordancers, dictionaries, cloze-builders, customisable word lists, and self-quizzing features based around several different corpora. As evidence of the effectiveness of such methods, Horst et al. (2005) report an experiment to teach large amounts of vocabulary to learners on an EAP course using the resources of the *Compleat Lexical Tutor*, including access to corpus information via a concordancer. As a result of various opportunities to meet words in novel contexts through the concordance and cloze-building features, they found that students learned vocabulary more successfully than through other methods.

Check My Words: using corpora as a reference tool

Where students are encouraged to explore a raw corpus or are guided by either specific materials or online tools that filter the output, corpora are essentially used as *research tools* to promote greater awareness of language use. An alternative, and equally innovative, classroom methodology, however, is to treat a corpus as a *reference* tool by offering writers an effective way to search for words and phrases at the point when they need them most: when they are actually completing an assignment. In this section, I discuss a program that enables students to access online language resources as they compose and proofread: *Check My Words* (Milton, 2006).

Check My Words (http://mws.ust.hk/cmw/index.php) is a suite of programs that seeks to integrate concordancing software into the writing process. While the program includes links to didactic references such as online dictionaries, thesauruses, encyclopedia and an English grammar guide, the heart of the software is the access it provides to corpus-based resources. The program installs a toolbar in a word processor which enables writers to highlight a phrase in their document to retrieve information about it (Figure 15.1). Other buttons in the toolbar allow writers to get definitions and translations of words, to hear stretches of text spoken aloud, to highlight potential errors in their document and to get example sentences which can help them select the appropriate phrasing.

The *resources* button pulls down a list of potentially useful websites, and gives access to several corpus tools and specialized corpora. '*Word Neighbors*' brings up collocations of the target word with a specified number of words to the left and right or within a target span of words. *JustTheWord* displays collocates identified statistically and clustered by word class and sense from the British National Corpus, and access to *Google Search* from a dialogue box which automatically creates appropriate search syntax.

JustTheWord provides a summary of the collocations of a target word, assisting students to choose between words that have similar meanings. While a thesaurus can provide information on near synonyms, phraseological considerations restrict combinations which sound natural and so constrain the choices which are appropriate in any context. *JustTheWord* exploits technology by Sharp Industries to statistically analyze 80 million words of the British National Corpus (BNC), providing information on the words which most commonly associate with a target word.

FIGURE 15.1 *Check My Words* toolbar

Thus, a student may have written 'he speaks with a big accent' and be unsure about the correct adjective to use. He or she can simply highlight the word and call up *JustTheWord* to generate a display of collocations. Figure 15.2 shows how this clusters combinations by approximate meaning and indicating, by an adjacent green bar, the strength of the connection based on a t-score. A larger t-score means the combination occurs more frequently than by chance given the frequency of the two items. As the student is interested in finding an appropriate adjective to use with 'accent', he or she needs to click the ADJ N* link in the right-hand part of the speech frame of the screen. This takes the user to the relevant cluster of adjectives that have a similar meaning to '*strong*' and which can be used in collocations with '*accent*'. Students can then click on a potential candidate collocation and see pages of KWIC concordance lines of the combination and decide if this is the meaning they intended. The results, therefore, combine the information provided by a thesaurus and dictionary while indicating the degree of idiomaticity of choices.

Users can also find longer combinations involving two words by typing them into the search box or discover how likely a combination is by hitting the 'Suggest Alternatives' button. The program will then respond with an idea of how likely it is to find these words together in the corpus, a red bar indicating

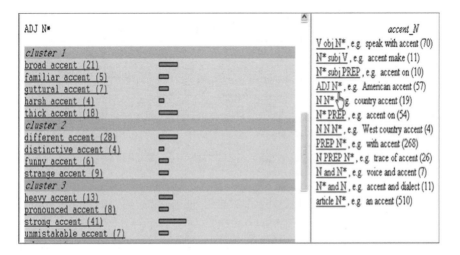

FIGURE 15.2 *JustTheWord* clusters for adjective + accent

that the combination is unlikely and some suggestions for alternatives. More than this, *JustTheWord* replaces each word in the input with a related word and indicates the strength of association between them. A blue bar represents the similarity between the original word and its replacement.

The main corpus resource in the program, however, is *Word Neighbors,* a concordance tool which can also be downloaded as a separate toolbar or used as an integral part of *Check My Words.* Figure 15.3 shows the options available on the opening search screen. Users enter a word or phrase in the central box and can optionally select the part of speech of the item, the number of words to the left and right of it, and the span to show the occurrence of words in any phrase. There is also the option of searching the entire 141 million word databank or selecting a particular genre or register.

Thus, if a writer is unsure whether 'go to shopping' or 'go shopping' is correct he or she might delete the problematic *to* in the search phrase, select a span of '3' to see if any other word occurs in the phrase, and uncheck the 'show all word forms' button. The results will confirm, of course, the overwhelming use of 'go shopping' with a few instances of 'go out shopping'. Similarly, to determine whether *possible to* or *possible that* expresses the writer's intended meaning in an academic essay, entering the word *possible* with the instruction to search one word to the right helps to disambiguate the different uses. Instead of overwhelming the student with pages of concordance lines, the results screen simply shows the number of words requested grouped by all the parts of speech the word can have with all the parts of speech of words that normally follow it. Figure 15.4 shows that the target word with the immediate right collocates distinguish *possible that* from *possible to,* both grammatically and as collocates.

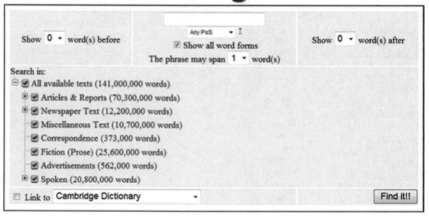

FIGURE 15.3 *The Word Neighbors* search screen

Word✱Neighbors

	possible	
Show 0 ▾ word(s) before	Any PoS ▾ 2 ☐ Show all word forms The phrase may span 1 ▾ word(s)	Show 1 ▾ word(s) after

Search in:
⊞ ☑ All available texts (141,000,000 words)

☐ Link to [Cambridge Dictionary ▾]   [Find it!!]

Patterns/Words			Frequency
ADJ ⊡ + NOUN ⊡:	e.g. "possible way"	Show results	11003
ADJ ⊡ + TO ⊡:	e.g. "possible to"	Show results	7837
ADJ ⊡ + PREP ⊡:	e.g. "possible for"	Show results	5348
ADJ ⊡ + CONJ ⊡:	e.g. "possible that"	Show results	3839
ADJ ⊡ + ADJ ⊡:	e.g. "possible future"	Show results	1529
ADJ ⊡ + DET ⊡:	e.g. "possible the"	Show results	738
ADJ ⊡ + ADV ⊡:	e.g. "possible only"	Show results	681
ADJ ⊡ + VERB ⊡:	e.g. "possible is"	Show results	564
ADJ ⊡ + PRON ⊡:	e.g. "possible we"	Show results	377
ADJ ⊡ + INT ⊡:	e.g. "possible Yeah"	Show results	6

Total Expressions: 31922

HELP   REPORT PROBLEMS   LANGUAGE LEARNING EXERCISES

NOTE: The division of words into classes (e.g. noun, verb, etc.) by a computer program is NEVER 100% accurate. For example, when you click on "Show results" for a verb, you may see some nouns displayed. The classification given here is a close approximation of the characteristic ways that the word behaves. However, you must use your human judgment in deciding the class of the word.

FIGURE 15.4 Results for a search on 'possible' in *Word Neighbors*

Further, by pressing the 'Show results' button for the target form, users are directed to contextualized authentic examples from the selected corpora (Figure 15.5), making it possible to distinguish the epistemic meaning of 'possible that' from the deontic modality of 'possible to'.

Check My Words was devised by a teacher at a university in Hong Kong for undergraduates whose first language was not English and it has subsequently been taken up by institutions in several countries around the world. While a useful tool to access language information on the fly, users also have the option of completing language exercises in a more conventionally didactic, *research* oriented way. The *Check My Words* website suggests a number of exercises using *Word Neighbors* which help raise students' awareness of the importance of phraseology in English and of particular useful collocates at the same time as helping them to learn the use of the tools. For example, one exercise encourages students to discover how certain delexical verbs like *have, make, give* and *take* can be used with a noun as a substitute for a single verb (e.g. *have an argument*) by looking up *have* + 1–4 words after it to find common collocates in newspaper texts. Another task is to search for often

Word&Neighbors

NOTE: The division of words into classes (e.g. noun, verb, etc.) by a computer program is NEVER 100% accurate. The classification given here is a close approximation of the characteristic ways that the word behaves. However, you must use your **human judgment** in deciding the class of the word!

	Search results for **possible that (ADJ CONJ)**	Text Type
1	However, it is still possible that hoteliers, nightclub owners etc. may decide to change their facilities making them permanently unavailable. ...**more**	Advertisements BNC-AMW
2	It is quite possible that the results of strategic benchmarking may indicate a need to revisit the organization's vision statement, which may look puny when compared to what others are accomplishing at present. ...**more**	Articles & Reports (Business & Administration) Mgmt process improvement.TXT
3	It's possible that you'll have to buy extra licenses for them to use the same software on their home machines. ...**more**	Articles & Reports (General) z1.txt
4	The Bull Court at Knossos is not well preserved, but it is possible that a fence of some kind ran round its edge; a fragment of fresco found in the Labyrinth shows a strongly made three-rail wooden fence with a ...**more**	Articles & Reports (Humanities & Social Science) BNC-CMP
5	Therefore, it is possible that a database opened in shared mode may approach the performance levels of a database opened in exclusive mode. ...**more**	Articles & Reports (Instructions) JETLOCK.TXT
6	IS IT POSSIBLE THAT WE MIGHT REVISIT THE WISDOM OR THE SCOPE OF THE COURT'S EARLIER RULING AS TO THOSE CRIME SCENE BLIPS IF WE WERE ABLE TO PROVIDE THOSE VIDEOTAPES TO THE PROSECUTION? ...**more**	Articles & Reports (Law) OJ_TRIAL.TXT
7	This is because it is quite possible that the laws in both cases may be much the same. ...**more**	Articles & Reports (Science & Engineering) BNC-A6S
8	If an adviser elects not to infuse capital into, or purchase a depreciated instrument from, a fund to compensate investors for their losses (or is prohibited from doing so), it is possible that dissatisfied investors may redeem their shares, causing ...**more**	Correspondence Letter from Chairman.txt

FIGURE 15.5   A context page for 'possible that'

confused pairs (*above/over, every/each, although/however, actually/really*, etc.) to see contextual meanings. Whether used for research or as a writing resource, there is considerable potential in the program for assisting students towards a familiarity of idiomatic phraseology.

Reflections

This software tool represents an interesting and useful application of corpora for novice writers which shows the advantages that might be gained by providing access to real texts but without expecting learners to become applied linguists in the process. *Check My Words* overcomes the limitations both of current CALL programs, which are often autocratically didactic, and existing print materials, which cannot supply this kind of information. The program not only puts user-friendly concordance tools in the hands of student writers, but also builds on current research on feedback and autonomy through point-of-need assistance. Its strength lies in its integration of accessible concordance output with more conventional online resources to enable students to query target-text uses from within their word-processor.

This kind of immediate online assistance can be extremely useful in raising students' awareness of the meanings of particular word combinations at the time when they need it most. As the program author, John Milton, observes:

> The approach provides students with the means to check and improve their language by referring to copious, authentic, and comprehensible resources during the writing process. This access, combined with resource-rich feedback from their teachers, can greatly increase the amount of positive and negative evidence available to students. Many researchers believe such evidence promotes acquisition, and if this approach can help students become more confident, responsible, and independent in selecting forms and patterns that are accurate and appropriate, it can also help relieve teachers of the need to act as proofreading slaves. (Milton, 2006: 125)

To be successful, however, such an approach has to be integrated into the curriculum and potential resistance overcome. Innovations invariably threaten cherished learning theories and challenge established practices.

The software described here is based on a procedural model of learning rather than a more familiar declarative model, and so makes new demands on learners and questions assumptions about how languages and writing should be taught. Students are not always comfortable revising without explicit reformulation of their errors, particularly in Hong Kong, and teachers themselves may be uneasy about a degree of learner autonomy which threatens more traditional teacher roles. Server logs tracking student revisions and surveys of teachers using the program, however, suggest that students eventually use the resources effectively and that rates of successful revisions increase (Milton, 2006). Most of what we know of language as users is based on our repeated encounters with words in natural settings – by our informal analysis of collocation – and resources that assist students to explicitly recognize collocation may be a step towards the development of more effective and autonomous learning.

Conclusions

It is always dangerous to discuss an innovation in education as heralding a paradigmatic shift that will greatly improve teaching and learning. We have been disappointed in the past and should be cautious in the present. I have mentioned some of the potential problems of introducing corpora innovations to effect changes in teaching and learning languages in the preceding discussion, but among the most obvious is the fact that access to 'real language' does not, by itself, promote learning. Corpora supply decontextualised, atomized bits of language that must be recontextualised for classroom purposes, making it real and usable for learners. There is also a need to consider *what* language is included in our teaching corpora. An exclusive emphasis on the specialized writing of disciplinary experts or of native speakers may devalue the language of non-native English speakers and restrict communicative competence to limited specialized settings. Nor should frequency be allowed to dominate what we teach. There is a place for introspection and intuition, and for the saliency of items in what is selected for teaching purposes, otherwise we risk teaching students to simply parrot the clichéd and the trite.

Many of these points will be obvious to teachers and those wishing to use corpora as teaching tools, but we certainly need to guard carefully against the tyranny of frequency and convention and avoid a tendency to valorize expert and native speaker discourse. I hope to have shown in this short chapter, however, something of the potential of corpora for innovation in language education. Among the most far reaching of these are a shift in seeing language as composed mainly of idiomatic forms rather than grammatical rules, and how large samples of language, made accessible and relevant for students, might contribute to new ways of learning.

I would like to thank McNeill, Center for Language Education, Hong Kong University of Science and Technology, for permission to reproduce the screenshot from *My Words* in this chapter.

Key readings

Flowerdew, L. (2012). *Corpora and language education*. London: Palgrave. A comprehensive discussion of the approaches and applications of corpora to teaching language.

Hunston, S. (2002). *Corpora in applied linguistics*. Cambridge: Cambridge University Press. A theoretically situated overview of corpora applications in applied linguistics, including teaching.

Sinclair, J. (ed.) (2004). *How to use corpora in language teaching*. Amsterdam: Benjamins. Practical guidance in the practicalities of using corpora, interpreting the results and applying them to the classroom.

References

Atkins, S. & Rundall, M. (2008). *The Oxford guide to practical lexicography*. Oxford: Oxford University Press.

Barker, F. (2010) How can corpora be used in language testing? In O'Keeffe, A. and McCarthy, M. J. (eds.) *The Routledge handbook of corpus linguistics*. Abingdon, Oxon: Routledge, pp. 633–645.

Biber, D., Johannson, S., Leech, G., Conrad, S. and Finnegan, E. (1999). *Longman grammar of spoken and written English*. London: Longman.

Carter, R. A. and McCarthy, M. J. (2006). *Cambridge grammar of English*. Cambridge: Cambridge University Press.

Chambers, A. (2010). What is data-driven learning? In A. O'Keefe & M. McCarthy (eds.) *The Routledge handbook of corpus linguistics*. London: Routledge, pp. 345–358.

Collins COBUILD advanced learner's English dictionary (2003)

Conrad, S. & Biber, D. (2009). *Real grammar: a corpus-based approach to English.* London: Longman.

Cook, G. (1998). The uses of reality: a reply to Ron Carter. *ELT Journal,* 52 (1): 57–63.

Coxhead, A. (2000). A new academic wordlist. *TESOL Quarterly,* 34 (2): 213–238.

Flowerdew, L. (2012). *Corpora and language education.* London: Palgrave.

Hinkel, E. (2002). *Second language writers' text: linguistic and rhetorical features.* Mahwah, NJ: Lawrence Erlbaum.

Horst, M., Cobb, T. & Nicolae, I. (2005). Expanding academic vocabulary with an interactive on-line database. *Language Learning & Technology,* 9 (2): 90–110.

Hunston, S. (2002). *Corpora in applied linguistics.* Cambridge: Cambridge University Press.

Hyland, K. (1996). 'I don't quite follow': making sense of a modifier. *Language Awareness,* 5 (2): 91–100.

Hyland, K. (2004). *Disciplinary discourses: social interactions in academic writing.* Ann Arbor: University of Michigan Press.

Hyland, K. (2008). As can be seen: lexical bundles and disciplinary variation. *English for Specific Purposes,* 27 (1): 4–21.

Johns, T. (1991). Should you be persuaded: two examples of data-driven learning. *English Language Research Journal,* 4: 1–16.

Jones, M. & Schmitt, N. (2010). Developing materials for discipline-specific vocabulary and phrases in academic seminars. In N. Harwood (ed.) *English language teaching materials: theory and practice.* Cambridge: Cambridge University Press, pp. 225–250.

Krishnamurthy, R. & Kosem, I. (2007). Issues in creating a corpus for EAP pedagogy and research. *Journal of English for Academic Purposes,* 6 (4): 356–373.

Lee, D. & Swales, J. (2006) A corpus-based EAP course for NNS doctoral students: moving from available specialized corpora to self-compiled corpora. *English for Specific Purposes,* 25(1): 56–75.

Louw, B. (1993). Irony in the text or insincerity in the writer? The diagnostic potential of semantic prosodies. In M. Baker et al. (eds.) *Text and technology.* Amsterdam: Benjamins, pp. 157–176.

McCarthy, M. & McCarten, J. (2012). Corpora and materials design. In Hyland, K., Chau, M-H. & Handford, M. (eds.) *Corpus applications in applied linguistics.* London: Continuum, pp. 225–241.

McCarthy, M.J., McCarten, J. & Sandiford, H., (2006). *Touchstone.* Cambridge: Cambridge University Press.

Milton, J. (2006). Resource-rich web-based feedback: helping learners become independent writers. In K. Hyland & F. Hyland (eds.) *Feedback in second language writing.* Cambridge: Cambridge University Press, pp. 123–139.

Mindt, D. (2000). *An empirical grammar of the English verb system.* Berlin: Cornelsen.

Mudraya, O. (2006). Engineering English: a lexical frequency instructional model. *English for Specific Purposes,* 25 (2): 235–256.

Nation, P. (2001). Using small corpora to investigate learner needs: two vocabulary research tools. In M. Ghadessy, A. Henry and R. Roseberry (eds.) *Small corpus studies and ELT.* Amsterdam: Benjamins, pp. 31–46.

Oxford Dictionary of English (2010). Oxford: OUP.

Partington, A. (1996). *Patterns and meanings: using corpora for English language research and teaching.* Amsterdam: Benjamins.

Römer, U. (2010). Using general and specialized corpora in English language teaching: past, present and future. In M. Campoy-Cubillo, B. Bellés-Fortuño & M. Gea-Valor (eds.) *Corpus-based approaches to English language teaching.* London: Continuum, pp. 18–38.

Schmitt, D. & Schmitt, N. (2005). *Focus on vocabulary: mastering the academic word list.* London: Longman.

Scott, M. & Tribble, C. (2006). *Textual patterns: keyword and corpus analysis in language education*. Amsterdam: Benjamins.

Sinclair, J. McH. (1991). *Corpus, concordance, collocation*. Oxford: OUP.

Sinclair, J. McH. (2004). *Trust the text: language, corpus and discourse*. London: Routledge.

Thurstun, J. & Candlin, C.N. (1998). *Exploring academic English: a workbook for student essay writing*. Sydney, Australia: NCELTR.

Tucker, G. (2001). Possibly alternative modality. *Functions of Language*, 8 (2): 183–216.

Walsh, S. (2010) What features of spoken and written corpora can be exploited in creating language teaching materials and syllabuses? In A. O'Keeffe and M. J. McCarthy (eds.) *The Routledge handbook of corpus linguistics*. Abingdon, Oxon: Routledge, pp. 333–344.

Widdowson, H.G. (2003). *Defining issues in English language teaching*. Oxford: Oxford University Press.

Willis, D. (1990). *The lexical syllabus: a new approach to language teaching*. London: Harper Collins.

Yoo, W. H. (2009). The English definite article: what EFL/ESL grammars say and what corpus findings show. *Journal of English for Academic Purposes*, 8 (3): 267–278.

16

INNOVATION IN THE YOUNG LEARNER CLASSROOM

David Nunan

Introduction

Arguably, the two standout innovations in ELT at present are technology enhanced language learning, and the teaching of English to young learners (TEYL). Private language schools, commercial publishers and Ministries of Education around the world are implementing policies to introduce the teaching of English as a foreign language at earlier and earlier ages. In this chapter, I propose two things. First, to review the current literature on the teaching of English to younger learners, and to look at what empirical research has to say on the question of the optimal age at which to introduce foreign languages in school. Second, to present two case studies of pedagogical innovations in TEYL involving technology. Case study 1 looks at an innovative online programme in North America that met with only limited success. Case study 2 is based on a pilot study in Korea of a new global ELT series for young learners. If the results of the pilot study are confirmed when the materials are introduced, it looks as though this innovation will be successful.

The chapter aims, therefore, to provide a balanced overview of TEYL, looking at the issue from theoretical, empirical and practical perspectives. In writing the chapter, I will draw on published data sources as well as carrying out original research drawing on elicited data from questionnaires and interviews as well as case studies and classroom observations.

Key ideas and concepts

In this chapter, I do not propose to engage in a lengthy discussion of 'innovation' and 'change', as these concepts are dealt with exhaustively in

Section 1 by Kennedy, Markee, Holliday and Gong, and Waters and Vilches. Rather, I want to look at the confluence of two major trends in language education: the Teaching of English to Young Learners (TEYL) and the use of technology in language education (both of which can be seen as 'innovations' in their own right).

The teaching of English to young learners

In thinking about young learners, we need to bear in mind that the term covers a large chronological age span: from around three years of age to 15, although chronological age is just one of the variables that needs to be taken into consideration:

> Some writers and researchers try to segment learners strictly according to age: 3–5 year olds, 6–8 year olds and so on. While, as we shall see, children do exhibit different mental and social characteristics at different ages, a strict segmentation is not particularly helpful. As Pinter (2006:2) points out, all children are unique, and two children at the same chronological age can exhibit markedly different characteristics. (Nunan, 2011: 2)

As indicated in the introduction, a major trend worldwide is to introduce the teaching of English as a foreign language at earlier and earlier ages (Cameron, 2001). In an extensive survey of the impact of English as a global language on polices and practices in the Asia-Pacific region, I found that in all countries surveyed, the starting age of instruction had been, or was about to be, lowered (Nunan, 2003).

This lowering is based on the assumption that younger equals better. However, there is little empirical support for this position. In the late 1980s, in a book-length review of the empirical research available at the time, Singleton concluded that:

> There is no consistent support in the literature for the notion that younger second language learners learn more efficiently or successfully than older learners. (Singleton, D. 1989: 37)

At about the same time, in a somewhat different review, Ellis (1985) also concluded that in foreign language situations, if all other factors such as amount of exposure and instruction are constant, teenagers do better than young children and adults. Subsequent reviews have generally supported this position.

Does this mean that we should NOT teach English to young learners? Not necessarily. We need to ask a number of questions that have relevant bearing on the issue. These include the following:

- Was the curriculum and methodology age / developmentally appropriate? If the curriculum model and teaching methods are not appropriate to the age and developmental stages of the learners, then it is not surprising that learners do not do as well as older learners.
- Were the teachers specifically trained to teach languages to young learners? In the course of a review into the impact of the emergence of English as a global language on policy and practice in the Asia-Pacific region, Nunan (2003) found that most EFL teachers of young learners were neither specifically trained to teach young learners, nor to teach language. In fact, in many private schools, they had no teacher training of any kind.
- What was the intensity of instruction? In many educational systems, the amount of time devoted to foreign language instruction is tokenistic – sometimes as little as forty minutes a week (Nunan, 2003). Although we do not have a great deal of evidence on how much time is needed to support measurable gains in proficiency, we can be pretty certain that forty minutes a week is certainly not enough.
- Did the instruction cater to ALL of the learners' needs: cognitive, physical, psychological and social? Linse (2005) argues strongly for a 'whole learner' approach in the young learners' classroom. She points out that the teacher of English to young learners is often the first to identify physical or psychological factors as the underlying cause of learning disability.

Even if all of these issues – age and developmental appropriacy, appropriately trained teachers, intensity of instruction, and whole person teaching – are satisfactorily addressed, it should come as no surprise that young learners do not perform as well as adolescents and adults in acquiring a foreign language. We do not expect them to do as well in the acquisition of mathematical concepts, developing academic reading and writing skills in their first language, or carrying out science experiments, so why should foreign language acquisition be any different?

The need for instruction to be developmentally appropriate is particularly crucial (Linse, 2005; Nunan, 2011). Many years ago, the Swiss child psychologist Jean Piaget identified the following four, broad developmental stages through which children pass in the first 12–15 years of life.

Stage 1: Sensori-motor

This stage extends from birth to approximately two years of age. During this period, the child learns to interact with the environment by manipulating objects. In his / her first language, the child begins the transformation from proto-language to real language. The rapid development of vocabulary is a notable feature of child language development at this stage.

Stage 2: Pre-operational

This period extends from around the age of two to seven. In its first language, the child develops and consolidates his / her grammar. Socially, at this stage, children are egocentric, thinking that the world revolves around them. Psychologically, their ability to think logically is extremely limited.

Stage 3: Concrete operational

From approximately seven to eleven years of age, children are in the concrete operational stage. At this time, they are beginning to develop the ability to separate the self from the environment and to think logically. They have limited ability to make generalizations from concrete experiences.

Stage 4: Formal operational

From eleven years onwards, the child enters the final developmental stage – that of formal operations. They are now able to generalize beyond immediate context, extrapolating from the instance to the general. Abstract thinking develops. Puberty also occurs, although increasingly, children are entering puberty at earlier and earlier ages. Brain lateralization[1] also occurs, although the concept of lateralization and its implications for language learning is quite contentious in the literature. (For many years, it was believed that after the onset of puberty and brain lateralization, it was impossible to develop native-like facility in a second or foreign language, but some researchers now dispute this.)

These stages have particular relevance for language education. They suggest, for example, that abstract grammatical explanations are likely to be of limited use to learners who have not reached the stage of formal operations.

Technology in language education

A second key trend in language education has been the use of technology. There have, however, been surprisingly few innovations using technology with young learners, although this chapter will discuss two programmes that are exclusively technology-based.

A question (more rhetorical than real) that loomed large over the field of language teaching not too many years ago, was 'How can someone learn a language by interacting with a machine?' These days the issue is no longer whether or not it is possible to learn languages through technology, but how technology can be integrated into a variety of learning arrangements to maximize the effectiveness of instruction.

I see four principal roles for technology in language learning, although not all of these will be equally pertinent for younger learners, particularly those at the lower end of the chronological scale. These roles are as follows:

- As a carrier of content;
- As a language practice tool;
- As a learning management tool; and
- As a communication medium.

As a provider of content, technology allows access to a wide range of aural, written and visual input. For older learners, it can also provide information on language itself through online dictionaries and similar resources.

Technology is ideal for providing the extensive, repetitive practice required for successful mastery of the target language. Learners are able to practice at their own pace, and to receive instant feedback on their performance. The self-paced, individualized opportunities afforded by technology take much of the drudgery out of classroom-based practice and this feature seems particularly relevant to the learning needs of young people. When the computer provides opportunities for learners to practice the language by doing spoken and written drills, completing comprehension questions, carrying out grammar exercises and so on, it is acting as an instructional tool.

Technology can also relieve teachers of much of the tedium inherent in print-based management systems. All steps in the curriculum process, from needs analysis to assessment, can be facilitated through technology-based systems. Examples of the kinds of tasks that can be facilitated through technology are to:

- administer and collate needs analyses data from students
- allow teachers to post course information, handouts and other materials for students to download
- enable students to submit assignments and for teachers to grade and return assignments electronically
- document student achievements and archive learner portfolios containing samples of spoken and written language
- administer, analyze, collate and store the results of classroom quizzes
- administer, collate and present student evaluation of teaching questionnaires.

As a communication medium, technology enables learners to connect with and communicate with native speakers of the language or with other learners. This provides older learners with opportunities for authentic communication, opportunities that rarely, if ever, existed prior to the ubiquitous appearance of technology. These four functions of technology are as relevant to TEYL as they are to teaching adults. That said, the way that they are exploited in instructional programmes will vary. For example, there is little point in presenting grammar deductively to learners who are not developmentally ready to process grammar in this way. This is generally thought to be around the Piagentian stage of formal operations (Nunan, 2011).

As has been discussed, technology has the potential to provide young learners with essential environmental support in the learning process. If appropriately designed, it can offer multimedia platforms that stimulate young learners and encourage them to use their curiosity, develop their creativity and nurture their imagination to actively explore the learning environment. Technology provides teachers and developers with the chance to create classroom materials and tasks that are not only interactive, but also allow variation in the pace, organization and decision-making in order to hold the attention of young learners. Equally, technology can provide systematic routines for young learners to follow and to reinforce their learning through repetition of familiar activities. Finally, technology also meets the needs of young learners to feel a sense of achievement and satisfaction with their work by giving them instant feedback and summarizing their learning progress and effort. While these opportunities can be provided in other ways, few approaches allow all of them to be offered together. For further elaboration on the roles and functions of technology in education, see Beatty (2010).

Case studies

In this section, I describe two case studies in which technology plays a central role in the delivery of English language instruction to young learners. The first case study describes a programme that met with only limited success, while the second describes a successful programme.

Case study 1: 'MyEnglish'

Background and context

Based in North America, over a period of years, the MyEnglish organization developed a highly successful online programme for teaching English to adults.[2] This success prompted the organization to develop an online programme for teaching English to young learners.

Two teams of professionals made up the bulk of the employees. One team consisted of language professionals who knew a lot about language teaching but very little about technology. The other team consisted of technicians, who knew just about everything there was to know about computer programming, but virtually nothing about language teaching. Most of the language specialists were former teachers, who wanted a change of scene. Although one or two had textbook authoring experience, most did not. They therefore had a lot to learn about curriculum development, syllabus design and materials writing.

My involvement with the company came about when I was contacted by Edward, the team leader. I had known Edward for several years. A former teacher and editor, he was one of the few people at MyEnglish who knew the business end of materials writing. Edward asked me to run a series of practical workshops on syllabus design and materials writing. At the beginning of the initial workshop, I asked the group, 'So what is MyEnglish? Is it a publishing venture or a language school?' Members of the group looked at each other in puzzlement. Clearly, this was not a question they had ever contemplated. After some discussion, they decided that it was probably both.

Things were (and still are) changing rapidly in the world of language pedagogy. A global explosion in the demand for English, increasing competition in all sectors of the industry, the drive for profits, and the growing importance of technology are changing the field out of all recognition. Neat distinctions between entities such as 'schools' and 'publishers' are morphing, and hybrid forms are beginning to emerge. Not so long ago, the largest language publisher in the world established a chain of language schools for teaching young learners in China.

The innovation

Against this background, the leadership at MyEnglish decided that they needed a new product. They evaluated the market, and identified the young learner market as the sector with the fastest growth and the greatest potential. They planned to align two significant innovations: the teaching of English to young learners, and technology, to create a unique product, and one they hoped would capture a large chunk of the market. While they needed to answer to their shareholders, they were not totally driven by the bottom line. There were several idealists and visionaries in the management team, and they genuinely wanted to change the way that the world learns English. A considerable budget was allocated to the project.

A small team was assembled to create the product. The team leader was Steve, a large, prematurely balding young man who had worked for the company for several years as a technician, but who was looking for a change of direction. The other key player was Paula, a freelance educational software developer. Neither Steve nor Paula had any experience as language teachers, and knew next to nothing about language.

At this point, my role within the company had been restricted to advising on the content of the adult courses. However, one day I was invited, along with several others to a meeting to showcase the prototype unit for the kids' product which had tentatively been entitled *Zak's English*. Zak was the central character in the course. He was an alien who visits earth and has a series of adventures.

Before we got to see the prototype unit, Paula gave us a short lecture on the educational philosophy underpinning the course.

The secret to teaching young learners, she said, *is to make sure they're having fun. Young learners get bored easily, and need to be entertained. They also have short attention spans and so the activity focus has to be constantly changing. And that's why the gaming approach is so successful. Learners think they're having fun – they're not even aware that they're learning. Learning happens by stealth.*

With that, she activated the computer projector, and took us through the prototype unit for *Zak's English*. The materials are certainly engaging. The amusing cartoon characters, Flash animation and cutting-edge technology have been artfully deployed to create high interest and challenging tasks.

At the end of the presentation, Paula got a round of applause. Beaming, she asked if there were any questions.

What level is this material designed for? I asked.

Well, this is the beginners' level, she replies, looking slightly puzzled.

I'd like to look at the scope and sequence.[3]

Scope and sequence? She looks even more puzzled. Clearly, there was no scope and sequence.

Later, I asked Edward about his involvement in the project. He replied that he was not involved, that, like me, he was seen to be part of the adult team. Steve and Paula were in complete control of the project.

What's the problem? he asked.

Where do I start? The language level is way too high, and there's no pedagogical focus. The language structures are all over the place, the audio is way too fast, and the vocabulary doesn't seem to have been graded in any way.

You'd better have a word to Ray, said Edward.

Why don't you? You're in charge of all things pedagogical.

This is a different project. We have a very flattened structure to the organization. You just don't go fishing in someone else's pond. This is Paula and Steve's pond. They wouldn't like it if I interfered. His frustration was clearly evident, and I was not surprised when a short time later he returned to conventional publishing.

I made an appointment to speak to Ray, the CEO of the company, and outlined my concerns. Being a consultant can be frustrating. Advice, hard-won over a considerable number of years, is more often than not ignored. In this case, however, Ray shared my concern.

So what do we do?

Don't get me wrong – the materials are fabulous, but just not for beginning language learners. You need to get someone on the team who knows about language teaching.

A solution presented itself the following day. I received a call from Helen Chiu, a former colleague who planned to return to the States after many years in Asia. She had a master's degree in TESOL, and considerable experience as a teacher, materials writer and editor. And she was looking for work. I arranged for her to have a conversation with Ray, and she was offered a position on the *Zak's English* team as pedagogical consultant, with specific responsibility for creating the scope and sequence.

Halfway through the project, Helen abruptly resigned. Later, she recounted the daily struggles that she had with Steve and Paula. *They just didn't want to listen,* she said.

The course was eventually finished. Although I still had concerns about the level and the uneven progression of the language, overall, the product was pretty good. It was innovative and represented a novel approach to the teaching of English to young learners, making use of cutting edge graphics and animation through flash technology and other technological innovations found in computer games while drawing on games theory and experiential learning. A sales force was put in place in Asia, and the product was launched. I spoke at several of the launch events in China, Korea and Japan. The audiences seemed favorably impressed, and it looked as though the product was off to a good start. Within a year of the launch, however, it became clear that the product failed to gain traction in the marketplace, and was permanently shelved.

Reflection

So, what went wrong? I put this question to Ray one day when we met up for a drink. (By this stage, he had also left the company.) He sighed and said, *when it became clear that we weren't meeting our targets, we did some market research – which we should have done in the first place. We'd pilot tested the product, of course, and although some problems remained with the level and progression, we were pretty satisfied. The kids loved the materials, and we had trouble getting them to stop at the end of the piloting period. So we thought we were on to a winner. What we didn't factor in was the view of the parents. There was a widespread belief that if the kids were having fun, they couldn't be learning. They just didn't recognize the pedagogical value of games. There were other problems, of course, in some markets, we picked the wrong partner, but getting too far ahead of the market was our main mistake.*

In summary, then, here are three observations that flow from this case study:

1. When one is engaged in innovation, make sure that the people involved know what they are doing. (This seems obvious. However, it is a principle that is overlooked surprisingly often.) Identify the skills that are needed and put together a team that contains a mix of skills. Make sure you pick people who can work as a team, and who acknowledge and respect the unique skills of other team members.
2. If the innovation involves technology, make sure that technology serves the needs of pedagogy and not the other way round. In a company dominated by technicians and engineers, this is always likely to be a challenge. The temptation to incorporate the latest cool technological advance is often too great to resist.
3. Know the market, and don't get too far ahead of it. It can be extremely frustrating, having to retreat from the cutting-edge, when introducing an innovation. However, if you want your innovation to gain traction in the marketplace (and there seems little point in doing it if this is *not* your intention), then it is important not to get too far ahead of the market. Determining what the market is ready to accept requires market research, judgment and educated guess work.

The next case study also involves the use of technology in the instruction of young learners, but this was approached very differently.

Case study 2: 'The English First Academy'

Background and context

This case study took place in South Korea, in a small, private language school in Gyeonggi-do (province) about one hour south of Seoul. The institute, known as an English 'Hahk-won' (literally 'study-institute') in Korean, was a stand-alone business rather than a 'chain-institute' belonging to one of the ubiquitous chains which are prevalent throughout Korea. The institute had been struggling due to curriculum and management issues and was seeking a new direction.

The school had about 40 students, a number which had fallen from 75 at the same time the previous year, and the previous Director of Studies had moved on, leaving behind reduced class sizes and a need to recruit new students. A decision was made to expand into classes for younger students including kindergarten-aged students. The institute owner was a professor at a university. The owner approached Aaron, a native English-speaking colleague, for help in re-establishing the reputation of the school through curriculum innovation in the young learner area.

The owner and Aaron discussed potential strategies and agreed to target the five-to-ten year age group (pre-K to grade 3) with a blended programme based on second language literacy.[4] The project appealed to Aaron for two reasons: first, he had significant experience in blended literacy programmes which meld extensive reading and CALL; second, the young learner literacy movement was an expanding sector of the market in Korea as many parents became aware of the idea of starting young second language learners on the path to reading through children's literature.

Korea had seen a growing interest in literacy through 'watered down' language arts programmes with extensive reading components, sometimes with book libraries (some of which included eBooks). The institute owner felt that despite the falling number of students in the older age groups at the institute, there was a market in the local area (32 apartment buildings surrounded the institute, and there were more than 100 within a two block radius) for a pre-K, kindergarten and G1-3 literacy based Primary Language School after-school programme.

The existing staff included one foreign teacher and a Korean teacher who had lived in the United States for a number of years. Such teachers were common in PLSs because of their bilingual abilities. There was also a Korean general manager. The owner asked Aaron to work with him to build a 'brand' curriculum based on Aaron's design with his support. Initially, Aaron was invited to work on a part-time basis teaching model classes and training staff, but very quickly things developed to the point where he was asked to become full-time Director of Studies.

The innovation

Through his work with Korea TESOL as a teacher training and conference and workshop organiser, as well as with the Extensive Reading Special Interest Group (SIG), the Young Learners SIG, and through organizing conferences for CALL, as well as authoring and presentation work, Aaron had developed an extensive knowledge of the young learners' field in Korea. Additionally, for four years he had run an after school programme through a university research institute featuring literacy based instruction with an Extensive Reading programme involving CALL technology for motivation, performance tracking and assessment. When Aaron started managing the university programme, which functioned basically as a kind of 'fancy language school' in the words of the parents (since parents would not sanction their children being involved in a programme unless it replaced a PLS in their children's schedules), there were 35 students, a number that grew to 120 after two years of blended programme innovation. In this innovative programme, technology fulfilled three of the four roles outlined in the section preceding the two case studies: that is, as a provider of content, a practice tool and a learning management system.

The rich literacy components provided students with considerable meaningful input and aided rich vocabulary development. The CALL component allowed students to work both in the classroom (five hours a week) and at home online (two to five hours a week). Both literacy development and more general 4-skills language learning were delivered online. The main literacy programme is called 'Fast-Forward' (NS Learning Korea) – which is a brain-based phonemic awareness-phonics-fluency-vocabulary programme. This is supplemented with a component entitled 'Reading Assistant' – which builds oral fluency and comprehension. Exposure to levelled texts is deepened using the Reading A-Z (RAZ Kids) online eBooks Learning Management System.

The 4-skills coursebook world is also delivered online. Though the development of these materials was still at the pilot stage when the innovative programme described in this case study was being implemented, there was sufficient content to introduce the children to the 'world' and stimulate their interest in self-directed online learning. None of this would be possible, of course, without a small CALL lab for learner training. Here, the Korean bilingual teacher, as well as Aaron's own high-intermediate to advanced bilingual skills, were important factors in motivating learners (and gaining parental commitment to the programme).

At the time of the innovation described in this case study, the owner had been in the field a long time. He had academic credentials as well as teacher training experience, and thought the programme was ideal. Despite less than ideal financial circumstances, he agreed not only to back the programme but to help plan, implement and market the programme. There is no doubt that the comparative success of the programme was due, at least in part, to the enthusiastic backing of the leadership of the school.

Results

Despite a difficult beginning, the programme was successfully implemented and students, parents and teachers in the five-to-ten year old programme were delighted with the results. The youngest classes (five-to-six-year-olds) saw students master the alphabet within six weeks as well as rapidly developing phonemic awareness. These young students gained confidence through their immediate success and this transferred into their story book based 'speaking' class as well. The middle group (seven-to-eight-year-olds) began to read simple online ebooks independently within three months and their parents were amazed at the progress. The oldest group (nine-to-ten-year-olds) had more mixed results, although one boy in the group made such outstanding progress and demonstrated such enthusiasm, that he inspired the other students.

Nine year-old Jihwan, a shy grade 3 boy, was so taken by the online ebook programme he spent five to eight hours a week reading ebooks, taking quizzes and accumulating points in the Learning Management System. The transformation in his language skills was remarkable. His reading fluency and speaking ability improved dramatically, and his attitude to learning changed dramatically, not only at the institute but also at his regular school. His mother called the institute and was effusive in her praise. After garnering 10,000 points in a single week, a party was held for him. As a result of this and the amazing results with the youngest group, almost instantly a feeling of 'gifted' learning was created at the institute and enrolments increased – especially in the classes aimed at the two youngest age groups.

Likewise, there was considerable progress in the professional development of the teachers. Initial reservations about having to learn how to use the new tools soon gave way to enthusiasm.

One of the foreign teachers employed by the school commented:

> Initially I was reticent to commit fully to the programme, because of previous bad experiences with online learning and extensive reading. However after seeing the results with the kids, especially seeing the change with Jihwan and the boys in his group, I am a believer. The teacher has to let go of the idea of always 'teaching' and see themselves as a facilitator in the online area, and if they do kids can go so far themselves. Through managing the online reading of my students I gained new insight into what programme innovation looks like.

The Korean bilingual teacher learned a great deal about how literacy instruction works through coaching the children with the online programme. She was committed to enrolling in an online literacy training course and would continue to teach literacy through CALL in private teaching in the area where she lives. She felt it would be difficult to find another teaching job in the area at this time in English education where this kind of programme innovation is encouraged.

She commented:

> It was a real challenge to learn how to run an online literacy class. I was only used to 'teaching' students rather than 'training' them too. In the blended programme I was introduced too, with the youngest kids, I had to train the kids as well as their parents, and that was tough initially. However, in the end I was really amazed about how much could be achieved so quickly if the right conditions for efficient use of homework time are created. Also I love using the language (computer) lab during class time. This idea revolutionized my teaching. If I ever manage my own school in future there will always be offline and online class time too.

However, after four months, despite this great success and an increasing enrollment in the younger classes targeted by this programme, the institute closed due to continuing student attrition in the higher level, older-aged 'traditional' offline styled institute classes. The innovative pre-K to grade 3 classes were so popular with parents that they were devastated at the closure. Several children's parents promised that they would enroll their children's younger siblings. Unfortunately, the severe depletion of older students made continuing unviable. The owner said that if this programme had been implemented about a year earlier when there were many more 1st grade, 2nd grade and 3rd grade students and before the institute had lost many of its older students then the business would have been a major financial success.

On the final day, Jihwan's mother came to the institute in tears describing how much her boy loved the programme, the teachers and how much his school teacher had commented on his improvement in English class. She said his whole attitude to learning had changed because of his exposure to our 'gifted' style programme.

Reflection

Blended programmes combining early literacy instruction with CALL based programmes for literacy and 4-skills development can create ideal conditions for language acquisition. However, several factors are crucial. All the stakeholders must take ownership of the programme, which means teachers need to be trained and feel that they are developing professionally as a result, parents must gain an early and in-depth understanding of how literacy works and why CALL is critical to their children's success. Students, for their part, must feel that the programmes are fun, and they must experience the early success that builds instant confidence. The key here is in effective management of the programmes by more qualified staff pursuing professional development in CALL and literacy as well as with publishing and curriculum design companies promoting and delivering effective programmes. Finally, it is crucial that parents understand the rationale behind the innovation and are prepared to throw their support behind it.

Conclusion

The innovations described in the case studies in this chapter were both focused on the young learner, and both had a very strong technology component. Overall, the pedagogical and technical quality of the materials and resources were outstanding. Despite this, one of the innovations was relatively more successful than the other. Interestingly, it is possible to identify a set of related factors that impeded the innovation in Case Study 1, and facilitated the innovation in Case Study 2. Critical to the success of the innovation were the enthusiastic support of the leadership, buy-in by parents, active engagement by the children, and ongoing professional development on the part of the teachers.

Key readings

Linse, C. 2005. *Practical English Language Teaching: Young Learners.* New York: McGraw-Hill. This book provides an accessible introduction to TEYL. Although relevant research is covered, the book is essentially practical, with many examples from textbooks as well as classroom extracts.

Nunan, D. 2011. *Teaching English to Young Learners.* Anaheim: Anaheim University Press. This book aims at providing a balanced coverage of theoretical, empirical and practical aspects of the teaching of English to young learners. A wide range of topics are covered including the use of technology in the classroom.

Pinter, A. 2006. *Teaching Young Language Learners.* Oxford: Oxford University Press. This book provides the most comprehensive coverage of the theory and research of teaching language to young learners. Through vignettes and examples, the book takes the reader into classrooms where children are being taught foreign languages.

Notes

I would like to thank Aaron Jolly for providing input for Case Study 2.

1   Brain lateralization refers to the process by which the two hemispheres of the brain become separated, and mental functions such as language learning and use become confined to one or other hemispheres.

2   All names in this case study have been changed to preserve the anonymity of the institution and the people involved.

3   'Scope and sequence' is the term used by publishers to refer to syllabus content underlying a textbook or course. This is usually set out as a chart at the beginning of the textbook.

4   A 'blended programme' is one in which instruction is delivered through technology as well as through face-to-face teaching.

References

Beatty, K. 2010. *Teaching and Researching Computer-Assisted Language Learning* (2nd edn). London: Pearson Education.

Cameron, D. 2001. *Teaching Languages to Young Learners.* Cambridge: Cambridge University Press.

Ellis, R. 1985. *Understanding Second Language Acquisition.* Oxford: Oxford University Press.

Linse, C. 2005. *Practical English Language Teaching: Young Learners.* New York: McGraw-Hill.

Nunan, D. 2003. The impact of English as a global language on educational policies and practices in the Asia-Pacific region. *TESOL Quarterly*, 37, 4.

Nunan, D. 2011. *Teaching English to Young Learners.* Anaheim: Anaheim University Press.

Pinter, A. 2006. *Teaching Young Language Learners.* Oxford: Oxford University Press.

Singleton, D. 1989. *Language Acquisition: The Age Factor.* Clevedon, Avon: Multilingual Matters.

17

TECHNOLOGICAL INNOVATION AND TEACHER CHANGE: IT IN TEACHER PROFESSIONAL DEVELOPMENT

Lillian L. C. Wong

Introduction

Rapid advancement of information technology (IT) is a powerful force for social, economic and educational change. Education systems around the world have introduced initiatives to respond to the IT imperative and to meet the demands of global knowledge economy in the IT-driven information age. Many scholars (e.g. Voogt & Knezek, 2008) observe that the use of new technologies is contributing to the rapid changes schools are facing. The investment and expectations in new technologies for teaching and learning are high and the challenges for teachers are numerous and complex. Teachers are not only expected to keep up with new technologies but also to integrate IT into their curricula and classroom practices to equip students with the skills of the information age.

This chapter reviews the factors that affect the incorporation of technological innovation in language teaching and the impact it has on teachers. Based on a two-year longitudinal study of a successful innovative programme by the Hong Kong government to help over 1,800 English teachers develop IT skills, it argues that the decisive factor for successful change lies with the teachers who implement changes in the classroom. The findings point to important relationships between pedagogy and technology as well as between the adoption of the technological innovation and teachers' beliefs and practices.

Technological innovation, teacher change and professional development

The incorporation of technology in language education, like other educational innovations, occurs at various levels and is affected by different factors. Kennedy

(1988, p. 332) uses a 'wheel within wheels' diagram to demonstrate the complex relationships – innovation in the classroom forms the core of the wheel, and institutional constraints, educational issues, administrative concerns, political issues and cultural factors are the levels that form progressively outer circles. Within these complex and dynamic systems, the decisive factor for effective and successful change is humans. As Paisey points out:

> Most crucially, an educational organization is operated by the persons who are themselves the instruments of change. Without their willingness and participation, there will be no change. (cited in White, 1988: 116)

At the heart of an innovation in education are teachers who implement changes in the classroom. A number of writers (e.g. Hall & Hewings, 2001; Hargreaves & Fullan, 2008; Lamie, 2005) have emphasized the importance of teachers in educational change and this includes technological innovations. As Marcinkiewicz (1993: 223) asserts:

> Full integration of computers into the education system is a distant goal unless there is reconciliation between teachers and computers. To understand how to achieve integration, we need to study teachers and what makes them use computers.

There has to be a match between teachers' beliefs about language teaching and learning and what they see as the capabilities of technology to support the successful introduction of technology in the classroom (Levy & Stockwell, 2006). Teachers' beliefs indicate their planning, organization, classroom decisions and practices, thus, their beliefs and principles are contextually significant to the implementation of innovations (Ertmer, 2005). The importance of introducing and understanding an innovation for its effective implementation from teachers' perceptions is highlighted by a number of studies (Fullan, 2007; Rogers, 2003; Wedell, 2009).

Breen et al. (1989: 118), for example, note the demands that teachers experienced in adopting an innovation in an in-service programme for teachers of English as a foreign language in secondary schools in a European country:

> By its nature, innovation entails teachers in the processes of personal readjustment and gradual accommodation in thinking and practice. The teacher needs time to make the ideas and practical suggestions his or her own; to interpret them and adapt them to particular classes and pupils ... to have time and means to evaluate any changes they bring to their classrooms from training.

The literature on the subject of innovation in education with technology shows that the greatest difficulties met by teachers are philosophical and pedagogical ones (Legutke, 2005). Technology often involves teachers changing their concepts of teaching and learning and their perceptions of their role as teachers. As a result, some researchers emphasize the value of IT adoption within the training experience itself (Mitchem et al., 2003), while others stress the value of situated learning experiences (Egbert et al., 2002) and mentoring by teachers with IT experience (Ward et al., 2002). Deep conceptual change is the focus of a new kind of professional development.

An essential element of successful change is the development of teachers (Richards & Farrell, 2005). Sociocultural perspectives of teacher learning focusing on inquiry-based approaches in supporting the professional development of teachers has been advocated in recent studies (Burns & Richards, 2009; Johnson, 2009). Active steps need to be taken to help teachers transit to the new mode of teaching and approach to pedagogy. Professional development has to assist teachers to explore and understand their own situations, the phenomenology of technological innovation and curricular change and to draw on their knowledge and skills to work out the most appropriate plans for their own classrooms and their own professional development.

The present study attempts to contribute to a better understanding of the process of change and adoption of the technological innovation of in-service secondary English teachers.

Case studies of teacher change and technological innovation

Context of the research

Information technology has become a powerful force for educational change in Hong Kong as in the rest of the world. In English language teaching and learning, preparing learners for the changing socio-economic demands resulting from advances in information technology was specified as one of the two overall aims of the Hong Kong English Language Education Curriculum Framework released in 1999 (Curriculum Development Council, 1999). As a consequence of this policy, many English teachers reported that up to 20 percent of their timetables might be allocated to Computer Assisted Language Learning (CALL) activities. As part of this IT initiative in English teaching, the Centre for Applied English Studies at the University of Hong Kong was commissioned by the Education Bureau to conduct a fifteen-hour in-service teacher training course on information technology for secondary-level English teachers. The course was run for three years, and about 1,800 teachers were trained; more than one in every four secondary English teachers.

The course was organized into five, three-hour topical sessions in Multimedia Learning Centres (MMLCs) and aimed at enhancing secondary school English teachers' knowledge, skills and strategies in using IT in teaching and learning. In the course, teachers were introduced to classroom uses of IT resources, including CALL CD-ROMs, the Internet, bulletin boards, chat rooms, *PuzzleMaker, D-Film, Hot Potatoes, Blackboard* and *HyperStudio*.

I was interested in the impact of this initiative on teachers' use of IT in their teaching after the course: specifically, in their perceptions of the value and role of technology in teaching and learning, and the impact of technological innovation on their pedagogical practices and belief systems.

Research design

The research was a two-year study using a case study approach to gain in-depth understanding of the process of IT integration in the particular contexts in which the teachers worked. Case studies have been found to be useful for studying educational innovations and evaluating programmes (e.g. Merriam, 1998). In this sense, a case study approach was particularly suitable for exploring the adoption and change process of the technological innovation.

The study comprised four stages: pre-course, during-course, end-of-course and post-course stages and a variety of methods were employed for collecting data:

- Pre-course: questionnaire
- During-course: end-of-lesson reflections in diary
- End-of-course: questionnaire and focus group discussions
- Post-course:
  - ○ video-recorded classroom observations, audio-recorded end-of-lesson interviews, analysis of lesson plans and teaching materials, teacher reflections in journals, email and telephone communications over a six month period immediately after the course
  - ○ a round-up interview following the analysis of the data
  - ○ a final interview and a final post-course questionnaire one year later.

I remained in regular contact with five volunteer teacher participants from the final cohort of the course for eighteen months after the course. I will now focus on two of these five teachers to explore their implementation of IT in their teaching contexts. Their contrasting experiences offer particular insights into the process of teacher change and adoption of the technological innovation.

Case studies

Ben, the subject of the first case study, is a Cantonese-speaking teacher who was fifty-two years old, with twenty-three years of teaching experience when he took the teacher training course. Patsy, the subject of the second case study, is a New Zealander who was fifty-five years old, also with over twenty years of teaching experience. Both sought to implement IT with one Form 3 (Grade 9) English class. Ben's school was a well-known high band English-medium school while Patsy's was a low band Chinese-medium school. Students in Ben's class were academically very strong and were highly proficient in English in general, while Patsy's class had a lower range of abilities in English. Ben's school was an IT pilot school, which was among the twenty leading schools in IT development in Hong Kong, while Patsy's school had standard infrastructure and support resources.

Ben and Patsy began from no experience using IT in teaching. On questionnaires administered at the beginning of the course, both Ben and Patsy rated themselves as 'not confident' with their IT skills and 'trying to learn the basics' while admitting frustration in using computers. At the end of the course, both rated themselves more highly and stated that they were 'beginning to understand the process of using technology' and felt more comfortable with IT. However, in the eighteen months that followed, Ben reported a drop in confidence in using IT; on the other hand, Patsy reported steady gains in confidence and having reached a high level of adoption of technology and integrating IT into the curriculum. As I will show in the case studies, this reflects the fact that Patsy experienced more success than Ben in her efforts in the process of change and the adoption of technological innovation.

Case study one: Ben

Ben graduated from a traditional elite English-medium secondary school and had a Teacher Certificate majoring in English. When he began the in-service teacher training course, he had been teaching in his current school for one year. Ben reported that he had some experience using word processing, but he had not used IT in teaching before the course.

In the six months that followed the course, Ben used the school MMLC twice to introduce two programs presented in the teacher training course to his students. On both occasions, he brought a teaching assistant to the class for technical support. In the first observed class, Ben spent a double lesson demonstrating the use of *Hot Potatoes*. This is a program that includes six applications for creating interactive exercises on the Internet, such as multiple-choice and gap-filling exercises. In the second observed class, Ben presented *D-Film* (a web-based animation program) for students to create animated dialogues. In between the two classes, Ben used a laptop twice in the classroom follow-up on the *Hot Potatoes* and *D-Film* activities.

In these classes, Ben stressed the use of the programs in a step-wise procedure but provided students with no guidance on language to develop meaningful content. Students were given very little time to work in class and they were requested to hand in their products as homework. As Ben said in the interview after the second observed class, 'I asked them, forced them to finish the product for me, to create the two exercises as homework'. Ben did not understand the interactive purposes of the programs and simply saw the class as an opportunity for practice exercises. His use of IT was simply for the sake of using it.

Ben's style of presenting the programs and requesting students to submit their work displays his teacher-centred approach to teaching. Classroom interactions largely involved Ben presenting and the students listening before doing individual work and receiving teacher's comments. During his presentation, Ben always sat down in front of the teacher computer and had the technical assistant lock all the students' computers. It was only after he had finished his presentation that students were allowed to use their computers. Instructions like 'You have no choice, the computers are locked, so stop pressing your keyboard' were noted repeatedly in the observed classes. Ben used the 'lock/unlock' function of the system to control students' behaviors in the MMLC.

This kind of teacher control was also observed in the classroom. As in the MMLC lessons, Ben sat down at the teacher's desk and spoke with a microphone. He was often serious and much involved in his own presentation of materials. In a double lesson, Ben lectured with three PowerPoint slide-shows and students were asked to do six pages of rewriting sentence exercises; each time no more than five minutes were given. Students reacted negatively to Ben's reliance on repetitive practice exercises and Ben was upset when students did not follow what he asked.

Ben's strong teacher-centred style of teaching was also revealed in his emphasis on correcting students' mistakes and checking all students' work. He explained that he needed to see students' 'real' work by asking them to print out the online interactive exercises they created in the first observed class:

> This is something I need *to have, very practical, very real* because what they have done just now, I don't know what sort of mistakes they have made, I don't have any idea, so I need to have a real copy of their exercise, and then I can *correct the mistakes* for them.

It can be seen that Ben perceived his teacher-centred teaching approach as appropriate and he was pleased with himself as an experienced teacher who could discipline his students to pay attention to his teaching. However, his classroom teacher-lecturing style and his maintaining of strict classroom discipline did not complement the use of IT.

Using IT in teaching was a big add-on to Ben and he needed to spend considerable time on preparation. Ben said he felt 'relieved' after the first class and described the process of preparation as 'torture' – it gave him 'a lot of pressure and frustration' putting the time, energy and effort needed in his technical preparation for the lessons using IT. He was aware of his limited IT knowledge and skills, and reported spending a week preparing a lesson. Indeed, it was noted that not only did his lack of IT knowledge and skills create negative feelings, but his choosing to use relatively technically complicated programs the first times using IT in teaching also intensified the whole situation. He was upset and did not know what to do when there was an Internet problem in the second observed class. He commented that he was 'really very weak' at computers. Ben's awareness of his limitations was evidenced throughout his implementation of IT and comments like this were common:

> I have a feeling that *I know so little* but it's not a negative feeling, it's just I feel if I could know better, *if I know more, then maybe things can be done better...*

Ben perceived using IT in teaching as 'to do and try new things' as he stated in the interview after the second observed lesson. The pressure he felt in using IT was because it was about learning new skills and knowledge in teaching and his awareness that his students were more capable than him:

> Sometimes I *look very stupid* because I *don't understand something even my students find that it is so simple (laughs)* then it is something *very frustrating.* The reason why such thing happens is because *my basic knowledge about computer is weak.* This is the *very, very cruel fact.*

His view of such 'very, very cruel fact' further revealed his strong teacher-centred belief as it seemed a face-losing issue to Ben.

In the final interview eighteen months after the training course, Ben admitted that he was 'a very traditional teacher' who had many years of teaching experience, and he would not change much of his practice. Moreover, he stated that his 'belief in teaching never changes' when he was asked about his experience in using technology:

> *Whether there is IT or not, will never affect my belief in teaching. IT is something luxurious, I can still teach very successfully without IT. I'm a language teacher, I have a lot of experience, I have a lot of material to help my student to learn English* and *I know how to make them feel interested in my lesson, without IT I can do this job very easily and successfully.* Of course I would say that *it is helpful* because the world is changing. I *always believe in IT because I know that this is a new, advanced technology,* the fact is only that I'm not good at it and then I'm *happy to learn it* and sometimes, maybe I feel sorry because *my skill is not as good as students,* some of the students are really good at it at computers.

This reflection shows that Ben had considerable confidence in himself as a teacher and a belief in the value of IT at the conceptual level. He believed in IT because it was a common trend to use computers and his students were good at computers; however, at the practical level, he felt his inadequate IT skills for teaching.

That Ben did not change his practice although he had positive beliefs about IT in teaching and learning might be because he did not recognize it as an integral part of the curriculum. Ben stressed a few times in the final interview:

> *IT is just a skill, a tool,* it's *just a way of another way of* teaching the language; it's nothing more.

To Ben, IT was a supplement, an add-on to him and to his teaching. As we will see in the next section, Patsy, the second case study teacher participant, appeared to have integrated IT into her teaching and experienced more success in her attempts to use IT.

Case study two: Patsy

Patsy was educated in New Zealand with a BA in Education and English as well as a Post-graduate Diploma in Second Language Teaching. She was a NET teacher (Native English Speaking Teacher) and Assistant Coordinator of the English Department and had been teaching English in her current school for three years when she began the in-service teacher training course. At the beginning of the course, Patsy reported that she had some experience of word processing, email and chat and that she had used the web to search for teaching materials, but she had not used IT in the classroom. Patsy also had strong beliefs about language teaching and her detailed resume emphasized her teaching approaches and philosophy:

> I am skilled in the *communicative approach* to language, and stress student involvement, participation and interaction ... I am committed to the use of *authentic materials* in the classroom and aim to ensure all teaching is appropriate, relevant and focused on *student needs and abilities.*

Integration of IT into the curriculum and concerns for students' needs were important aspects of using IT for Patsy. They were her goals in adopting IT from the beginning. After the course, Patsy prepared a well-planned and clearly focused scheme of work to implement IT using the Internet. The plan reflected her desire to use authentic materials that related to students' daily lives in her teaching. In the eighteen months that followed the course, Patsy used the Internet to extend topics covered in the school textbook, holding twelve classes on four topic-based units such as Vegetarianism, The Phantom of the Opera, Job hunting and Visiting Hong Kong in the first six months of implementation. In the three classes on the fourth topic of 'Visiting Hong Kong', for example, the students located websites on travel to Hong Kong, noted information on areas like weather, hotels, restaurants and shopping, and made PowerPoint presentations for the class. Patsy always prepared lesson plans and task sheets for activities for each unit.

Patsy incorporated authentic materials from the Internet into her teaching throughout and confirmed her belief in using authentic materials and perceived the benefits of the Internet in enhancing her students' learning:

> Oh definitely worth doing. Students find information that they want, they go to the vegetarian restaurants, they now know the websites, the sort of food, how much does it cost, and I want them to *learn the skills*, so that they could *apply them in their real life*. It's *authentic life experience*.

Patsy had a fairly clear idea of the role that the Internet could play in her students' learning by providing vast amounts of up-to-date and authentic information. Patsy also realized that students were using more English when they focused on activities using IT:

> They are *not speaking in mother tongue but using English*, using English in class from the start to finish, we may say we need to move on the curriculum, then they are still working with English, *they are really using the language, it must be useful*.

When asked at the end of the third observed session why she had chosen to focus on Internet activities, Patsy said:

> Oh, because I've been thinking about IT when I'm designing the programme… and I think *adding something to what they've been doing with the textbook*. I think, it adds to the *enjoyment*, to the *interest* they have and their willingness to work.

She believed her students were more motivated to learn and more focused on their learning when using computers. The positive learning atmosphere and attitude in turn contributed to good class discipline as remarked in the class observation notes that students were often all settled down within five minutes in the MMLC.

Her familiarity with the Internet, however, appears to have been the main factor in her choice of focus for units of work:

> It's not that difficult actually, once you get into it, you start thinking about it, I did the same thing, I thought I need somebody to give me a programme to use, *after the IT course I realized I could actually do things with IT, that doesn't involve spending money* …

Patsy credited the in-service teacher training course for helping her realize that she did not need to use specially designed software, but could build upon her existing IT knowledge. The fact that she did not need to experiment with various new software increased Patsy's confidence.

Patsy's strong belief in the student-centred approach was also displayed throughout her IT implementation. As in the interview after the third class observation, Patsy stated:

> So no matter the ability or capability of the teachers, *students bring a lot of knowledge themselves to the development,* we don't have to worry about seeking help, they know all that, they are better than I, I always think it's useful if you use what students know, and *they can help each other* ... I think it's really important.

Her student-centred style matched her beliefs about the role of IT in enabling students to become responsible learners.

> I feel more comfortable ... I'm not afraid to use the knowledge I learnt in the IT course ... I *feel comfortable with the students ... they were the experts.*

Such positive outcomes seemed to be owing to Patsy's openness and belief in student-centred learning and this was consistently demonstrated across all her lessons by her role as a facilitator in providing a supportive learning environment for students to explore and experience learning through IT. The class observation notes show that Patsy usually prepared task sheets for activities, and appeared comfortable teaching in the MMLC, giving clear instructions and guidelines, moving freely around the classroom to observe students' performance and offering help.

In the final interview a year after the implementation of IT, Patsy evaluated her success in using IT by reflecting on students' positive responses:

> I think with computers, *classes change from more teacher-centred to more student-centred.* It *helps with the interactions* between students because *they do help each other.* I'll get them to work and to encourage them to talk. But they do the discussion and make the decision ... And it gives me a chance to *walk in the environment around to work with individual students.*

Patsy realized the change of roles that IT required of the teacher and students, confirming that it could support student-centred learning, encourage collaboration among students, and enable more teacher support for individual students. These roles that IT facilitated thus aligned with Patsy's teaching beliefs and philosophy.

This positive attitude helped her to overcome various obstacles in implementing IT, such as, technical breakdowns, frustration with the layout of and access to the MMLC, the difficulty of the language that students found on the Internet, and a lack of interest and collaboration from other teachers. Patsy's attitude to problem-solving in the MMLC was reflected in a series of self-reflection comments that she wrote at the end of the first six months of implementation:

> *Development of confidence* in my use of MMLC and the use of IT with the students. From my observation of the videos of my lessons, I felt there was a *definite change in my ability* to present the lesson to the students, to explain what I wanted from them and to *actively participate in helping students in a positive way.*
>
> *Improved programme planning* as I developed the different units. I think I was unrealistic in what I expected students to complete in a lesson at the beginning of the programme and at first very little was actually finished. I need to improve further on this and keep the units of work simple and short while remaining challenging for students.

Patsy therefore viewed obstacles and problems as opportunities for learning and her engagement with IT as a process of development.

In the final interview conducted eighteen months after the training course, Patsy reported that she was using IT regularly and that it was now well-integrated with her teaching:

> I see IT integration as *using IT as an integral part of the programme, but not just a set of tasks.* It's used throughout the programme.
>
> I believe I have *enhanced my programme and improved my relationship with the students* ... it has *helped my professional development as a teacher.*

Patsy's successful adoption of IT and change exemplify the positive cyclical interactive effects among the teacher factors, student factors, and teacher professional development course.

Reflection

Ben and Patsy both learned a lot from their experience during and after the in-service teacher training course but by the end of the eighteen months after the course, Patsy had clearly been the more successful of the two in integrating technological innovation. While Patsy appeared to have become comfortable in using IT in her teaching, Ben felt frustrated and was struggling with many problems. As very experienced teachers who had taught for over twenty years, IT integration involved deep processes of change at both the professional and personal levels. Patsy seemed to have been far more open to change than Ben, and the obstacles to IT integration seemed bigger for him. It is important to recall, however, that both Ben and Patsy took on the initiative to adopt IT voluntarily and enthusiastically and they saw similar potential benefits for their students and themselves.

The two case studies indicate that the effectiveness of the integration of technological innovation is mediated in substantial ways. Teachers' beliefs about the roles and values of technology, about teaching and learning and about classroom roles are key influences in the extent an innovation is adopted.

Patsy had a strong commitment to student-centred learning with clear beliefs of how IT could be used to support this. She valued IT as the means to achieve her pedagogical goals and saw the importance of the opportunities and potentials that IT offered in enhancing teaching and learning. She perceived IT as an integral part of their teaching practices. There was an intimate connection between IT and her pedagogical beliefs: IT reinforced the kinds of beliefs she had about teaching and learning.

In contrast, Ben possessed teacher-centred transmission-oriented beliefs and did not see how he could use IT effectively. His belief in a regimented approach to teaching English was translated to his use of IT. Although he was interested in using IT to make a change to his teaching and believed in the benefits of IT for student motivation, he faced difficulties in understanding how technology-oriented activities could complement his curricula. His use of IT was to involve students learning about computer operations and software applications, so IT remained a separate activity unconnected to teaching English. He also struggled in organizing activities in a room full of computers for individual student access which were related to a sense of loss of teacher control in the classroom and a threat to his centre of authority. It appeared that despite being in an IT pilot school with considerable access to technology, Ben continued to see IT as abstract knowledge which he could not reconcile with his classroom .

Problems in using IT were seen as technical problems, and connected to his lack of IT skills but in fact, his difficulties were more related to his lack of understanding of the roles and potential of IT in teaching and learning in general and the IT tools he used in particular. His choice of IT applications showed that he simply found the tools attractive and believed that they could make his lessons more interesting. He tried relatively advanced and complicated programs in the very first lessons without a good understanding of their characteristics or pedagogical value and this simply intensified the technical and logistic problems he encountered. To solve this he switched to other tools, but these frequent changes meant that he constantly needed to face new problems and old problems in new contexts. Thus, Ben encountered a 'vicious circle' with more and more problems piling up. Lack of skills and knowledge, and the concomitant negative experiences in his initial tryouts with IT in teaching dampened enthusiasm and explained the ineffective IT adoption of Ben.

It is important to recall that both Patsy and Ben started with low IT skills and lack of IT experience in teaching. However, rather than trying various tools, Patsy chose to focus on the Internet, a technology that fitted her pedagogical beliefs of the communicative approach to language teaching and student-centred learning. Furthermore, she recycled tools and activities, with which she became more familiar progressively. Whenever she encountered technical problems, she knew that she could rely on her students who were IT 'experts': this was in principle with her beliefs in student-centred learning. Thus, Patsy appeared to have experienced fewer problems and obstacles at the beginning of her adoption of IT. Despite not having the expertise in IT, the initial positive experiences, which built up Patsy's confidence and enthused her to make greater exposure to teaching with IT, were directly linked to her fast rate of development and change.

As the discussion has shown, Patsy had clear student-centred learning briefs but Ben did not share pedagogical beliefs which aligned with using IT, they engaged in very different processes of change. IT integration for Patsy seemed a matter of coming to grips the way in which IT could support her clearly conceptualized pedagogical beliefs. However, for Ben, it was a matter both of coming to grips with IT and finding a pedagogical purpose for using IT meaningfully. Thus, IT integration was a much more complex process for Ben whose pedagogical beliefs did not relate to student-centred learning that is embedded in the changes with the adoption of IT.

Conclusion

This chapter shows that changes brought by technology challenge teachers' established beliefs and values, habits and practices. The analysis of the two case studies suggests that the effectiveness of integration of technological innovation into teaching and learning is closely linked to teachers' beliefs and pedagogical expertise. When the technology is aligned with teachers' pedagogy, the efforts in using technology are more likely to yield positive effects. In other words, when IT fits into teachers' frameworks of beliefs and practices, the integration is much more effective.

Technology in itself cannot transform classrooms; it is the pedagogical use of technology that can enhance teaching and learning. Thus, comprehensive professional development for technology should include not only the development of technological knowledge and skills, but also strategies for technology-enhanced teaching and learning, and for classroom management and practice. It should support teachers to understand the changes in teaching and learning process and the roles of teachers and students in the new technology-mediated environments. It should also help teachers develop theoretical and pedagogical competence in applying technology to facilitate meaningful learning and student-centred practices in their classrooms, and equip teachers for 'best practices' in IT integration, so technology will become a powerful tool that is useful to teachers in making the pedagogical shift from being the 'sage on the stage' to mentors who are 'guides on the side'. The emergence of new information technology provides an opportunity and a necessity for change. Teacher professional development plays an essential role in facilitating the process of change.

Key readings

Davison, C. (Ed.). (2005). *Information technology and innovation in language education*. Hong Kong: Hong Kong University Press. This book presents an investigation and critical analysis of developments and issues in the use of information technology in English language teaching internationally.

Hubbard, P. & Levy, M. (Eds.). (2006). *Teacher education in CALL*. Amsterdam; Philadelphia, PA: John Benjamins Publishing Company. This volume reports on experiences of CALL teacher education around the world. It includes research, theories, policies and practices in a wide variety of contexts.

References

Breen, M., Candlin, C., Dam, L., & Gabrielsen, G. (1989). The evaluation of a teacher training programme. In R. K. Johnson (Ed.), *Second language curriculum* (pp. 111–135). Cambridge: Cambridge University Press.

Burns, A., & Richards, J. C. (2009). *Cambridge guide to second language teacher education*. Cambridge: Cambridge University Press.

Curriculum Development Council. (1999). *Syllabuses for secondary schools. English Language (Secondary 1–5)*. Hong Kong: The Education Department.

Egbert, J., Paulus, T. M., & Nakamichi, Y. (2002). The impact of call instruction on classroom computer use: a foundation for rethinking technology in teacher education. *Language Learning and Technology*, 6 (3): 108–126.

Ertmer, P. A. (2005). Teacher pedagogical beliefs: the final frontier in our quest for technology integration? *Educational Technology Research and Development*, 53(4): 25–39.

Fullan, M. (2007). *The new meaning of education change (Fourth Edition)*. New York: Teachers College Press.

Hall, D., & Hewings, A. (Eds.). (2001). *Innovation in English language teaching*. London: Routledge.

Hargreaves, A. & Fullan, M. (Eds.). (2008). *Change wars*. Bloomington: Solution Tree.

Johnson, K. E. (2009). *Second language teacher education: a sociocultural perspective*. New York: Routledge.

Kennedy, C. (1988). Evaluation of the management of change in ELT projects. *Applied Linguistics*, 9(4): 329–342.

Lamie, J. M. (2005). *Evaluating change in English language teaching*. Basingstoke: Palgrave Macmillan.

Legutke, M. K. (2005). Redesigning for foreign language classroom: a critical perspective on information technology and educational change. In C. Davison (Ed.), *Information technology and innovation in language education* (pp. 127–148). Hong Kong: Hong Kong University Press.

Levy, M. & Stockwell, G. (2006). *CALL dimensions: options and issues in computer-assisted language learning*. Mahwah, New Jersey: Lawrence Erlbaum Associates.

Marcinkiewicz, H. R. (1993). Computers and teachers: factor influencing computer use in the classroom. *Journal of Research in Computing in Education*, 26: 220–237.

Merriam, S. (1998). *Qualitative research and case study applications in education*. San Francisco: Jossey-Bass Publishers.

Mitchem, K., Wells, D. L. & Wells, J. G. (2003). Effective integration of instructional technologies (IT): evaluating professional development and instructional change. *Journal of Technology and Teacher Education*, 11(3): 397–414.

Richards, J. C. & Farrell, T. S. C. (2005). *Professional development for language teachers: strategies for teacher learning*. New York: Cambridge University Press.

Rogers, E. M. (2003). *The diffusion of innovations* (Fifth Edition). New York: The Free Press.

Voogt, J. & Knezek, G. (Eds.) (2008). *International handbook of information technology in primary and secondary education*. New York: Springer.

Ward, J. R., West, L. S. & Isaak, T. J. (2002). Mentoring: a strategy for change in teacher technology education. *Journal of Technology and Teacher Education, 10* (4): 553–569.

Wedell, M. (2009). *Planning for educational change – putting people and their contexts first*. London: Continuum.

White, R. (1988). *The ELT curriculum: design, innovation and management*. Oxford: Blackwell.

18

INNOVATION IN ASSESSMENT: COMMON MISCONCEPTIONS AND PROBLEMS

Chris Davison

Introduction

Assessment for learning (AfL), a concept first used in the UK in the late 1980s, and widely promoted through the work of the Assessment Reform Group (Assessment Reform Group, 1999, 2001; Black & Wiliam, 1998), refers to any assessment in which the primary purpose of the information being collected is to improve learning. AfL has been adopted as educational policy in a wide range of educational systems around the world, including in English language education. However, the process of initiating and implementing such innovative assessment approaches, especially in very traditional exam-oriented educational systems, can pose particular challenges.

Drawing on data from a range of questionnaires, interviews with key stakeholders and teachers, and the analysis of policy documents collected as part of a number of recent research and development studies undertaken by the author in Hong Kong, Singapore, and Brunei, this chapter will explore some of the common misunderstandings and conceptual confusions that arise in educational communities during the process of assessment innovation, arguing that although the current emphasis on the teacher as an agent of change in educational innovation is important, there also needs to be a focus on the educational system itself as a mediator of change. The implications of the findings for research, policy and practice will also be discussed.

The nature of the innovation: assessment for learning

Assessment for learning (AfL) is a core component of assessment policy in a number of educational systems internationally, including Australia and New Zealand, Canada, and the United Kingdom (e.g., Cumming & Maxwell,

2004; Learning and Teaching Scotland, 2006; New Zealand Education Gazette, 2002; Saskatchewan Learning, 1993), and in some states of the USA (Stiggins, 2008). It is also increasingly being adopted as national educational policy in Asia (e.g. Curriculum Development Institute, Hong Kong, 2002; Ministry of Education, Singapore, 2008; Ministry of Education, Brunei, 2011) as well as in many developing countries.

The term AfL was coined to ensure 'a clear distinction be made between *assessment of learning* for the purposes of grading and reporting, which has its own well-established procedures, and *assessment for learning* which calls for different priorities, new procedures and a new commitment' (Assessment Reform Group, 1999, p.2). The key characteristics of 'assessment' in AfL include:

1. assessment is embedded in teaching and learning;
2. learning goals are explicitly shared with students and students are taught how to know and to recognize the standards they are aiming for;
3. students are engaged in continuous peer and self-assessment;
4. constructive qualitative feedback helps students to recognize the next steps needed for learning and how to take them;
5. teachers, parents and students regularly review and reflect on assessment data;
6. it is assumed every student can improve (adapted from the Assessment Reform Group, 1999: 7).

The term 'assessment for learning' is often used synonymously with the term 'formative assessment', but recently many researchers have been calling for a sharper distinction to be made between the two terms (Kennedy et al., 2006; Roos & Hamilton, 2005; Taras, 2005). Traditionally, formative assessment is perceived as informal and fairly frequent, the gathering of information about students and their needs while they are still learning, in contrast to 'summative' assessment, the more formal planned assessments at the end of a unit or term/year used to evaluate student progress and/or grade students. In an assessment *of* learning culture, formative and summative assessment are distinctly different in both form and function, and teacher and assessor roles clearly demarcated, but in an assessment *for* learning culture, even summative assessments of the students' language skills can and should also be used formatively to give constructive student feedback and improve learning (for example, see Biggs, 1998; Carless, 2008; Davison, 2007; Davison & Hamp-Lyons, 2009; Hamp-Lyons, 2007; Harlen, 2005; Kennedy, 2006). Kennedy (2006, p.4) proposes that in this more inclusive model of assessment:

1. All assessment needs to be conceptualized as assessment *for* learning.
2. Feedback needs to be seen as a key function for all forms of assessment.

3. Teachers need to be seen as playing an important role not only in relation to formative assessment but in all forms of summative assessment as well – both internal and external.
4. Decisions about assessment need to be viewed in a social context since in the end they need to be acceptable to the community.

Kennedy argues that 'the continuing bifurcation between formative and summative assessment is no longer useful, despite the fact that such a distinction has resulted in some excellent research and development work on formative assessment' (p.14). He disputes Roos and Hamilton's view (2005) that summative assessment as a procedure is too deeply entrenched to become, in their words, to become 'a valid activating mechanism for goal-directed educational activities', supporting Biggs (1998) who also argues that an exclusive focus on formative assessment leaves many negative summative assessment practices uncontested, a major problem at the systemic level given summative assessment has such a significant influence on student learning, often negative backwash undermining any of the positive impacts of formative assessment. In fact, as has been well-documented in systems such as Hong Kong and Singapore (e.g., Cheah, 1998; Hamp-Lyons, 2007), it is extremely difficult to sustain any significant teacher-based formative assessment practices in most traditional examination-dominated cultures, hence the call for greater consideration of tests as productive learning opportunities (Carless, 2008).

'Formative' assessment itself is also being problematized (Black & Wiliam, 2009; Leung, 2004). In AfL, formative assessment has two key functions: informing and shaping the decisions about what to do next, by helping both the teacher decide what to teach next, and, even more importantly, the student understand what they have learnt and what they need to learn next (Black, 2001; Black & Wiliam, 1998; Black et al., 2003). The learner's role is crucial, for it is the learner who does the learning. However, as Torrance (1993: 340) argued some years ago, many teachers are at risk of assuming formative assessment is at best 'fairly mechanical and behaviouristic ... in the graded test tradition'; at worst summative, 'taking snapshots of where the children have "got to", rather than where they might be going next':

> The term 'formative' itself is open to a variety of interpretations and often means no more than that assessment is carried out frequently and is planned at the same time as teaching. Such assessment does not necessarily have all the characteristics just identified as helping learning. It may be formative in helping the teacher to identify areas where more explanation or practice is needed. But for the pupils, the marks or remarks on their work may tell them about their success or failure but not about how to make progress towards further learning (Assessment Reform Group, 1999, p.7)

Black and Wiliam (1998) convincingly demonstrate the learning gains that can be achieved through well-focused, teacher-based formative assessment, claiming no other strategy has such potential for enhancing student learning across age levels and in different contexts. In a more recent meta-study of major influences on educational achievement, Hattie (2009) also found that formative practice, in particular self-assessment and feedback, had the highest effect sizes (i.e., impact on student outcomes) out of more than 100 different instructional and contextual factors. Because of this and other very compelling research, AfL has been taken up in so-called 'mature' assessment cultures (for example, see DET NSW, 2008). However, somewhat paradoxically, under the influence of the OECD (2005), AfL has been embraced much more strongly as the centrepiece of assessment reform in a range of traditional examination cultures, including Brunei, Hong Kong and Singapore. Increasingly, through 'top-down', or 'imposed change' (Fullan, 2001), English and other teachers in these small nation-states are being called upon to plan and/or implement appropriate assessment procedures to monitor and evaluate student progress in their own classroom, including designing and implementing their own classroom-based assessment tasks, actively engaging learners in self and peer assessment and incorporating critical but constructive feedback into the assessment cycle (Davison, 2007; Davison & Leung, 2009). The next section will briefly explore the background and context to these assessment reforms, as well as their overarching goals and rationales, and implementation strategies, through a comparative case study of three nation-states.

A comparative case study: assessment for learning in Hong Kong, Singapore and Brunei

Although they vary in size of population, Hong Kong, Singapore and Brunei have many commonalities, all post-colonial societies but still with strong educational influences and ties to Britain, hierarchical cultures with relatively conservative governing structures which predispose them towards top-down, rather than bottom-up, processes of educational change. With few natural resources (other than ever-diminishing oil reserves in Brunei), all are striving to develop twenty-first century skills and high levels of English language competence to ensure strong employment and economic growth. Thus, they have been particularly receptive to OECD calls for the establishment of assessment for learning as a way of raising student achievement, improving literacy skills and enhancing global competiveness.

In Hong Kong, assessment for learning (AfL) underpins the recent development of a school-based assessment (SBA) component in secondary English language teaching (Davison, 2007; Davison & Hamp-Lyons, 2009). The stated purpose of SBA is to provide a more comprehensive appraisal of learners' achievement by assessing aspects of English language learning that cannot be easily assessed in public examinations whilst at the same time enhancing teaching and learning. The initiative marks a shift from traditional norm-referenced, externally set and assessed examinations, towards a more student-centered, teacher-based assessment system that draws its philosophical basis from the assessment for learning movement discussed above, officially adopted as educational policy in Hong Kong in 2002 (Curriculum Development Institute, 2002: 5):

> Based on the beliefs that every student is unique and possesses the ability to learn, and that we should develop their multiple intelligences and potentials ... there should be a change in assessment practices and schools should put more emphasis on 'Assessment for Learning' as an integral part of the learning, teaching and assessment cycle ... teachers should use assessments (e.g. as simple as effective verbal questioning, observation of student behaviour) and provide immediate feedback to enhance student learning in everyday classroom lessons. The focus is on why they do not learn well and how to help them to improve rather than just to use assessments to find out what knowledge students have learned.

In SBA, teachers are involved at all stages of the assessment cycle, from planning the assessment programme, to identifying and/or developing appropriate formative and summative assessment activities right through to making the final judgments. In-class formal and informal performance assessment of students' authentic oral language skills using a range of tasks and guiding questions and the use of teacher judgments of student performance using common assessment criteria are innovative aspects of the new school-based assessment scheme, as is the insistence on students playing an active role in the assessment process, with self and/or peer assessment and feedback vigorously promoted (see SBA Consultancy Team, 2005, 2008, 2010 for more detail).

In Singapore, assessment for learning was adopted as educational policy in 2008 as an integral component of the new English language syllabus (Ministry of Education Singapore, 2008: 3):

> For teaching and learning to be effective, teachers will identify and monitor pupils' changing needs, abilities and interests so that they can modify or adapt their teaching methods to help pupils improve their learning. Teachers will also give timely and useful feedback to pupils and provide them with opportunities to act on the feedback to improve their learning. Together, the processes of diagnosing pupils' needs, abilities and interests, monitoring pupils' learning progress, and feeding-forward to improve learning constitute Assessment *for* Learning (A*f*L).

However, in Singapore, unlike Hong Kong, there have been relatively few changes to the traditional examination system thus far, but a much larger investment in curriculum and professional development to establish assessment for learning communities at the school level.

In Brunei, the adoption of a new educational policy, called SPN 21, in 2008, led to the introduction of school-based assessment in the first two years of secondary school, but without any fundamental change in the use of assessment information or the mode of assessment, and no 'move away from a summative system to a more educational purpose of assessing student progress or achievement' that had been so strongly advocated (MOE Brunei, 2008). Hence, from early 2010, assessment for learning has been systematically integrated into school-based assessment to promote a change in the philosophy, termed SBAfL, to integrate assessment with teaching and learning, ensure students take more responsibility for their learning and provide teachers and students with qualitative information on how students are progressing in English, as well as in five other core subjects (MOE Brunei, 2011: 8):

> At the informal end of the continuum, assessment of student progress is purely formative, often spontaneous actions by the teacher and focused on the learning process. Teachers may use various strategies such as prompting to help scaffold the student towards their personal best. Here students are provided with low-stakes activities as they are not graded for summative purposes. As we move up the continuum, the assessment activities and tasks begin to take on a more formal character, but are still low-stakes ... At the very formal end of the continuum, assessment tasks are prescribed and are both formative and summative in nature. These ... Brunei Common Assessment Tasks (BCATs) ... have formative purposes as well (with) self and peer assessment and teacher feedback before and after each BCAT assessment.

Assessment in SBAfL encompasses a variety of modes such as research projects, practical experiments, oral presentations, drama performances, role-play, portfolios, video productions, listening tasks, discussion leading and journal writing, where the learning outcomes cannot be assessed through conventional written tests. Teachers design lessons and assessment tasks to cater for all student learning levels, ensure that students are aware of the learning outcomes, develop rubrics for the assessment tasks and explicitly share them with the students; encourage self and peer assessment, give effective feedback to students (i.e. where they are on their 'learning journey' (a term also used in Singapore), what the next level of achievement is and what they need to do to reach that next level); make valid and reliable judgments of students' achievements and share student samples with other teachers during social standardization meetings.

In all three systems, the widespread concern about lack of student engagement in learning and the dominance of the exam-oriented curriculum provided the initial spark for the introduction of assessment for learning, with each nation borrowing and improving on the others' assessment innovations. Substantial resources were provided for professional development and for curriculum materials, but the implicit assumption at the system level was that having provided the incentive, the input and the professional development, adoption of the innovation would then be relatively straightforward, but this was not the case. This raises the whole issue of the nature of educational change and the problems of implementing assessment for learning at a systemic, not just classroom level.

Assessment innovation: common misconceptions and problems

With increased focus on larger scale reform, government agencies are becoming more adept at combining 'pressure and support' forces in order to stimulate and follow through in achieving greater implementation (Fullan, 2001: 87), but there were still problems in the early stages of assessment reform in Hong Kong, Singapore and Brunei. Data from a range of questionnaires, interviews with key stakeholders and teachers, and the analysis of policy documents collected as part of a number of recent research and development studies undertaken by the author identified recurring common misunderstandings and conceptual confusions in all three educational communities as assessment for learning was introduced on a system-wide scale. Some of these problems were predicted by the literature on educational change, others seemed to be particular to the nature of the innovation itself. These misconceptions and problems will be elaborated below.

First, as predicted in the literature, there was some initial confusion as to the nature of the innovation with superficial adjustment in the format, frequency and feedback of assessments, Fullan's (2001) 'false clarity', followed much later by more fundamental changes to the purposes of assessment (i.e., more emphasis on enhancing learning and teaching) and teacher and student roles (i.e., involving learners more actively in evaluating and improving their own learning). Teachers also vary significantly in how quickly and easily they will grasp the central concepts of AfL. One Hong Kong English teacher reported in the midst of the early assessment reform in 2006: 'It's a good piece of assessment, but it's not a good piece of....ah.....it doesn't actually help them. *It helps us to assess them, but it doesn't help them to progress,*' but many other Hong Kong teachers are still grappling with what it means to enable students to demonstrate their best long after AfL is assumed to be standard practice (Davison & Hamp-Lyons, 2009).

In Brunei, some teachers report assessment practices already aligned with AfL, other teachers struggle to break free of their marking 'mindset'. Research shows that such variation is normal, and that innovations are always implemented in various ways and with varying levels of quality (Roy & Hord, 2004). This highlights the danger of adopting a fidelity approach to educational innovation which assumes the task for the teacher is to faithfully implement an already developed innovation in the way the developer intended. Rather, research shows change is often a result of adaptations and decisions made by teachers as they work with new ideas and materials. However, the innovation's key characteristics and actual uptake (ranging from ideal implementation to non-use along a continuum) need to be identified, so we can know what the innovation looks like in practice, and whether quality implementation has occurred, to create an image of the innovation that we can carry in our minds and a vision toward which the system can move. Even then, research shows it takes at least three years for early concerns to be resolved and later ones to emerge (Hall & Hoard, 2001).

Second, also as predicted, there was an inevitable lack of understanding among those initiating the assessment reform of the nature and extent of support needed and the time required to set up quality, teacher-based assessment, including the development of differentiated assessment tasks, much more difficult and time-consuming to construct than traditional testing and/or impressionistic marking (Fox, 2008), and mechanisms to ensure teachers (and students) are making consistent and trustworthy assessment decisions (Davison 2004; Davison & Leung, 2009; Rea-Dickins, 2007). For AfL to be successfully implemented, teachers need access to a range of models, exemplars and work samples and the establishment of structured opportunities to share practices and benchmark with other classes, schools and even educational systems through face-to-face and online communities of practice. Research shows that a fundamental requirement for the successful implementation of any educational innovation is a supportive environment, including time, materials, and organizational structures that encourage people to experiment and that establish collaborative structures for professional dialogue (Penney & Fox, 1997).

However, the greatest stumbling block to assessment reform in these three different educational systems was the initial misconception among policy makers that assessment for learning simply meant changes in assessment practice, when what was required was a change in the whole assessment culture (Davison & Leung, 2009). Contrary to most predictions, teachers were not the 'problem'. As soon as the new assessment systems were piloted, student enthusiasm seemed to provide most teachers with the impetus for change, with many teachers commenting that even though the innovation greatly increased their workload, it was worth it because of the significant improvement in student engagement and in learning outcomes. Their students' positive response to the change in assessment practices encouraged teachers to rethink their attitudes to assessment, and to gradually adopt new beliefs and processes, which then led to even greater uptake of the assessment innovation, a pattern reported more widely in the literature on educational change (Stein, McRobbie, and Ginns, 1999), and further confirmation that teachers' attitudes are crucial in determining the success or failure of innovation (Hargreaves, 1994; Hargreaves et al., 2001).

However, teachers do not work in isolation; their attitudes and beliefs about change are inextricably linked to those of other members of the educational community, not just colleagues, but supervisors, parents and students. In particular, Fullan (2001) highlights the role of the school leaders, including principals and district administrators, in legitimating change and providing teachers with both psychological and material support (see also Wideen, 1994). They are the people most likely to be in a position to shape the organizational conditions necessary for success, such as the development of shared goals, collaborative work structures and climates, and procedures for monitoring results. When illustrating the problems that a principal might confront, Fullan (2001: 83) argues that:

> The subjective world of principals is such that many of them suffer from the same problem in 'implementing a new role as facilitator of change' as do teachers in implementing new teaching roles: What the principal should do specifically to manage change at the school level is a complex affair for which the principal has little preparation. The psychological and sociological problems of change that confront the principal are at least as great as those that confront teachers. Without this sociological sympathy, many principals feel exactly as teachers do: Other people simply do not seem to understand the problems they face.

Fullan (2001) concludes that whether or not implementation succeeds depends on the congruence between the reformers and local needs, and how the changes are introduced and followed through. The quality of the relationships between reformers and those impacted by the reform is crucial in supporting change efforts when there is agreement, and to reconciling problems when there is conflict among these groups: between ministries, and local school boards, administrators, and teachers; between state departments and local districts; and between project officers and local authorities. Fullan argues that the difficulties in the relationship between external and internal groups are central to the problem and process of meaning. Not only is meaning difficult to grasp when two different worlds have limited interactions, but misinterpretation, attribution of motives, feelings of being misunderstood, and disillusionment on both sides are almost guaranteed.

Such conflict is inevitable when the system itself is not seen as part of the reform process. In all three nation-states in this case study, there were distinct stages in the assessment reform when it became clear that there was a direct conflict between what was expected of teachers in their 'new' approach to assessment in the classroom, and what was still entrenched as assessment practice at the system level. As one teacher in Brunei posted so eloquently on a common website set up to assist assessment reform:

> How can we go on with our efforts on focusing on students' needs
> when accountability is still an issue every teacher has to deal with?
> Accountability such as in submitting marks every single week to an
> authorit(y) and then *if no marks are submitted, we are thought to be
> doing nothing in the class?*

In Hong Kong, the examination system needed to change so it was more
closely aligned with AfL principles, with 'marking criteria' made public and
standards–referenced assessment introduced with reports in profiles and
levels. In Singapore, the traditional examination system proved less open to
change which meant the initial approach adopted to the introduction of AfL
had to be revised and instead AfL systematically integrated into the curriculum.
In Brunei, not only was there an initial lack of alignment with the examination
system, but the inspectorate was also shackled with an outdated monitoring
and evaluation system which no longer matched the expected assessment
practices, and the delay in the development of an outcomes-oriented
curriculum meant initial efforts to introduce AfL were limited by a lack of
common standards and expectations.

In all systems there were initial delays in communicating the nature of the
assessment reforms to key stakeholders, especially principals and parents, in
ways which provided them with a sense of clarity and control. Examples of
direct conflict between the expressed aims of the assessment reform and the
ways in which the reform was implemented at the system level were endemic,
and far more difficult to change than teacher practice. At the same time, these
entrenched systemic structures and practices inhibited and blocked what
teachers and their students could actually implement in terms of AfL at the
chalkface. In other words, ironically, the greatest stumbling block to assessment
reform was a failure of policy makers to practice what they preached.

Reflection on assessment innovation

This short case study demonstrates that to implement assessment for learning,
systemic assessment reform needs to start with the institutional assessment
culture and work backwards to the school communities and individual
learners and teachers. Thus, the key questions to guide AfL reform should
focus on what kind of learners, teachers and school communities does the
system value and want to develop. If the response is, as it is most likely to be,
'self-regulating, independent, creative, critical, engaged learners', policy
makers need to ask what kinds of learners, teachers and school communities
are in the assessment system now, and how can they be supported to move
forward. In other words, what kind of system-level structures and processes
of change can be adopted for the implementation of AfL that are theoretically
and philosophically consistent with assessment for learning, and that can
model desired outcomes and lead – by example – to sustainable improvements

in assessment, learning and teaching at the same time ensuring maintenance of community confidence in the assessment system. Hence, I propose a parallel set of key characteristics of 'assessment' reform for the introduction and development of AFL at the system level, adapted from the original tenets of the Assessment Reform Group (1999: 7), that is:

1. AFL is embedded in curriculum and assessment institutionally and pedagogically;
2. assessment reform goals are explicitly shared with all stakeholders and stakeholders together work to identify how to know and to recognize the standards they are aiming for;
3. all stakeholders are engaged in continuous peer and self-assessment;
4. constructive qualitative feedback helps stakeholders to recognize the next steps needed for reform and how to take them;
5. all stakeholders regularly review and reflect on assessment data;
6. it is assumed every school, teacher and student can improve.

In such a system, AfL is not just a target of assessment reform but a mediating influence, in fact, a driver of how to achieve such reform. This is the overarching framework for assessment reform now being adopted in Singapore and Brunei to ensure that all parts of the system align or cohere. In Hong Kong it will need to be the basis of any evaluation of assessment reform, so that it is not individual teachers or even schools that are held accountable for the ultimate success of any educational innovation, but the system itself.

Implications for research, policy and practice

There are several implications of this case study for research, policy and practice. In terms of research, this case study suggests that it is misleading, even dangerous, to look at only one component of assessment reform, that many factors and processes need to be taken into account in designing and evaluating new assessment systems and that the assessment culture, not just assessment practice, need to be examined. As Hargreaves and Evans (1997) argue, theories of educational change which focus primarily on technical factors are the product of a positivist epistemology that assumes 'a set of logical rules of explanation, independent of the world and its social practices' (Usher et al., 1997, p. 176), failing to recognize that knowledge is personal, subjective, developed and interpreted within a unique social context. The importance of programs, policy, directives, school regulations and recommendations to the successful implementation of change needs to be acknowledged, but educational change is fundamentally shaped by what teachers believe, by what their peers and leaders believe and do, and by the culture they create together.

For policy makers wanting assessment reform, it is clear that they need to model and practice the kinds of attributes they want to inculcate in their teachers and students if reform is to be successful. This means not only providing appropriate professional development and making significant changes in pre-service education to support assessment reforms, but changing all the other components of the systems including curriculum and syllabus documents, external examinations, teacher performance appraisal systems, inspection and accountability procedures and decision-making structures. At the classroom level, teachers also need to ensure their practices model the behaviors they want their students to demonstrate. Such changes will also help develop the other vital ingredient in successful assessment reform, that is, the quality of relationships among the various stakeholders. As Fullan (2009) argues, if policymakers and practitioners are ignorant of each other's subjective worlds, then innovation and implementation will fail.

The author would like to thank her colleagues who contributed so much to these cross-national research perspectives, in particular Kalthom Ahmad, Cheri Chan, Brian Galbraith, Liz Hamp-Lyons and Wendy Leung.

Key readings

Glasson, T. (2008). *A practical guide to assessment for learning*. Melbourne: Curriculum Corporation. This book and accompanying DVDs provides practical guidance for teachers to help them use assessment for learning effectively in the classroom. It explains how a focus on learning intentions, success criteria, effective teacher and peer feedback, strategic questioning, student self-assessment and the formative use of summative assessment, helps teachers to encourage students to take more responsibility for their learning, thereby improving performance. The book supports the Assessment for Learning website, www. assessmentforlearning.edu.au.

SBA Consultancy Team (2010). *2012 HKDSE English Language Examination: Introduction to the School-based Assessment Component*. Hong Kong: HKEAA, http://www.hkeaa.edu.hk/DocLibrary/SBA/HKDSE/Eng_DVD/index.html. This multimedia resource is aimed at Hong Kong teachers to help them use assessment for learning effectively in the classroom as part of the SBA component of senior secondary English. It describes and illustrates the key characteristics of AfL and provides a number of video-case studies and interviews with leading AfL practitioners, including Dylan Wiliam and the author.

References

Assessment Reform Group. (1999). *Assessment for learning: Beyond the black box.* Cambridge: University of Cambridge School of Education. Retrieved 2 February 2012 from http://arg.educ.cam.ac.uk/AssessInsides.pdf
Assessment Reform Group. (2001). *Assessment for learning: 10 principles.* Retrieved 2 February 2012 from http://www.assessment-reform-group.org.uk.
Biggs, J. (1998). Assessment and classroom learning: A role for formative assessment? *Assessment in Education: Principles, Policy and Practice*, 5(1): 103–110.
Black, P. (2001). Formative assessment and curriculum consequences. In D. Scott (Ed.), *Curriculum and assessment.* Westport, CT: Ablex Publishing.
Black, P. & Wiliam, D. (1998). Assessment and classroom learning. *Assessment in Education*, 5(1): 7–74.

Black, P. & Wiliam, D. (2009). Developing the theory of formative assessment. *Educational Assessment, Evaluation and Accountability, 21*: 5–31.

Black, P., Harrison, C., Lee, C., Marshall, B. & Wiliam, D. (2003). *Assessment for learning*. New York: Open University Press.

Carless, D. (2008). Developing productive synergies between formative and summative assessment processes. In M. F. Hui & D. Grossman (Eds.). *Improving teacher education through action research* (pp. 9–23). New York: Routledge.

Cheah, Y. M. (1998). The examination culture and its impact on literacy innovations: The case of Singapore. *Language and Education, 12*(3): 192–209.

Curriculum Development Institute (2002). School policy on assessment: Changing assessment practices. In *Basic education curriculum guide: Building on strength, Chpt 5*. Hong Kong: Curriculum Development Institute.

Cumming, J. J. & Maxwell G. S. (2004). Assessment in Australian schools: Current practice and trends. *Assessment in Education, 11*(1): 89–108.

Davison, C. (2004). The contradictory culture of classroom-based assessment: Teacher-based assessment practices in senior secondary English. *Language Testing, 21* (3): 304–333.

Davison, C. (2007). Views from the chalkface: School-based assessment in Hong Kong. *Language Assessment Quarterly, 4* (1): 37–68.

Davison, C. & Hamp-Lyons, L. (2009) The Hong Kong Certificate of Education: School-based assessment reform in Hong Kong English language education. In L-Y. Cheng and A. Curtis (Eds.). *English language assessment and the Chinese learner*. London: Routledge.

Davison, C. & Leung, C. (2009). Current issues in English language teacher-based assessment. *TESOL Quarterly, 43* (3): 393–415.

Department of Education (NSW). (2008). Assessment for Learning in the new Years 7–10.Syllabuses. Retrieved 9 Feb 2011, from http://arc.boardofstudies.nsw.edu.au/go/sc/afl/.

Fox, J. (2008). Alternative assessment. In E. Shohamy & N. H. Hornberger (Eds.). *Encyclopedia of language and education: Language testing and assessment* (2nd ed., vol. 7, pp. 97–108). New York: Springer.

Fullan, M. (2001). *The new meaning of educational change*. New York: Teacher's College Press.

Fullan, M. (Ed.). (2009). *The challenge of change: Start school improvement now!* (2nd edn). Thousand Oaks, CA: Corwin Press.

Hall, G. E. & Hord, S. M. (2001). *Implementing change: Patterns, principles, and potholes*. Boston: Allyn and Bacon.

Hamp-Lyons, L. (2007). The impact of testing practices on teaching: Ideologies and alternatives. In Cummins, J. & Davison, C. (Eds.). *The international handbook of English language teaching, Vol. 1*. (pp. 487–504). Norwell, MA: Springer.

Hargreaves, A. (1994). *Changing teachers, changing times: Teachers' work and culture in the postmodern age*. London: Cassell.

Hargreaves, A., Earl, L., Moore, S. & Manning, S. (Eds.). (2001). *Learning to change: Teaching beyond subjects and standards*. San Francisco: Jossey-Bass and Barcelona: Octaedro.

Hargreaves, A., & Evans, R. (1997). Teachers and educational reform. In R. Evans (Ed.). *Beyond educational reform: Bringing teachers back in* (pp. 1–18): Buckingham; Philadelphia: Open University Press.

Harlen, W. (2005). Teachers' summative assessment practices and assessment for learning. Tensions and synergies. *The Curriculum Journal, 16*(2): 207–223.

Hattie, J. (2009). *Visible learning: A synthesis of over 800 meta-analyses relating to achievement*. New York: Routledge.

Kennedy, K., Chan, J. K., Yu, F. W. M. & Fok, P. K. (2006). *Assessment for productive learning: Forms of assessment and their potential for enhancing learning*. Paper presented at the 32nd Annual Conference of the International Association for Educational Assessment, Singapore, 21–26 May.

Learning and Teaching Scotland. (2006). *Assessment is for learning programme.* Retrieved on 2 October 2007 from http://www.ltscotland.org.uk/assess/about/index.asp.

Leung, C. (2004). Developing formative teacher-based assessment: Knowledge, practice and change. *Language Assessment Quarterly, 1* (1): 19–41.

Ministry of Education, Brunei (2008). *SPN21 Interim Guidelines.* Brunei: Ministry of Education.

Ministry of Education, Brunei (2011). School Based Assessment for Learning Brunei Darussalam SBAfL Guidebook for Years 7 and 8 Core Subjects. Brunei: Curriculum Development Department.

Ministry of Education Singapore (2008). *2012 English language syllabus.* Singapore: Government Printer.

New Zealand Education Gazette. (2002). *Better assessment likely.* Retrieved on 2 July 2009 from http://www.edgazette.govt.nz/articles.php/show_articles.php?id=6155.

OECD. (2005). Formative assessment: Improving learning in secondary classrooms. Paris: OECD.

Penney, D. and Fox, B. (1997). 'At the wheel or back seat drivers?': The role of teachers in contemporary curriculum reform. *Queensland Journal of Educational Research, 13*(2): 14–27.

Rea-Dickins, P. (2007). Classroom-based assessment: Possibilities and pitfalls. In Cummins, J. & Davison, C. (Eds.). *The international handbook of English language teaching, vol. 1.* (pp. 505–520). Norwell, MA: Springer.

Roos, B., & Hamilton, D. (2005). Formative assessment: A cybernetic viewpoint. *Assessment in Education, 12*(1): 7–20.

Roy, P., & Hord, S. (2004). Innovation configurations chart: A measured course toward change. *JSD, 25*(2): 54–58.

Stiggins, R. (2008). *An introduction to student-involved assessment for learning* (5th edn). Upper Saddle River, NJ: Pearson Merrill Prentice Hall.

Saskatchewan Learning. (1993). *Learning assessment program.* Retrieved on 2 March 2006 from http://www.sasked.gov.sk.ca/branches/cap_building_acct/afl/docs/plap/foundation.pdf.

Taras, M. (2005). Assessment – summative and formative: Some theoretical reflections. *British Journal of Educational Studies, 53*(4): 466–478.

Torrance, H. (1993). Formative assessment: Some theoretical problems and empirical questions. *Cambridge Journal of Education, 23*(3): 333–343.

Usher, R., Bryant, I. & Johnston, R. (1997) *Adult education and the postmodern challenge. Learning beyond the limits.* London: Routledge.

Wideen, M. (1994). *The struggle for change.* Bristol, PA: Falmer Press.

SUBJECT INDEX

AUTHOR INDEX